Protecting
the Home Front

ALSO BY OR EDITED BY
MICHAEL SCHEIBACH
AND FROM MCFARLAND

*Atomics in the Classroom: Teaching
the Bomb in the Early Postwar Era* (2015)

*"In Case Atom Bombs Fall": An Anthology of
Governmental Explanations, Instructions
and Warnings from the 1940s to the 1960s* (2009)

*Atomic Narratives and American Youth:
Coming of Age with the Atom, 1945–1955* (2003)

Protecting the Home Front

Women in Civil Defense in the Early Cold War

MICHAEL SCHEIBACH

McFarland & Company, Inc., Publishers
Jefferson, North Carolina

Library of Congress Cataloguing-in-Publication Data

Names: Scheibach, Michael, 1949– author.
Title: Protecting the home front : women in civil defense in the early Cold War / Michael Scheibach.
Other titles: Women in civil defense in the early Cold War
Description: Jefferson, North Carolina : McFarland & Company, Inc., Publishers, 2017 | Includes bibliographical references and index.
Identifiers: LCCN 2017040486 | ISBN 9781476672120 (softcover : acid free paper) ∞
Subjects: LCSH: Civil defense—United States—History—20th century. | Women and war—United States—History—20th century. | Sex role—United States—History—20th century. | United States. Federal Civil Defense Administration—History. | Cold War—Social aspects—United States.
Classification: LCC UA927 .S34 2017 | DDC 363.35082/0973—dc23
LC record available at https://lccn.loc.gov/2017040486

British Library cataloguing data are available
ISBN (print) 978-1-4766-7212-0
ISBN (ebook) 978-1-4766-3063-2

© 2017 Michael Scheibach. All rights reserved

No part of this book may be reproduced or transmitted in any form or by any means, electronic or mechanical, including photocopying or recording, or by any information storage and retrieval system, without permission in writing from the publisher.

Front cover images © 2017 iStock

Printed in the United States of America

McFarland & Company, Inc., Publishers
  Box 611, Jefferson, North Carolina 28640
  www.mcfarlandpub.com

For all the women who have made
a difference in my life.

Table of Contents

Women's Civil Defense Prayer	ix
Preface: "We Are Going to Win"	1

Part I: Call to Duty
1. Women's Challenge	10
2. *"Georgia Women in Civil Defense"*	20
3. *"Challenge for Security and Survival: Manual for Women in Civil Defense"*	28

Part II: Beyond Containment
4. Gender and the FCDA	32
5. *"President Truman's Message to Congress on the Federal Civil Defense Administration"*	46
6. *"Katherine Howard's Speech on Security at Home"*	48

Part III: Organized Support
7. Members in Good Standing	58
8. *"Pledge for Home Defense"*	72
9. *"Texans on the Alert for Civil Defense and Disaster Relief"*	76

Part IV: On Guard
10. Serving the Community	84
11. *"This Is Civil Defense"*	100
12. *"The Warden's Handbook"*	108

Part V: Aid and Comfort
13. Joining the Ranks	114
14. *"Police Services"*	126

15. *"The Nurse in Civil Defense"*   135

Part VI: Be Prepared

16. Home Protection and Preparedness   144
17. *"Women in Civil Defense"*   156
18. *"Get Acquainted with the Home Defense Corps"*   161
19. *"Individual and Family Preparedness"*   164

Part VII: Out of the Kitchen

20. Feeding Family and the Masses   170
21. *"Emergency Mass Feeding Instructor Course"*   184
22. *"Basic Course in Emergency Mass Feeding Handbook"*   192

Conclusion: The "Home" in Home Front   197
Appendix: Selected Chapters from "Civil Defense in Outline"   205
Chapter Notes   227
Bibliography   237
Index   245

Woman's Civil Defense Prayer

O Heavenly Father, grant unto the women of this nation understanding that they may learn to serve both their country and their homes; so that in working for the one they may not sacrifice the other. Help them to choose the path that is right, and to follow it through to the end. And let the love they cherish for their homes and the tolerance and courage that has come to them through their work go forth to ease the discord in this world, remembering always that they can have no strength without Thy Power. Amen.

Georgia Women in Civil Defense (c. 1952)

Preface: "We Are Going to Win"

Although less than 1 percent of households had televisions in 1948, more than 55 percent of Americans—some 26 million households—had televisions by 1954 and spent their evenings sitting in front of 12-inch black-and-white screens watching an ever expanding choice of programs.[1] The three television networks—ABC, CBS, and NBC—offered everything from mysteries, westerns, and light-hearted variety programs, to game shows, news and commentary, and family-oriented comedies. This also was the era of dramatic teleplays, however, presented under the aegis of *Ford Theater, Fireside Theater, Studio One, Playhouse 90, Armstrong Circle Theatre,* and *The Motorola Television Hour,* to name a few. On Tuesday, May 18, 1954, viewers tuning in to *The Motorola Television Hour's* presentation, titled simply "Atomic Attack," soon became engulfed in a one-hour drama that, despite its fictional premise, took on the verisimilitude of Cold War tensions that had escalated since the United States and the Soviet Union each had developed a hydrogen bomb—a bomb a thousand times more powerful than the atomic bombs used to destroy Hiroshima and Nagasaki, Japan, in August 1945.[2]

"All Marylanders concerned with the problem of survival under H-bomb attack are urged to see the ABC-TV network program," announced Sherley Ewing, director of the Maryland Civil Defense Agency, in a public statement. One newspaper called it "a vivid, terrifying and powerful play, depicting what can, and might, happen were Manhattan to be attacked by enemy atomic bombs. Recommended for its excellent treatment, its sensitive characterizations, and, practically, for the valuable information it reveals about Civil Defense organization." Another newspaper declared it too intense, but acknowledged that "the basic idea was to teach civil defense and show that it is preparing for the unhappy possibility of such a blast." In an effort to avoid panic, as Orson Welles had caused in 1938 with his radio broadcast of *War of the Worlds,* the network even issued an advance warning carried by newspapers nationwide that the program was not real. Donald Kirkley of *The Baltimore Sun* wrote, "[A]t this moment in history, with many citizens living

Women were often portrayed as the protector of family and home, as illustrated here from the Alert America promotional brochure, published by the Federal Civil Defense Administration in cooperation with the Valley Forge Foundation in 1952.

in dread of being annihilated by an unexpected blast from the sky, a television counterpart of the Welles thing could be catastrophic." With this in mind, the network preceded the program with yet another warning to reassure viewers that the story was fictional.[3]

As "Atomic Attack" opens, Gladys Mitchell (played by Phyllis Thaxter) is finishing breakfast with her family in their suburban home some fifty miles outside of New York City. When her husband leaves for work and her two daughters for school, Gladys turns her attention to cleaning the kitchen and doing laundry. Then, at precisely 10:50 a.m., she is startled as the house shakes violently. Listening intently to the radio for updates, Gladys hears that a hydrogen bomb, possibly launched by a submarine equipped with guided missiles, has destroyed the city. In a moment of panic, she throws on her coat and opens the front door, ready to retrieve her daughters from school. Just at that moment, however, the radio announcer tells listeners to tune it to CONELRAD at 640 and 1240 on their dials, the emergency broadcasting system, and Gladys promptly follows the instructions.

The CONELRAD announcer urges all civil defense workers to report immediately to their emergency stations. He then continues: "Stay where you are unless you're in immediate danger. Do not attempt to join your children if they're at school. They are being well taken care of where they are. Do not try to telephone. Remember, radioactivity may make food and water in open containers dangerous. Do not attempt to inquire about progress in New York as yet there is no information." At this point, without much hope that her family has survived, Gladys becomes overwhelmed at the unfathomable situation; and, in a moment of desperation, she screams as the scene ends.

Many historians of the 1950s have focused on the media's portrayal of women as wife, mother, and homemaker without the experience, capability, or confidence to escape gender constraints—a portrayal that reflected socially acceptable traditional gender roles for women in an era often viewed as heralding the status quo and conformity. Betty Friedan's landmark 1963 book, *The Feminine Mystique*, labeled this situation the "problem that has no name," which resulted from women being seemingly happy as suburban housewives but, at the time, being conflicted and quietly depressed because they lacked the commitment or ability to escape.[4] Elaine Tyler May, in her book, *Homeward Bound: American Families in the Cold War Era*, also focuses on women's restrictive roles in the 1950s. She draws a correlation between the military and political policy of containing the atomic bomb and the containment of women within their "sphere of influence"—the home—where dangerous social forces might be "tamed." Although she acknowledges that the government's civil defense strategies gave new meaning and importance to women's traditional roles, in so doing, she argues, it helped to fortify the home as a place of security. "Even in the ultimate chaos of an atomic attack," May writes, "appropriate gender roles would need to prevail. A 1950 civil defense plan put men in charge of such duties as firefighting, rescue work, street cleaning, and rebuilding, while women were to attend to child care, hospital work, social work, and emergency feeding."[5]

In contrast, Susan Hartmann argues that May and other historians have overlooked "decision makers and opinion shapers" who promoted more expansive opportunities for women. "In an era dominated by the celebration of domesticity and women's traditional roles," Hartmann writes, "experts and opinion leaders ... sought to adjust public opinion and public policy to accommodate women's greater participation in the public sphere."[6] Laura McEnaney has expanded on Hartmann's viewpoint, rightfully arguing that even though the civil defense program reinforced women's domestic skills, it simultaneously offered women the power and opportunity to expand upon those skills.[7] In this view, the government's emphasis on family self-help was a means to personalize the Cold War and give Americans, male and female, a sense of ownership in their survival. "What emerged from this feminization of civil defense," contends McEnaney, "was no less than a militarist-maternalist women's movement that worked both collaboratively with and independently of government planners to spread the gospel of home protection, anticommunism, and 'woman power.'"[8] A woman, the "military housewife," had four critical tasks: to learn the basic rules of modern warfare; to train her family in how to survive potential disasters; to ensure that her home was prepared for both attack and recovery; and, perhaps the most important task, to make sure her family contained their panic and fear.[9]

Containing panic and fear is demonstrated in the next scene of "Atomic Attack," which opens at 11:30 a.m. with the CONELRAD announcer reporting that hydrogen bombs have hit cities from coast to coast, including Washington, D.C., Boston, Philadelphia, Seattle, and Los Angeles. Over the next ten days, as the United States and "the enemy" fight a nuclear war, with millions of casualties, Gladys not only maintains her composure; she also cares for her daughters, who escaped the blast but have been exposed to radioactivity, and encourages her daughters and her neighbors not to panic but to cope in the nuclear aftermath. While not rejecting her traditional roles as mother, nurturer, and home protector, she exhibits the strength and perseverance necessary to carry on—to survive.

A month later, on June 14, 1954, millions of men and women had an opportunity to experience a similar situation during the Federal Civil Defense Administration's Operation Alert, a hypothetical nuclear attack on the United States, with forty-two cities struck by atomic bombs and nine million people killed and another four million left homeless. The purpose behind Operation

Alert, which became an annual event until it ended in 1961, was to test the readiness of the nation's civil defense program. Ironically, a civil defense block warden—described in the FCDA's *Warden's Handbook* as "the direct link between the police and the local civil defense organization"—comes to Gladys's house in "Atomic Attack" and tells her, "Civil defense. Some folks thought it was a kid's game. Lots of laughs. Just a game." "Some game," Gladys replies. "Some laughs."[10]

Operation Alert was meant to bring more awareness and more seriousness to civil defense—to diffuse the notion that it was just a game. And, in this sense, it succeeded. More than 300 newspapers covered the event and 233 cities held civil defense drills, including the "target cities" of Boston, New York City, Houston, Kansas City, and Chicago. According to the FCDA, 62 million Americans lived in the areas where civil defense exercises took place. Many cities tested their sirens, warning of an impending attack, and conducted public drills. In New York City, buses pulled to the curb, subways stopped underground, office workers walked to shelter areas, and broadcasters instructed people to tune in to CONELRAD. Portland, Oregon, officials stopped traffic and handed out leaflets. Milwaukee school children took shelter as the city conducted a civil defense drill. Other cities, such as Houston, Texas, and Spokane, Washington, conducted evacuation drills.[11]

In its 1954 annual report, the FCDA stated that the widespread public participation made millions of Americans "ask themselves just what they would do if there were an actual attack." Unfortunately, the report continued, "too few answers were forthcoming in the relatively brief period during which public attention was captured."[12] The same could be said of the nation's civil defense program, which began in 1951 with the establishment of the FCDA by President Harry S Truman, and continued into the 1960s and beyond, although at a steadily declining level.

No attempt is made here to confirm the effectiveness of civil defense, its acceptance, or its ultimate success or failure. The historical record is clear that most Americans remained apathetic or just indifferent to civil defense, perhaps because they thought "what's the point!" Nor is there an attempt to ascertain the actual number of women who participated directly or indirectly in civil defense during the 1950s and early 1960s. It is impossible to confirm this number. Rather, the following pages explore the numerous and diverse opportunities for women not only to become involved in the nation's civil defense program, but also to become an essential component. In so doing, it reinforces and expands upon the argument—as offered by Hartmann and McEnaney, among others—that women, albeit primarily as volunteers and often utilizing skills associated with traditional gender roles, contributed significantly to civil defense, from protecting their homes and families, to serving their local communities, to participating in state and national programs and activities.

It is safe to say that millions of men and women had some involvement in or exposure to civil defense, such as a civil defense drill or mass feeding demonstration; a community civil defense exercise, such as Operation Alert; a civic presentation or religious gathering; or an exhibit, such as the government's traveling Alert America display, featuring booths on a wide range of atomic-related topics.[13] Mothers of school-aged children heard about duck 'n' cover drills; learned about "atomics" being taught in history, science, and other classes; and attended school programs related to the atomic bomb or atomic energy. Women in the workforce—some 30 percent of all women in the 1950s—read informative civil defense posters on buses and office walls, and picked up civil defense publications in building lobbies and retail stores. Women members of such organizations at the American Red Cross, Parent-Teachers Association, National Federation of Business and Professional Women's Clubs, American Home Economics Association, and American Legion Auxiliary attended meetings, workshops, and presentations on civil defense. Businesswomen, doctors, nurses, and other professional women contributed to civil defense. Women also received training and served as block wardens, medical aides, transportation workers, and auxiliary police officers. The list goes on.

Protecting the Home Front explores women's involvement with civil defense during the early Cold War, and includes original text and illustrations from FCDA and government publications that help to better understand and appreciate the scope of this involvement. Part I sets the stage by examining the government's challenge to women to join civil defense. Part II focuses on the Federal Civil Defense Administration's mission to enlist women into civil defense, and examines its approach to so-called traditional gender roles in its various programs, policies, and publications. Part III looks closely at the plethora of women's organizations—national, state, and local—that actively promoted civil defense at conferences and meetings, as well as by forming committees and distributing publications and other civil defense materials. Part IV then details the myriad ways women served their communities, from being plane spotters for the Ground Observer Corps to protecting their neighborhoods as block wardens. Part V explores women's significant role in the government's police and nursing services. Part VI chronicles women's essential role in protecting the family and the home. Finally, Part VII looks at women's responsibility to maintain an adequate and safe food supply at home, and to plan and make preparations for the mass feeding of survivors after an atomic attack. Each of the book's seven parts begins with a discursive chapter, followed by two or three FCDA civil defense publications complete with original cover design.

Unquestionably, the nation's civil defense program identified the protection of family and home as its priority mission, and Gladys Mitchell exemplifies a woman as family and home protector. In the beginning of "Atomic Attack," she is seemingly a happy suburban wife, mother, and homemaker living in a nice house with a husband who has a good job in the city and two lovely daughters. She also is someone lacking awareness and knowledge about civil defense, as we soon discover. Yet by the story's conclusion, she has accepted the fact that she has to persevere after the death of her husband, along with millions of others; care for her daughters; confront the dangers of radioactivity; and help her neighbors deal with the aftermath of a nuclear war. As the teleplay ends, Gladys is a stronger and more committed woman. After her youngest daughter asks whether the country has won the war, Gladys replies, "Not yet, darling. But we're going to. I promise you that. We are going to win." If there were a next scene, perhaps a few weeks later, no doubt Gladys would be seen talking with the block warden and asking how she can volunteer for civil defense. It would be her way of assuring her daughters—and herself—that the country would, indeed, ultimately win.

Part I
Call to Duty

1. Women's Challenge

> If atomic bombs are to be added as new weapons to the arsenals of a warring world, or to the arsenals of nations preparing for war ... [t]he people must unite, or they will perish.—*J. Robert Oppenheimer, Head, Los Alamos Laboratory, Manhattan Project*[1]

"Women of today can ill afford to be lulled into an unjustified feeling of security when there is a seeming easing of the international situation, as long as the underlying tensions and threats remain," wrote Major General Erwin Hostetler in *Challenge for Security and Survival: Manual for Women in Civil Defense*. Hostetler, then director of civil defense and emergency planning for the state of Ohio, acknowledged that the initiative and planning for civil defense had to come from a broad base of professional competence and leadership; he made clear, however, that the main task of civil defense rested with women. He then encouraged directors of local civil defense organizations to take advantage of women's interest and enthusiasm, their willingness to work, and "their quick and ready response to anything affecting the family and home."[2]

Hostetler's focus on the necessity for citizens, especially women, to participate in the nation's protection and survival mirrored those expressed beginning in the 1940s, during World War II, and continuing through the 1950s, as the Cold War intensified. What is notable about Hostetler's comments, though, is that they appeared in 1965, when the nation had seemingly turned its attention away from the threat of nuclear war to new social and military challenges, specifically the escalation of the war in Vietnam and the repercussions of racial violence and civil rights protests.

In March 1965, President Lyndon Johnson had dispatched 3,500 Marines (two battalions) to Vietnam, becoming the first United States combat troops, although more than 20,000 "military advisors" were already there. The United States also began air strikes against the North Vietnamese. On July 28, Johnson sent more troops, bringing the total to 125,000. By the end of the year, close to 200,000 American combat troops were on the ground in Southeast Asia in a war that lasted a decade and took the lives of more than 58,000

This poster was designed to encourage civilians, especially women, to join civil defense and, ultimately, to train others (National Archives).

Americans. Anti-war protests occurred in the nation's capital and soon spread throughout the country.

The civil rights movement had gained momentum in the 1950s, propelled forward by the Supreme Court's 1954 ruling in *Brown vs. Board of Education* that struck down the "separate but equal" doctrine, and intensified by the 1957 Little Rock (Arkansas) Central High School confrontation, when nine African American students enrolled in the all-white school, followed by the 1960 Greensboro, North Carolina, sit-ins of African American youth in all-white establishments. In both Little Rock and Greensboro, positive results eventually prevailed with new integration policies, thus giving the civil rights movement more confidence. President Johnson's support for civil rights, and the growing support among many Americans, white and black, ultimately led to passage of the Civil Rights Act of 1964, which outlawed discrimination based on race, color, religion, gender, or national origin. Unfortunately, it also led to more violence with the murders of four civil rights workers in Mississippi in the summer of 1964 and the spread of riots across the nation, including the August 1965 riots in the Watts section of Los Angeles.[3]

Yet despite these social and political realities, *Challenges for Security and Survival* illustrates that nuclear annihilation remained a very real underlying threat to which the American people had to remain vigilant. This was never more evident than during President John F. Kennedy's watch, when the nation twice had ventured to the nuclear precipice.

The first confrontation, the Berlin Crisis, occurred in October 1961 and involved the Soviet Union's demand that Western troops (representing the United States, United Kingdom, and France) withdraw from West Berlin, located some 100 miles inside the East German border—an effort that failed when the U.S. forced the Soviet Union to back down. A year later, in October 1962, the U.S. came close to war during the Cuban Missile Crisis before President Kennedy's threat of nuclear retaliation forced Soviet Premier Nikita Khrushchev to remove the missiles positioned in Cuba, just 90 miles from the nation's borders. Addressing the American people on television, the president stated his position in unmistakably clear terms: "It shall be the policy of this nation to regard any nuclear missile launched from Cuba against any nation in the Western Hemisphere as an attack on the United States, requiring a full retaliatory response upon the Soviet Union."[4]

The peaceful resolution of the Cuban Missile Crisis, followed by passage of the Limited Test Ban Treaty in 1963 eliminating atmospheric and underwater atomics tests, had eased international tensions between the two nuclear superpowers—tensions that had continuously escalated since August 1949, when the Soviet Union successfully exploded its first atomic bomb. Long before the Soviet Union's entrance into the atomic age in 1949, however, the communist nation had become an adversary of the United States, even though the two countries were allies during World War II.

Almost immediately following the conclusion of the war in August 1945, newspapers, magazines, books, radio programs, school classrooms, community meetings, and even church gatherings emphasized the apocalyptic consequences of another world war fought with atomic weapons—with most Americans acknowledging the inevitability of the Soviet Union developing an atomic bomb. Speaking in 1946, David Lilienthal, head of the Atomic Energy Commission, summed up the situation by proclaiming that "the awful strength of atomic power ... directly affects every man, women, and child."[5] And Americans soon became exposed to—and influenced by—the scientific principles of atomic energy and inundated with warnings about its destructive power. National polls conducted in 1946 and 1947 found that some 80 percent of Americans believed other countries either already possessed the atomic bomb or would develop one within five years; and 64 percent believed atomic bombs would eventually be used against the United States. Historian Paul Boyer, in his seminal study of America in the late 1940s, *By the Bombs' Early*

Light, documents how Americans' celebratory mood following the final victory over Japan descended quickly into the frightening realization that the new atomic age presented unprecedented perils to the nation and to civilization. "[P]rimal fear of extinction cut across all political and ideological lines," wrote Boyer.[6]

This fear intensified as the Soviet Union strengthened its hold in Eastern Europe by drawing what Winston Churchill called an "iron curtain" across the European continent. The Soviet Union accentuated its intent on dominating Eastern Europe in June 1948 when it blockaded access by road, train, and water to the Allied-controlled areas of Berlin, located well within East Germany. Over the next year, the U.S. and its allies airlifted 2.3 million tons of cargo to the beleaguered city, until the Soviet Union reopened the corridors in May 1949, thus ending the "Berlin Airlift." A month earlier, on April 4, the U.S. and 12 European allies plus Canada formed the North Atlantic Treaty Organization (NATO) to prevent the spread of Soviet aggression. Four months later, on August 29, the Soviet Union successfully detonated an atomic bomb. On October 1, the world witnessed the fall of China, an important ally in World War II, to Mao Zedong and communism. Then, on June 25, 1950, the North Korean army crossed the 38th parallel, invading the democratic South Korea and creating a new and very real wartime threat of communist aggression.[7]

The escalation of the Cold War, now with an atomic-armed adversary, prompted President Harry S Truman to issue a twofold call-to-arms: first, the nation had to strengthen its military defense, prompting the president to authorize immediate development of a "super" atomic bomb; and, second, the government had to prepare the American people for the probable, if not inevitable, atomic war between the world's two postwar superpowers. This preparation, moreover, would focus initially on the home—the protective sanctity of the family and the domain of women.

The president formally implemented this call-to-arms in September 1950 by approving a National Securities Resources Board report recommending a massive civil defense mobilization program aimed primarily at women. The NSRB, which had been created by the National Security Act of 1947 and placed in the Department of Defense in 1949, had declared: "The civil defense program for this country must be in constant readiness because for the first time in 136 years an enemy has the power to attack our cities in strong force, and for the first time in our history that attack may come suddenly, with little or no warning."[8]

In October, W. Stuart Symington, NSRB chairman, met in Washington, D.C., with representatives from 53 women's groups to explain women's national defense responsibilities. This led to the presidents of fourteen of the largest women's organizations forming a national clearing house committee. These organizations included professional women in the American Association of University Women and National Association of Business and Professional Women's Clubs; employed women in Women of the American Federation of Labor and C.I.O.; women of faith in the National Council of Catholic Women, Young Women's Christian Association, and National Council of Jewish Women; and African American women in the National Council of Negro Women, to name a few.[9]

In its report, the NSRB emphasized that women would be needed as paid employees and as volunteers, with all aspects of civil defense open to qualified women, including leadership roles as directors and associate directors of state and local civil defense organizations. In addition, women could choose to work in control centers, public relations, transportation, engineering, light rescue, public health and city planning, and warden and welfare services. Or they could volunteer to be telephone operators, drivers, feeding and housing administrators, clerical workers, or airplane spotters. As one reporter wrote, "Officials believe that almost any woman could volunteer to do some work, even though it might be only part-time. Women are expected to offer any special talent, skill, or training to national defense at the federal, state, or local level. More than 50 percent of the manpower in civil defense will be women, with the need for women doctors, nurses, dentists, lawyers, draftsmen, dieticians, and administrative workers being in special demand."[10]

Responding to the government's program, states, cities, and towns across the country announced plans to recruit women volunteers. In October 1950, the U.S. Conference of Mayors and a conference of state officials were held in Washington, D.C., in part to receive additional information about the civil defense program. New York State announced the need for 418,000 wardens alone. In Philadelphia, Mayor Bernard Samuel declared, "Women have a clearly defined role in the city's civil defense organization, and we are wasting no time in clarifying the need to them." The mayor then announced that the city's civil defense program needed 100,000 women volunteers. Major General James Dozler, director of the civil defense program in South Carolina, announced that women formed "the greatest untapped resource of the manpower of the country" and would be needed to fill at least half the civil defense positions in the state. He went on to stress that women with proper training were quite capable of performing the same jobs as men.[11]

In December, in yet another move, President Truman announced the creation of the Federal Civil Defense Administration (FCDA) to "promote and facilitate the civil defense of the United States in cooperation with the several States."[12] Formerly launched in January 1951. the FCDA, headed by Millard Caldwell, former governor of Florida, was charged with preparing comprehensive civil defense plans and programs; conducting research to develop civil defense measures and equipment; conducting and arranging training programs; and disseminating civil defense information. Under Executive Order 10222, issued in March 1951, Truman effectively disbanded the NSRB, transferring its civil defense responsibilities to the FCDA.[13]

One of the FCDA's most challenging goals was recruiting some 17 to 20 million volunteers for the U.S. civil defense program, with not 50 but 80 percent expected to be women.[14] A civil defense pamphlet summed up women's importance: "The strength and courage of American women—traditional guardians of the home—is one of the Nation's greatest resources. If the women of this country will prepare with courage and determination, we will have the Civil Defense we need to be strong."[15] To achieve this goal, the FCDA worked with 4,000 national organizations representing some 100 million people. In May 1951, 1,000 representatives of 268 organizations met to discuss plans to distribute civil defense information and training. The American Hotel Association, for example, placed civil defense "Alert Cards" in close to 7,000 hotel rooms and published a special booklet on what to do if an atomic attack occurred while in a hotel; the American Legion printed and circulated civil defense materials to its 17,000 posts across the country; the American Red Cross coordinated blood collections, first-aid training, and home-nursing training programs; and a religious advisory committee was formed to coordinate civil defense programs sponsored by the nation's religious groups. Working in cooperation with the FCDA and state civil defense agencies, the Air Force also instituted recruitment efforts to enlist men, women, and youth into the re-formed Ground Observer Corps, a volunteer-based program to watch the skies for enemy aircraft.[16]

According to the FCDA's 1951 annual report, 87 percent of Americans living in major cities knew the basics of self-protection against atomic attack, largely the result of "billions of messages" delivered via newspapers, radio, television, magazines, and other media. An example is a 1951 pamphlet published by Columbia Broadcasting System. Titled *Homemaker's Manual of Atomic Defense*, it was based on Margaret Arlen's television program, "Course in Self Preservation," and covered the basics of first aid, radioactivity, shelter protection, and food provisions. The pamphlet offered simple advice: "An enemy who, by merely threatening, can terrify the homemakers of America has already won a large victory. We can fight panic with information."[17]

The FCDA, which published more than 50 million copies of civil defense publications in its first year, must be credited with fulfilling the government's objective to inform and to involve the public in civil defense. And over the next decade, the government's civil defense efforts emphasized the importance—even the necessity—of women helping their communities and their families prepare for and survive an atomic attack, and mastering the requisite skills needed to rebuild the nation in the aftermath of such an attack. Writes historian Susan Stoudinger Northcutt, "[T]he atom bomb, a weapon which was the domain of the military and the centerpiece of military strategy, was domesticated (shaped, altered, tamed) in the 1950s and early 1960s in the United States, largely as a consequence of civil defense, a government program that expanded 'nuclear reality' to directly include millions of civilians, especially women and families. The domestication was mass-based, gradual, and political."[18]

The FCDA appointed regional directors for women's affairs in its first year of operation. Then, in January 1953, newly elected President Dwight Eisenhower expanded this effort by naming Katherine Howard as assistant administrator of the FCDA to actively recruit women. That same year, the FCDA reorganized and expanded the National Women's Advisory Committee, formed under President Truman to evaluate the agency's civil defense program and offer advice on how to improve women's commitment to national security. The committee was composed of leaders of national women's organizations representing some 26 million women, as well as directors of women's civil defense activities at the federal, regional, and state levels.[19]

Although Howard resigned in 1954, citing personal reasons, during her short tenure at FCDA she made quite an impact by connecting women's civil defense activities with their "traditional" responsibilities involving family and home. In a speech at the 63rd Continental Congress of the Daughters of the American Revolution, she called civil defense "merely a prudent extension of existing proactive services" that women provided every day.[20] Howard often addressed women's importance, explaining that families' defense arsenal consisted of "love of family, loyalty to country, aid to others, faith in God, a fierce regard for freedom, and the will to work together in the traditional American ways."[21] Upon Howard's resignation, Eisenhower appointed Jean Wood Fuller as the FCDA's director of women's activities. Fuller, who had served in the Red Cross and Home Services Corp during World War II, became the new voice in the government's campaign to solicit women into civil defense. She, too, encouraged women to adapt their domestic skills to the Cold War, such as home nursing and first aid, on a practical level, and the art of persuasion and nurturing on another level.[22]

Howard's and Fuller's emphasis on the domestic aspects of women's contribution to civil defense must be acknowledged. This domestication—or feminization—of civil defense has been interpreted as reinforcing traditional gender roles and containing women in the home, as argued by Elaine Tyler May in her book, *Homeward Bound: American Families in the Cold War Era*. May based her conclusion in part on the government's focus on home protection exercises, home nursing and first aid practices, stockpiling food supplies, and an assortment of other life-protecting activities. Kristina Zarlengo also has addressed the domestication of civil defense, suggesting that the American household, under the management of a housewife, became an agency of the nation in the 1950s. Moreover, patriotism became a domestic duty and housework a civic obligation "with grave consequences." Women and children, in essence, formed a new class of soldier—deterrence soldiers—that reshaped peacetime behavior to complement the requirements for preventing war.[23]

But Zarlengo argues further that government literature on atomic warfare and atomic power generated new feminine ideals. "The American housewife," she writes, "inspired a whole canon of propaganda since the rhetoric of civil defense taught that the household was a bunker where women's expertise and competence were vital to a nation at risk—providing a refuge from the incipient city war zone." The American people, in other words, were inculcated with government rhetoric about the need for their contributions to national security, thus transforming their homes, their personal space, into a military sphere.[24] Susan Northcutt makes a similar point, suggesting that "homes and families became involved in atomic planning, catapulting women (as wives and mothers as well as household managers) to the forefront of civil defense."[25]

Women had been in the forefront before, fulfilling their responsibilities during World War II in government and military roles, as well as contributing to the nation's massive home-front industrial output. By the end of the war in 1945, women constituted 37 percent of America's workforce, and nearly one out of four married women worked outside the home. But the new atomic age required even more responsibility, and government officials, politicians, scientists, media professionals, educators, and assorted social commentators wasted little time in ratcheting up efforts to inform, enlighten, and even frighten the American populace—particularly families and children—about the power of the atomic bomb and the dire consequences ahead if they did not contribute to the nation's security and the preservation of civilization. Historian Mary Brennan, in her book, *Wives, Mothers, and the Red Menace*, traces the anti-communist movement during the 1950s, arguing that the FCDA encouraged women to embrace traditional gender roles but also to become active in the community in order to contrast their lifestyle with that of women in the Soviet Union. "Many of the plans the FCDA made revolved around the housewife," Brennan writes. "She was the protector of the home; she was the one who stocked the pantry; she kept the house free of dirt, germs, and clutter; most important, she was vital in helping individuals, the family, and the community survive a nuclear attack."[26]

If women failed to become informed and trained in civil defense, they jeopardized not only the survival of their family but the survival of their neighbors, their community, and their country, Brennan argues. As often pointed out, women had to remain informed and up-to-date on self-protection procedures, and be able to share their knowledge with others in case of an enemy attack. They had to know the civil defense plans in their community, and these plans affected their family and home. If they achieved these goals, they fulfilled their responsibilities; if they failed, they also failed their families, their neighbors, and their community.[27]

Women in Civil Defense, published in 1952, exemplifies the emphasis on every woman's critical role in civil defense, whether in the workforce or as a homemaker.[28] "Whether you are a housewife, secretary, business executive, or nurse," it reads, "civil defense looks to you, as a woman, to take an active role in protecting your home as safe as possible against the danger of enemy attack." Women could not stop there, though. Their second duty was to join or begin a community civil defense organization, considered essential for the nation's defense. If a woman failed in this responsibility, she must accept the blame for creating an untenable situation:

> If your community does not have an active civil defense organization, much of the blame must fall on you and your neighbors. Unless you, as a responsible American woman, take action, you are gambling with the safety of your family, your friends, your community, and your country.... When you have trained your family and prepared your home, you have more than doubled your chances for survival in an atomic attack. When you have joined in organizing your community, you have given the community and the Nation a far better chance to survive an enemy attack. But you will have done more than just prepare in case of war—you will have made a positive contribution to keeping the peace.... Getting America prepared on the home front is a responsibility that falls in large part on the shoulders of all American women. It's your job—and you have no time to waste.[29]

This responsibility was applied to teachers, as well, who were charged with educating America's children about the realities of the atomic age, both its destructive power and potential benefits. FCDA administrator Clara McMahon, for example, emphasized that schools had to adjust their curriculums for the atomic age, including the possibility of an atomic attack. In 1953 she wrote: "When these goals are compared with the concepts of civil defense—individual self-protection, extended self-protection, mutual aid, and mobile support—it requires no leap of logic to see how closely the concepts can be tied in with the aims of education; indeed, that they are actually an extension of these aims." According to McMahon, teachers had to ensure that their students understood the threat all Americans faced.[30] Much has been written about duck 'n' cover drills and the emphasis on "atomics" in school curricula during the 1950s[31]; however, what is often not discussed is the fact that by the end of the decade, 71 percent of elementary and secondary school teachers—the ones ensuring that school-aged children and youth were informed about and prepared for the atomic threat, and kept safe during an atomic attack—were women.[32]

As the FCDA's focus on teachers illustrates, the government viewed women contributing in a variety of ways to the nation's civil defense program. Historian Andrew Grossman correctly argues that the FCDA actually continued the same approach to home-front preparation and civil defense training as the approach taken by the Office of War Information and Office of Civilian Defense during World War II, which stressed that women could contribute to the national defense equally with men.[33] Grossman concludes that the FCDA did not produce a domesticated or paternalistic view of women but "saw women as essentially genderless human resources."[34]

Rather than overseeing a federal government hierarchy, the FCDA, through financial necessity as well as purpose, promoted the creation of state and local civil defense organizations; civil defense education in America's schools; involvement by national, regional, and state associations; and particularly the adoption of civil defense activities by established community and women's organizations. The FCDA also reached out to professional women; businesswomen; women in administrative and supervisory positions; and even rural women. These women, without regard to age, experience, or background, and without formalized restrictions, were encouraged to join all areas of civil defense and to contribute to their community's safety and preparation for atomic attack. In short, the FCDA provided many opportunities for women at all levels: national, state, and local. Moreover, although women undoubtedly utilized their "traditional" skills, they also greatly expanded these skills and, more important, developed new ones. In so doing, millions of women met the government's challenge to safeguard the nation's home front.

2. "Georgia Women in Civil Defense"

> *One of the Federal Civil Defense Administration's major objectives was the enlistment of states and localities into the national civil defense program; and, subsequently, states and local communities would assist in attracting women volunteers. In 1954, the Georgia Civil Defense Department, as part of its civil defense program, published* Georgia Women in Civil Defense, *which covered women's responsibilities in civil defense. Women's role as family manager and protector as well as their role in preventing panic are highlighted in this excerpt.*

As patriotic citizens, men and women share alike in partnership and responsibility for this job of Civil Defense.

Newton D. Baker once said: "The drama of war is on the fighting front and the strength is on the home front." Since men will largely predominate on the fighting front, we must depend upon women for action and strength on the home front. Both men and women will furnish professional leadership, with women doubtless furnishing the larger part of volunteer manpower. In England during World War II, 80% of the Civil Defense Corps was composed of women. In the event of another war, a large part of Civil Defense will rest squarely on the shoulders of the women of America.

Our whole Civil Defense program is based on using each individual at the job which he or she is best equipped to do. The individual woman's place in Civil Defense depends upon the situation and needs in her own community. The local Civil Defense office knows and can tell her what these needs are. Women's distinctive responsibility for the family in our society is recognized. The security of her family is perhaps the most vital concern of every woman. Women will want to be especially proficient in those things which give their children and their families a chance for survival.

There is a great deal women can do *now*. There are plenty of problems Georgia women—women everywhere, in fact—can solve by calm, quiet planning which, later on, may save time and confusion and tragedy. Fortunately, they are not so different from the problems you wrestle with every day. And you can

GEORGIA WOMEN IN CIVIL DEFENSE

start at home—by building a firm foundation under the unit without whose wholehearted support and intelligent cooperation the best Civil Defense program ever written is bound to fail.

That unit, of course, is your family.

Let us review the pattern of Civil Defense. It starts with the individual and with the family. No amount of organization, no investment of funds can build a bomb proof, panic proof umbrella over each individual and each family that will completely protect them from the terror weapons of modern war.

The individual must know what he is up against and what to do about it. The facts of survival must be learned well—in homes, in schools, in neighborhoods, and in every community.

Preparation—knowing what to do and how to do it—is the best guarantee of survival in an atomic attack. In an air raid your best defense, to put it in a word, is *YOU!* With proper instructions and training, the number of casualties in a bomb blast can be cut in half.

Think about that!

Ask yourself, "What can I do?" At the moment, maybe nothing exciting or glamorous. You can, however, enroll right now for a first-aid class. On what you learn will be built later training, further assignments, other jobs. First-aid is a good foundation for all Civil Defense work.

Try also to take a Red Cross course in Home Nursing. This training will be valuable, as it will teach you to recognize symptoms of illness and to carry out the physician's orders.

Simple emergency steps everyone should know for action in case of burns, shock, bleeding and broken bones will be found in the booklet, "Emergency Action to Save Lives."

The simple and practical knowledge to be gained from this training and study in Home Protection will be valuable—war or no war.

These are the things we should learn, even if we had a guarantee that nobody would ever drop an atomic or conventional bomb on our country. They are what we would need in a fire, earthquake, cyclone or any one of the dozen disasters which even in time of peace overtake cities and communities—and almost invariably find them utterly and completed unprepared.

Remember, there are no trifles in a total war. Training in these phases of survival may seem a small matter now—but there could come a time when they could mean the difference between life and death for a loved one.

Suppose your child was hit by flying glass and suffering from serious loss of blood, or from a severe burn—what would you do?

If you do not know, you had better do all you can to find out, because if an atomic bomb should fall, you cannot depend on calling a doctor or an ambulance.

The telephone lines would be down or be jammed with official messages. Doctors won't be in their offices—they will be hurrying to emergency stations. Many of them will be dead. Everyone will be entirely on his own—we will have to depend strictly on ourselves in the immediate emergency.

Think of it like this: If 10 persons are in a boat together and the boat turns over, the more of them who can swim, the better chance they *all* have of coming through it safely.

There is a good thing to remember: "If you never need what you learn in Civil Defense, you lose nothing; but if you never learn what you need in Civil Defense, you may lose everything."

The entire civil defense program depends upon the informed citizen who has read at least one defense manual, and understands the basic rules of self-protection; who knows that the difference between life and death may well be his ability to keep calm, and to keep others calm, and to avoid panic no matter what happens. Experienced Civil Defense men are fearful that if a bomb were dropped tomorrow on any target in the country, vast numbers of people would be killed as a result of panic.

Panic Prevention

There is a defense against the atomic bomb. It is not a total defense any more than there is a total defense against bullets or against arrows, but knowing what to do and how to do it can reduce casualties and property loss. It is fear of the unknown that destroys reason and causes panic.

We are crippled by fear. Today's Civil Defense program is directed toward preventing such panic episodes as the Orson Welles scare—if war comes and the population of a city has to meet the challenge of an atomic bomb attack.

The more we know about the *possibilities*, and *the more we know about what to do*, the less chance there is of panic. The more we feel part of a group that is organized to deal with a crisis, the stronger our confidence will be; the greater our capacity to survive. A psychology for survival requires us to build up a group in which we feel safe, in which we can share with others whatever comes. This knowledge and this working together will keep down panic.

Psychologists advise parents to remember that children can stand practically anything except "the collapse of their parents." They contend that parents must establish their own psychology for survival by being trained in the skills of survival in order to help their children feel safe in this age. Mothers have an *extra portion of responsibility* in this. *By their example*, and through knowing what to do in an emergency, they can give security to their children.

Protective Measures for Home and Family

Begin now to take training in self-protection so you can give emergency protection to yourself and your family. Sign up for the following free courses, study literature, see movies on:

a. Emergency First Aid.
b. Home Nursing.
c. Fire Protection for the Home.
d. What You Should Know About Biological Warfare.
e. What to Do in Event of Atomic Attack.

Organize your family as a self-sustaining unit in case of disaster:

1. Assemble a first aid kit and see that each member of the family knows how to use it. It is suggested that first aid material proposed in the Civil Defense Household First Aid Kit ... be bought, item by item, and that the family discuss the articles and place them in a box. In this manner, every member of the family knows what is in the box and how to use it in the event of an emergency.
2. Make sure that at least one adult member of the family knows first aid and home nursing.
3. Select the safest part of the home for a shelter area and equip that "safety spot" with:
    (a) Food and water supply for three days.
    (b) First aid kit.
    (c) Flashlight.
    (d) Radio (self-powered).
    (e) Small hand fire extinguisher.
    (f) Material to keep children occupied.
4. Teach each member of the family the alert signals.
5. Inform each member of the family as to what action to take in event of an attack and hold family practice drills.
6. Assign duties to various members of the family with provision for alternates in the event some are not at home.
7. Have the family learn home fire protection and eliminate all fire hazards in the home.
8. Make sure your children and all the family know your block warden. The more information and training your children have, the more security they will feel and there will be less danger of panic and hysteria.
9. Select a meeting point in a suburban area of the city or in a neighboring community in a direction away from the center of the city

for the family to meet in the event the home is destroyed. Instruct all family members to wait there at least 24 hours. This area should be understood by out-of-town relatives or friends who might want to contact the family after the attack in the event one occurs.

Instruct Your Family

There is no better time than right now to revive an old family custom which has been all but lost in our modern family living. I am referring to the family council.

You, the housewife, are the family's General Manager. Some evening when the children have no homework and your husband has no lodge meeting or work-shop puttering, you might say:

"There is a possibility that something might happen which would put us just where our forefathers were. We wouldn't have all these nice conveniences of gas and electricity. We wouldn't have a refrigerator or an oil burner. If we turned on the spigot, no water would come out. We couldn't drive to the store, because the roads would be crowded with people with business much more important than ours. Let's all put our heads together and see what we could do to make out for a while without all these things we've come to depend on."

"What things we're accustomed to doing *CAN'T* we do if we have no light, heat or power? How can we keep warm? How can we cook? What do we do about water? What sorts of clothes should we have for this emergency?"

You'll find the answers to these and other questions in booklets and instruction cards issued by the State and Federal Governments, and in newspaper and magazine articles. But—before you hunt up these general answers, *work out the solution that applies directly to you and your own household.*

Here are some other questions you might ask:

"How capable am I, or are we, if you are directing the questions to your family council—of taking care of our injuries? Remember, no power. Possibly no telephone. And your doctor will be at an emergency station, so it's up to you. *You're on your own.*

"What do you know about first aid? Is there a basic first aid kit in your house?"

Toss that one to your husband, or even better, at your Boy Scout son. It will test their male responsibility. And be sure to demand a full report at the next family council meeting. You're the General Manager, you know, so exert your authority.

By this time you should have caught the interest of every member of your family. "What about fire? Someone asks.

Fire, you agree, might be a problem. As a matter of fact, fire always is a problem in a home. Remember, no water; no telephone; no fire engines with howling sirens to rush to your aid. Again, you're on your own.

"What conditions in your house would feed a fire? Rubbish in the cellar or the attic? Inflammable liquids in confined spaces: Toy chests and closets jammed with combustible odds and ends like Fibber McGee's?" There's another good chance to keep the masculine members of your family busy. How many cans of useless paint has your husband squirreled away in his basement workshop? And those piles of newspapers and department store cartoons and matches in every drawer?

Do you know where the master electric, gas and oil burner switches are in your home? If you're like most of us women, you leave matters of that kind to your husband. Find out where those switches are and how they work. Ask your husband. He'll love to show you.

How many people, in addition to yourself and your family, could you shelter and feed during an emergency of, let's say, two days? Well ... there's that old army cot in the attic ... and that mattress you've been intending for so long to give away ... and.... But, there again, are questions to which you've had to work out your own answers. Put you mind to it. If worse comes to worst, you might have to throw some of your personal niceties out of the window. You'd do it, too, if homeless humans appealed to you for shelter. So think about it now.

If, in spite of all your efforts to keep calm, you find yourself slipping into foreboding, just think of your great-great-grandma and how she faced the threat of tomahawks, scalping knives and fire arrows. They were just as terrifying for her as atom bombs are to you. She met danger with courage. In her day, women worked along with their men folk to protect their families and their homes, and, at the same time they did everything they could to help their neighbors. Our ancestors didn't have a name for the mutual aid they gave in times of emergencies—neighbor helping neighbor. Today we call the things they did ... Civil Defense.

Join Hands with Your Neighbors in Community Participation

On a larger scale, we and our neighbors must learn how to work in organized groups so that we can bring trained help, if necessary, to stricken people and stricken areas. Civil Defense is a test of nation-wide community action. It is symbolic of the tradition in these United States of neighbor helping neighbor in time of peril and distress.

The principle of neighborhood groups working together in Civil Defense is one of the most important parts of the program—you can help in your community by urging your neighbors to learn all about Civil Defense activities, and by volunteering for the local organization.

No woman in the world wants war. But only when a nation is fully and adequately prepared, both on the battle-front and on the home-front, can there be real hope of preventing war. The only present guarantee of our nation's safety and freedom is strength and preparedness. These are the two factors which will delay aggression. Therefore, Civil Defense should be regarded as preparedness for peace in the widest sense.

The strength and courage of American women—traditional guardians of the home—is one of the Nation's greatest resources. If the women of this country will prepare with courage and determination, we will have the Civil Defense we need to be strong. And each woman who gives her time and effort to Civil Defense will be doing her part to keep the forces of Communism in check, to prepare us against attack, and to help keep the peace."

3. "Challenge for Security and Survival: Manual for Women in Civil Defense"

Even with the escalation of civil rights protests and riots, including one in the Watts district of Los Angeles, and President Lyndon Johnson's tragic decision to send U.S. ground troops to defend South Vietnam, the threat of nuclear war with the Soviet Union, and potentially with China, which had exploded its first atomic bomb the year before, remained very real in 1965. Despite continued apathy among the public and lack of adequate funding by Congress, the government's civil defense program also remained very real. That year, the Ohio Civil Defense department published a pamphlet, titled Challenge for Security and Survival: Manual for Women in Civil Defense, *outlining the important role of women in civil defense and the challenges they faced. The message was not new, however. Civil defense officials had expressed the same message since 1950, shortly after the Soviet Union had entered the atomic age. The following excerpt describes women's challenges.*

Unless you, as a responsible American woman, take action to become informed and trained in the simple procedures you can perform, and for which you should take responsibility, in order to be better prepared to do what you can toward safeguarding your families and homes in any emergency or disaster that may arise, you are gambling with the survival of your family, your neighbors, your community, and your country.

It is important that women act at once to become informed and to inform their families in self-protection measures against the hazards of an enemy attack by air. They need to keep abreast of Civil Defense plans as developed, to interpret such plans to their families, their neighbors, and the people of their communities, and to emphasize the responsibility of individuals to take part in local Civil Defense organizations.

On a realistic basis, should warning of an enemy air attack on our country be released tomorrow, the women of our families would be expected to know immediate procedures to follow—where to seek shelter, what radio

CHALLENGE for SECURITY and SURVIVAL

- Home Protection
- Adult Education
- Medical Self-Help
- Shelter Management
- Radiological Defense

Manual for Women in Civil Defense

State of Ohio
JAMES A. RHODES, Governor

channels to listen to, what first aid equipment and emergency food supplies to have on hand or to take along in case of evacuation, and to care for the family and make it as secure and comfortable as possible wherever it might be.

This is part of the tradition of the American family and of the American woman as far back as early pioneer days. Certainly it would be followed in any time of crisis that may arise for us. Therefore, we urge every woman to volunteer for at least a thorough briefing on Civil Defense plans; better still, to prepare for personal action as a sincere and conscientious member of a local Civil Defense organization.

When you have prepared your home and trained your family, you have more than doubled your chances for survival in a nuclear attack or any disaster that may strike. That is why all women must know and practice Civil Defense principles and procedures. That is why all communities must be organized in Civil Defense.

While Civil Defense is largely "Government in Emergency," to do the job, millions of dedicated, hard-working, well-trained volunteers are needed. Your community needs volunteers now and for years to come. The greater percentage of these volunteers will be women. At least 70 percent of Civil Defense volunteers must be women serving in hundreds of specialized Civil Defense jobs....

When volunteer plans are developed, understood, and practiced—the preservation of peace may someday hinge on the readiness of our cities and civilians to meet all-out attack and come back fighting—it is one of the greatest deterrents to war we can provide as civilians. If we are ready to meet an attack in our homes and in our cities—and our enemy knows it—the attack may never come. Preparedness in our homes, actually, can be one of the greatest deterrents to enemy attack that we can develop.

THIS IS TODAY'S CHALLENGE TO AMERICAN WOMEN!

Part II
Beyond Containment

4. Gender and the FCDA

> There is no complete protection against an atomic bomb attack. But there is a lot we can do to reduce the number of deaths and injuries and to check panic. We must organize ourselves in every city, factory, office, and home. Civil defense is a responsibility which begins with the individual. It begins with you.... It is shared with the city, the State, and the Nation.—*President Harry S Truman*[1]

Much has been written about the federal government's efforts to maintain, and reinforce, traditional gender roles—men as providers, women as nourishers—within its national civil defense program of the 1950s and early 1960s. And the Federal Civil Defense Administration, established in 1951, did clearly consider women as protectors of the family and the home, a view that coincided with the image of the "happy housewife" projected in advertising and the media and reinforced by popular culture. Moreover, civil defense brochures and pamphlets published during this era often emphasized a woman's responsibility in preparing her family for an atomic attack, quieting her family's fear and panic, and ensuring her home was ready in case of disaster.

Yet arguing that the government contained women within their traditional gender roles fails to consider two points: (1) the federal government's belief that women were essential to the nation's defense; and (2) the myriad ways women voluntarily contributed to civil defense programs and activities throughout the nation. Speaking in 1950, for example, William A. Gill, head of the Office of Civil Defense Planning, the precursor to the FCDA, stressed the importance of transcending gender stereotypes. "In considering the role of women in mobilization," Gill said, "the [National Security] Resources Board has in the past usually treated the question of manpower without regard to sex. Recognition has been given to the principle that women can do almost any wartime task for which men are capable, on the assumption that women are given the same amount of training or have equivalent background of experience."[2] The FCDA's 1951 annual report validated women's importance by declaring their role in civil defense could not be overstated. "First," read

Among the precepts of civil defense was a mother's responsibility to protect her children, the nation's future generation. Here, a young admirer looks up to Mr. Civil Defense, a character created by cartoonist Al Capp, which was the symbol of the Federal Civil Defense Association to help promote its mission to keep Americans "Alert Today, Alive Tomorrow" (National Archives).

the report, "there are many jobs in civil defense that can best be handled by women. Second, many areas of target cities, usually residential, must be defended to a great extent by women during daylight hours because the men who live there are away at work"—alluding to the fact that women made up only 30 percent of the workforce.[3]

Women, both homemakers and those in the workforce, not only represented a vital—even indispensable—component of civil defense; they also were proactive in defining how they would contribute. As historian Laura McEnaney points out, women "really took charge and they led the civil defense administration to define women's role. So it really came from the bottom up, not from the top down."[4] Historian Andrew Grossman has added that the FCDA's civil defense mobilization policies were not based on a "paternalistic and stultifying domesticated function for women. On the contrary, in the FCDA's world of nuclear war, women were expected to take on roles that made 'Rosie the Riveter' pale in comparison."[5]

The country's defense mobilization had become critical again by 1950, just five years following V-J Day, marking the end of World War II. As pointed out elsewhere, the Soviet Union had spread its influence across Eastern Europe and entered the atomic age. China had fallen to communism. And allied combat forces—90 percent of which were American troops—battled their communist enemies as well as sub-zero temperatures during Korea's "coldest winter" of 1950–1951. Six months earlier, on June 25, 1950, eight divisions and an armored brigade consisting of some 90,000 soldiers of the North Korean People's Army (NKPA) crossed the 38th parallel and attacked South Korea, a democratic state. The United States, under the auspices of the United Nations, responded, eventually sending 5.7 million troops to Korea over the next three years, with more than 100,000 wounded and 45,000 killed.[6]

President Harry S Truman, responding to the magnitude of the conflict, issued Executive Order 10186 on December 1, 1950, creating the Federal Civil Defense Administration in the Office for Emergency Management of the Executive Office of the President.[7] The FCDA's primary purpose was to prepare Americans for the possibility, even the probability, of an atomic war. Additional functions included the following:

1. To promote the development of and standards for civil-defense measures and equipment.
2. To disseminate civil-defense information and exchange such information with foreign countries.
3. To conduct or arrange for training programs in such areas as organization, operation and techniques of civil defense for the instruction of state and local civil-defense leaders and specialists.

4. To assist and encourage states and foreign countries to form mutual agreements or pacts (with the consent of Congress) to meet emergencies or disasters from enemy attacks that cannot be met or controlled adequately by the local forces.
5. To make appropriate provision for necessary civil-defense communications.[8]

Two weeks later, Truman issued "Proclamation 2914—Proclaiming the Existence of a National Emergency," which represented the culmination of nearly five years of ever-increasing friction between the Soviet Union and the United States. Not only did the Soviet Union's entrance into the atomic age intensify the Cold War; it served to intensify the government's military complex, its anti-communist rhetoric and actions, and its renewed emphasis on home-front civil defense. The proclamation acknowledged that the recent events in Korea and other parts of the world constituted a "grave threat" to peace, and that "world conquest by communist imperialism is the goal of the forces of aggression that have been loosed upon the world." The time had come, said Truman, for "all citizens to make a united effort for the security and well-being of our beloved country and to place its needs foremost in thought and action that the full moral and material strength of the Nation may be readied for the dangers which threaten us."[9]

Then, on January 12, 1951, Truman signed the Civil Defense Act of 1950, formally launching the FCDA, and named Millard Caldwell, former governor of Florida, to head the agency. The act also authorized the federal government to provide matching grants to states for building air raid shelters, to procure and stockpile medical and other disaster supplies, and to establish a national warning system (which later became CONELRAD).[10]

The FCDA had a daunting task. At the beginning of 1951, the Soviet Union represented a major threat that was quite capable, it was believed at the time, to launch an atomic attack with long-range bombers. Its presence in the Korean conflict, albeit behind the scenes, only intensified these fears, as American troops suffered setback after setback during the early months, with the Chinese Communist Forces (CCF) recapturing South Korea's capital, Seoul, in January 1951, just four months after allied troops had liberated it from North Korean forces. The war continued on as a stalemate until President Dwight Eisenhower, who criticized his predecessor's handling of the war, finally pressured the North Koreans to agree to a settlement—a stalemate—which was signed July 27, 1953.[11]

The same year, the FCDA, now in its third year of operation, expanded its mission to encourage individuals, families, and organizations to help protect the nation. The government calculated that more than 17 million were available for civil defense, with the FCDA responding with a call for women to volunteer for a wide array of positions, from block wardens to medical aides to transportation providers. This "privatization"[12] of civil defense placed the responsibility for confronting the nuclear threat, as well as the responsibility to triumph over it, squarely on families, as is evident in the following FCDA scenario.

An atomic attack destroys City X in the scenario. Tens of thousands of people are dead or dying, and more are homeless. Hundreds of fires are aflame, and rubble blocks city streets. Fortunately, civil defense is ready. Overall planning and training has taken place. Plus, emergency supplies and equipment necessary to distribute them are in place. The police and fire services have been expanded with trained auxiliary volunteers. Health, welfare, engineering, and transportation have been built around existing facilities and coordinated to meet the requirements of civil defense. The warden and rescue services, which do not have a civilian counterpart, have recruited volunteers. Continuing on:

> No city, probably no State, could deal adequately with such a disaster by itself. It would need trained men and women, supplies and equipment quite possibly from the farthest corners of the Nation. If we were the object of an all-out, smashing attack that struck a dozen of our cities at once and produced in each of them a disaster of the kind described above, then surely no man, woman, or child in the entire country would remain untouched in some manner by the consequences.
> This is why we need a strong civil defense—a systematic, efficient way of dealing with attack on our home front. A strong civil defense can save fifty percent of the lives that might otherwise be lost.... Civil defense can sustain the people and augment the will to survive against any attack by any aggressor.[13]

Millions of women embraced their responsibilities in civil defense, which they viewed as an opportunity to elevate their importance beyond wife and mother and become, along with men, quasi-soldiers defending the country. By 1957, forty-two states had created Women's Civil Defense Councils.[14] Even by the end of 1951, the FCDA's first year, every state and major city had established civil defense organizations, with total combined appropriations of $183 million. In addition, the FCDA had distributed nearly 1.5 million civil defense guides and technical manuals to more than 1.8 million Americans who had volunteered for civil defense programs. In addition, it published 54 million copies of nine civil defense pamphlets, which had been distributed nationwide as part of its campaign to alert civilians to the atomic threat—a campaign that included ongoing public-service activities and publicity through newspapers, radio, television (where available), and magazines.[15]

FCDA also called for women to join the warden service, which needed some four million volunteers. Mrs. John L. Whitehurst, assistant to the FCDA administrator, accented this point in July 1951 at a meeting of the board of directors of the National Federation of Business and Professional Women's Clubs. "Women will be asked to carry on 80 percent of all civil defense work during an emergency," she told the directors. "All categories of work are available to women if they are trained, except heavy fire-fighting and heavy rescue work." Among the categories were evacuation, mass feeding, warning service, mutual aid, mobile units, nursing, child care, stenographic work, and particularly the warden service.[16]

The reliance on women in the warden service is noteworthy because unlike the air-raid warden of World War II, wardens in the government's civil defense program of the 1950s needed to be specialists in first-aid, firefighting, and rescue techniques. Additionally, wardens needed to be well-informed and trained to know what to do in case of atomic attack—representing the link between the civil defense organization and the American populace. "It is well known," reads the report, "that in many fields there are not sufficient professional and technical people even in peacetime. After the Armed Forces take a sizable part of the doctors, nurses, engineers, communications experts, firemen, policemen, etc., from our present forces, the number remaining for civil defense work must be spread rather thin." The only way to offset this loss in expertise, according to the FCDA, was to train volunteers in civil defense tasks, including self-protection—training supervised by the warden service.[17]

To promote the warden service, the FCDA published an administrative guide in August 1951, followed by the *Warden's Handbook* in December, designed expressly to educate state and local volunteers on a warden's various responsibilities and functions. And plans were under way to publish a technical manual describing the methods and techniques to be used by fire wardens, evacuation wardens, and rescue wardens. In addition to these publications, the agency sponsored civil defense training schools, and several states and cities had organized their own warden training courses.[18]

The FCDA's 1951 booklet, *This Is Civil Defense*, outlined ten major volunteer services: warden service, fire service, police service, health service, welfare service, engineering service, rescue service, transportation service, staff service, and communications service. Although the booklet took a gender-neutral approach concerning who should volunteer, it did point out that women could be very beneficial to the transportation service because many had been drivers for the military and the Red Cross during World War II. The booklet also stressed the importance of women to the warden service, which represented "the source of neighborhood civil defense leadership before, during, and after an attack" whose main responsibility was helping people to safety before an emergency and restoring order after. Wardens had to be well known and respected in the community for their leadership ability. "The warden is the link between the specialized civil defense services and the people," the booklet read. "Outstanding men and women who can assume responsibility are urged to volunteer for the warden service." Then, acknowledging women's more traditional role, the booklet said that women, "and especially housewives, play an important part in the warden service. Most women are at their home posts day and night. Usually they know their own neighborhoods better than men can ever know them. Women should interest themselves in the warden service as a first step in the organization of civil defense for their neighborhoods."[19]

On April 24, 1952, Truman gave a summary report to Congress on the FCDA's first year. Although he highlighted the agency's many accomplishments, he also issued a clarion call for more financial support, which Congress had failed to provide. In fact, although Truman had requested $535 million for the government's civil defense program in the current fiscal year, Congress had appropriated just $75 million. Truman had asked for $600 million in the new fiscal budget, which he felt essential "if we are to get the job done right." The nation needed more volunteers, Truman said, as well as increased stockpiles of medical and other supplies. It needed to promote bomb shelters and develop civil defense training programs, especially in so-called target cities. All of this was needed immediately in order to be completely secure against an enemy attack and "make aggression an unprofitable business."

President Truman complimented Congress on passage of the Civil Defense Act of 1950, but he took note of its inadequate appropriations. Congress needed to provide enough funding to get the civil defense program under way, such as building shelters and stockpiling disaster supplies; and, if it did so now, said the president, the government would need less money for civil defense in the future. Truman attempted to make a case that civil defense had to be strong in order to deter the enemy. A weak civil defense only added "to the strength of a potential enemy's stockpile of atomic bombs."[20]

Truman's plea did not sway Congress, however, even with the ongoing Korean conflict and intensification of Soviet-American relations. Between 1951 and 1953, Truman asked for $1.5 billion for the FCDA, but Congress allocated $153 million, just 10 percent. President Dwight Eisenhower did somewhat better. He asked Congress for a total of $564 million between 1954 and 1958, with Congress approving $296 million. Of the $450 million in operating funds, the FCDA used half to stockpile medical, food, and other emergency supplies, and 45 percent to help local governments purchase civil defense rescue equipment and training materials. The remainder of its budget went for administrative costs.[21]

Despite its meager budget, though, the FCDA held firm to its mission to inform, instruct, and indoctrinate American men, women, and children about the dangers of the atomic bomb and the necessity to be "alert today, alive tomorrow." By 1952, the FCDA was working with some 70 national women's organizations representing millions of women, naming some of their leaders to the agency's National Advisory Committee on Women's Participation, which had 28 members. In addition, 36 national women's organizations participated in the voluntary registration campaign and sent the *Civil Defense Volunteer Registration Guide* to 55,000 women members. Twenty-eight states had volunteer civil defense advisory committees composed of leaders of women's organizations. At least 38 states had women serving in an executive civil defense capacity. The FCDA provided these various organizations with current civil defense information, civil defense programs, speakers, printed materials, and exhibits for national conventions.[22]

The following year, the American Women in Radio and Television (AWRT), a national group of women broadcasters, adopted civil defense as one of its projects. It created special information kits for its members on such topics as home protection, first aid, and firefighting. It also developed a monthly script, titled "Civil Defense News for Women," which 300 members broadcast each month.[23] AWRT represented one of nearly 100 women's organizations working with the FCDA, many of which adopted resolutions in support of civil defense activities for their members. FCDA gave presentations at 18 national women's conventions in 1953, and many more presentations at state and local gatherings. Twenty-four organizations distributed close to 80,000 civil defense materials at various women's activities. FCDA's work with women's organizations also included the following:

- Forty-six top women's officials from regional and state civil defense offices and 29 leaders from women's organizations met for a three-day conference in March.
- Women leaders in government, radio, and press, as well as national women's organizations, attended a training session in June at the Rescue School of the National Civil Defense Training Center in Olney, Maryland.
- In October, the FCDA's Women's Advisory Committee held a two-day conference with 46 leaders of women's organizations, representing some 25 million members, to discuss current civil defense objectives and to present recommendations for future civil defense activities.
- Eighty leaders of women's organizations from eight western states attended the Third Western Women's Training Conference in California to study civil defense and participate in exercises and demonstrations designed to help promote civil defense to their members.[24]

In addition to these events, women's organizations around the country sponsored attendance at civil defense training schools. The National Federation of Business and Professional Women's Clubs financed their members to attend such schools as the one in Oklahoma City, Oklahoma. One woman, after attending the Oklahoma City school, returned home to give a 15-hour civil defense course, with the help of Red Cross and other local instructors, to 670 men and women. Plus, she registered almost 15,000 women willing to take home-protection and community-protection training. In May, the Maine deputy director in charge of welfare and the dean of the University of Maine called for the training in 500 Maine communities of 15,000 women in the state's mass feeding program.[25]

In October 1954, the FCDA's National Women's Advisory Committee met again in Washington, D.C. Attendees included leaders of women's national organizations, regional directors of women's civil defense activities, and women serving in civil defense groups from around the nation. In addition, women representing the British Women's Voluntary Services also attended. The purpose of the meeting was to evaluate the FCDA's overall civil defense program, to review its relationship with women's organizations, and to suggest ways to improve these organizations' contribution to civil defense and national security. According to the FCDA's annual report, the conference was considered a success based on the fact that almost every state and many cities now had women's advisory committees.[26]

During the 1954 Operation Alert, an annual event in which a fictional atomic attack was launched against the entire nation, volunteer women auxiliaries in New Orleans, Louisiana, tabulated, manifested, and prepared shipping documents for the movement of supplies—even though there were no actual supplies. Also that year, women's civil defense groups from various states met to coordinate plans. The AWRT, which had introduced a civil defense project the previous year, voted to continue the project. Special radio and television kits were used, with special emphasis on evacuation. The FCDA reported a significant increase in public interest in civil defense as a result of AWRT's project as evidenced by what it called "unprecedented" requests for civil defense publications mentioned in the broadcasts. After one broadcast, for example, the FCDA received more than 5,000 requests for a booklet mentioned by the announcer. Complementing AWRT's commitment to civil defense was the New England Chapter of American Women in Radio and Television, which passed a resolution offering its services to the public affairs committee in each state.[27]

That year also saw the Federation of Women's Clubs, working with local Parent-Teacher Associations, sponsor a 15-minute skit on home protection. In Maine, the Daughters of the American Revolution, the Auxiliary of the

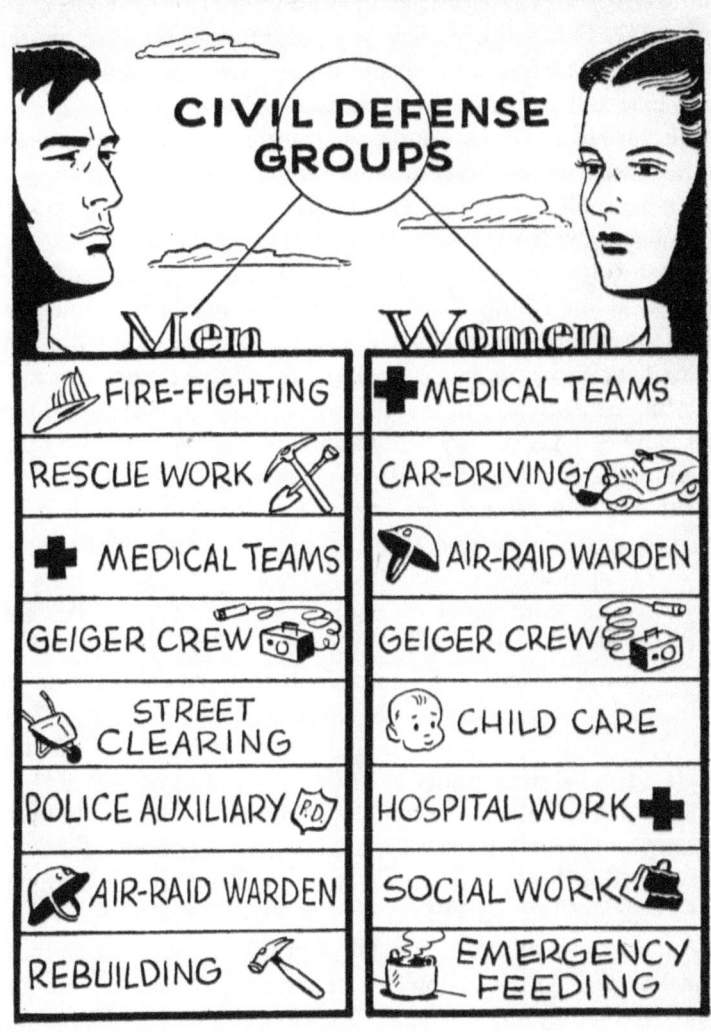

Civil defense jobs for men and women as outlined in *How to Survive an Atomic Bomb* (1950) by Richard Gerstell, a consultant to the Civil Defense Office, National Securities Board.

Veterans of Foreign Wars, and the Retail Grocers Association introduced a campaign encouraging families to maintain a three-day emergency food supply in "grandma's pantry." Throughout the year, the FCDA continued to sponsor and host events for women. In February, members of the American Legion Auxiliary from 40 states, Hawaii, Alaska, and Panama attended a five-day course at the National Civil Defense Training Center. The following month, regional directors of women's activities and their state counterparts met in Washington, D.C., for a three-day orientation and planning session with emphasis on ways to disseminate and discuss two new publications, *Home Protection Exercises* and *Home Nursing Course*.[28]

These types of meetings, events, and training sessions continued in subsequent years with the FCDA continually emphasizing women's importance. Although it did capitalize on women's traditional and acceptable gender roles, the FCDA also provided women with unprecedented opportunities to move beyond these roles and become active participants, and leaders, in civil defense. In 1956, for example, the agency held or sponsored some 100 meetings across the country with women's organizations, including the American Legion Auxiliary, Federation of Women's Clubs, Home Demonstration Clubs, and the Women's Auxiliary to the Veterans of Foreign Wars. Also that year, the American Legion Auxiliary held its annual training course on home protection, and the American Medical Association sponsored a special session on civil defense at its annual convention. Even the Future Homemakers of America discussed civil defense at its meeting that year in Chicago. In addition, the FCDA sponsored a special conference on emergency mass feeding; and the first youth conference on civil defense, with both girls and boys attending, was held in Battle Creek, Michigan.[29]

In 1957, the American Red Cross, continuing its cooperation with the FCDA, updated its *American Red Cross Textbook on First Aid,* reducing the standard course to 10 hours of instruction. That year, more than 500,000 people completed the shorter course, which emphasized life-saving practices deemed critical in an emergency situation. Cooperative courses in emergency mass feeding and care of the sick and injured, initiated by the Red Cross the previous year, were continued, with more than 137,300 people trained in the care of the sick and injured and some 10,000 trained in mass-feeding techniques. Another area of vital importance in the civil defense program was education—an area with a strong female presence as teachers and administrators, as well as mothers. The FCDA strengthened its bonds with the National Education Association that year by jointly publishing *Civil Defense Education Through Elementary and Secondary Schools* and distributing it to NEA members as well as civil defense directors. In other accomplishments, *Civil Defense and Vocational Education,* a publication developed in cooperation with the American Vocational Association, was distributed to civil defense directors and all AVA members; the National School Boards Association agreed to publish a similar booklet for school board members; the American Publishers Institute agreed to help add civil defense information to future textbooks; and the FCDA distributed "Civil Defense Information Sheets" to educators throughout the nation.[30]

In 1958, President Eisenhower consolidated the FCDA and Office of Defense Mobilization into a new agency, the Office of Civil Defense and Mobilization (OCDM), which continued its women's auxiliaries programs and work with the National Women's Advisory Committee. The OCDM's annual report stated that 50,000 women participated in more than 1,400 Home Preparedness Workshops, and that state and local civil defense groups continued to meet together and train for what many considered the inevitability of atomic war.[31]

As a new decade, and a "New Frontier," got under way, the government's civil defense program underwent substantial changes. President John F. Kennedy ended the OCDM in 1961, creating the Office of Civil Defense (OCD) and placing it in the Department of Defense. That same year, Kennedy asked Congress for $207.6 million to identify fallout shelters across the nation and stock them with food, water, first-aid kits, and other essentials. He then asked for an additional $35 billion for the defense budget. And in the shadow of the Berlin crisis, Congress passed the entire amount in just nine days. For fiscal 1962, in fact, Congress appropriated $306 million for civil defense, compared to a total of $532 million allocated over the previous 10 years.[32]

Kennedy believed in the value of fallout shelters, and eventually introduced the community shelter program. Addressing the need for such a program in a "fireside chat," Kennedy drew a parallel between two scenarios. In the first, tens of millions of Americans would die from a major nuclear attack because the nation had no program to avert such a catastrophe. "The only way by which we could protect ourselves from the direct effects of blast, heat, and firestorm," Kennedy said, "is by burying our cities deep underground." The other scenario, and the one Kennedy proposed, was a national community fallout shelter program, which would at least offer protection against radioactive fallout and, therefore, save millions of lives. When completed, in Kennedy's vision, 50 million shelter spaces stocked with adequate disaster supplies would be located in existing public buildings, tunnels, subways, schools, and other structures. He also called upon private industry to build shelters in new factories, offices, apartment buildings, churches, banks, and warehouses. Although Kennedy did not discourage the building of home shelters, which had never caught on to any degree nationwide and came under increasing criticism, community shelters formed the heart of his shelter program.[33]

As the government had maintained throughout the 1950s under Presidents Truman and Eisenhower, civil defense, said Kennedy, must involve all Americans, regardless of gender. "I hope that as many citizens as possible will join local defense activities," he said. "We have a big job to do in civil defense. But it is not the only job we have to do as a nation, and it must be held in proportion to the other responsibilities of the government. I know that we as a people can do it without risking the national frenzy which might persuade our friends that we regard war as inevitable and our enemies that we are engaged in a panic retreat from world responsibility. I know that we can do this job calmly, responsibly, and honorably."[34]

Opposition to the civil defense program by Congress and the public continued to mount after Kennedy's assassination in November 1963. President Lyndon Johnson, however, continued the program under his administration with the OCD reporting success. According to the OCD's 1965 annual report, for example, local governments had created public shelter spaces to protect some 51 million people, and had stockpiled these shelters with enough supplies to sustain more than 31 million people for two weeks. Another survey of available shelter space, however, found more than 151,000 structures capable of accommodating some 130 million people. Commenting on the importance of shelters, President Johnson said, "It is ... clear that without fallout shelter protection for our citizens, all defense weapons lose much of their effectiveness in saving lives. This also appears to be the least expensive way of saving millions of lives, and the one which has clear value even without other systems."[35]

Despite the steady decline of its annual budget after 1961, amounting to just $105 million in 1965, the OCD maintained its operation of three training schools offering courses to both men and women, including Civil Defense Management, Shelter Management Instructor, and Civil Defense Planning and Operations. It expanded its Civil Defense University Extension Program, in which the OCD contracted with land-grant colleges and universities in every state to conduct civil defense orientation and training courses; and it continued to work with a wide range of national organizations, providing guidance, materials, and other aids to develop civil defense preparedness programs that could be incorporated or added to an organization's events and programs.

As the OCD's activities suggest, and as the pamphlet *Challenge for Security and Survival*, published the same year by the Ohio Civil Defense Office, reinforces, civil defense remained a national concern well into the 1960s.[36] During the early Cold War era, the FCDA and its successors, OCDM and OCD, worked diligently to encourage Americans to participate in civil defense, and millions responded. It is also important to note, as historian Kathleen Johnson has suggested, that civil defense actually provided women with a foundation for more activism. "The national campaign to prepare for possible war allowed women to escape the narrow confinements of acceptable female behavior in the name of patriotism," she writes. "Women's prominent involvement in civil defense therefore challenges the notion that the 1950s remained a dormant period for women's activism in the United States."³⁷ This decade was anything but dormant for American women involved in civil defense. Moreover, it could be argued that women's participation in civil defense formed the foundation—and imbued them with confidence—for their activism during the socially and politically turbulent 1960s.

5. "President Truman's Message to Congress on the Federal Civil Defense Administration"

On April 24, 1952, President Harry S Truman submitted a message to Congress summarizing the work of the Federal Civil Defense Administration, which he had created through the Civil Defense Act of 1950. Although he thanked members of Congress for passing the act creating the FCDA, he went on to say that more was needed in the way of funding, suggesting that "every weakness in our civil defense adds to the strength of a potential enemy's stockpile of atomic bombs." Congress listened but failed to give the president the financial support he deemed critical for the civil defense program. Here is the statement from the Public Papers of Harry S Truman, 1945–1954, Harry S. Truman Library & Museum.

To the Congress of the United States:

I am transmitting herewith for the attention of the Congress the first Annual Report of the Federal Civil Defense Administration.

This is a comprehensive report on a most important subject. I hope it will be read and studied by every member of the Congress. Civil defense in this country is now a going concern—this report makes that very clear. A great deal has been accomplished by the Federal Government, the States, and our local communities to get the program under way. Over two million patriotic citizens have volunteered for civil defense work and a considerable number of them have already received specialized training in their jobs.

All that is good. But it is not nearly enough. This report shows the growing strength of our civil defense program. But it also shows the shortcomings—and these shortcomings are a matter of grave national concern. We have the skeleton of a good civil defense organization. Now we need to add millions more volunteers. We need vastly increased stockpiles of medical and other supplies. We need shelters. We need extensive training of our people in areas vulnerable to attack. We need all these things and need them fast before we can begin to feel reasonably secure about the defense of the United States—before we can say we have the kind of civil defense which helps to make aggression an unprofitable business, and thus supports our program for peace.

This calls for a far greater sense of urgency and for a better record of action by every citizen and at every level of Government—Federal, State and local—than has been given to civil defense up to this time.

The Congress itself has a real responsibility here. In January 1951, the Congress passed the basic legislation under which our civil defense program has been set up. It is good legislation. It provides a sound framework for doing the job. But ever since this law was enacted, the program has been starved for lack of adequate appropriations.

Naturally it costs more to get a program like this under way, building shelters, setting up the stockpiles, than it will cost to keep the operation going once this initial work is done. Ultimately, the annual cost of civil defense to the Federal Government should be only a fraction of what is needed now—provided we do not delay in carrying through with the initial buildup.

Last year I requested $535 million to build up our civil defense program in the current fiscal year. Instead the Congress provided only $75 million. This year $600 million has been requested as the Federal Government's share in speeding our civil defense work for the coming fiscal year. I earnestly hope the Congress will provide the full amount this time. It is essential if we are to get the job done right.

I want to be as clear about this as I can. We simply cannot afford a penny-wise-pound-foolish attitude about the cost of adequate civil defense. Everyone in this country—all of us—must face the fact that civil defense is, and will continue to be, just as vital to American security as our armed forces, our defense production and our aid to allies and friends abroad. Civil defense is another indispensable part of our total security program. I really believe that anyone who reflects upon this matter will understand why that is so. Every weakness in civil defense increases an aggressor's temptation to attack us. Every weakness in our civil defense adds to the strength of a potential enemy's stockpile of atomic bombs.

I hope that every member of the Congress will take time to think through the serious implications of this first Annual Report of the Federal Civil Defense Administration. I hope that every member will do his part to speed our progress on this vital [program].

President Harry S Truman

6. "Katherine Howard's Speech on Security at Home"

President Dwight Eisenhower appointed Katherine Howard as head of the women's division of the Federal Civil Defense Administration in 1953. Howard, who later became FCDA's deputy administrator, resigned the following year; however, during her tenure she traveled the country speaking before various state and local organizations. In October 1953, she spoke before the Assembly of Women's Organizations for National Security in Washington, D.C. Her speech, titled "Security at Home," provided the reasoning behind the nation's civil defense program. Although Howard often emphasized women's traditional gender roles in civil defense, this talk offered a more balanced approach to the need for women to participate in civil defense. (Retrieved from Alabama City Defense Assorted Papers, Civil Defense Archives, *https://civildefensearchives.org/ 2015/12/31/alabama-civil-defense-assorted-papers/.)*

Not long ago, at a Washington dinner party, a friendly foreign visitor was reviewing for an American official the things that had impressed him most about America in this age of peril in which we all live.

Our visitor was in accord with every defense measure we were taking, it seemed, except our nationwide civil defense program. Its importance was being blown up out of all proportion to the dangers we face on this side of the Atlantic, he thought. And he could not see why our plain ordinary citizens should be consulted about it, in any case.

"Look at my country," our visitor told his American listener. "We live right next door to the Russians. We would be the first to suffer if trouble came. Yet we are not nearly so concerned about our civilian populations as you are, here in the United States." But, of course, he added reflectively, "Our nation has been overrun many times in its centuries of history. Each time, homes have been destroyed and thousands of families have been separated. Helpless civilians have suffered injuries, starvation, even death. It is all very terrible, you understand, but that is what war does to one's homeland. By now our people are used to it."

Under the circumstances, the American's reply was a very well-considered one, I think. "That's just it," he pointed out politely. "Over here, we don't intend to get used to it."

And, of course, that is the crux of our concern for security here at home. Not only are we determined that we shall not be exposed to recurrent attacks on our homes and families, but we have been uniquely successful in fending off such attacks from beyond our borders for a full seven generations of American life.

Not for some 140 years has our nation been exposed to a foreign invader. That is a proud record, and in its pride lie both our historical strength and our present day weakness. For no one really knows any longer, ourselves included, just how we would react to mass attack on our own cities and towns and villages.

The question is one of skill and experience, of course, rather than one of national character. No one doubts the courage and resourcefulness of the American people in the face of a common danger. But it has been a very long time since the rifle and the plow played an equal part in opening up new lands for our pioneer ancestors. And there are very few Americans left alive who shared the everyday civilian tragedies and terrors of our War Between the States. Ruin and pillage have long passed from common experience in this great country of ours, happily enough, and we—who have had no shortage of military heroes abroad—have had little call of late to display civilian heroism at home.

Meanwhile the success of the American dream inevitably has brought us, a peaceful people, to the commanding heights of world power. Today, the winds of destiny blow strong against our exposed pinnacle, and dark clouds roll toward us from another quarter of the globe.

Our development of the A-bomb and the H-bomb, recently paralleled by the Russians, threatens our fondest hopes for international freedom and peace. And for the first time in almost a century and a half, our own great cities lie open to enemy attack.

All this has happened because a new force for conquest and destruction has come into being. As citizens of a free nation, we find it hard to understand the full implications of this destructive new force as it might be used against us by a few evil men at the head of a powerful military dictatorship.

It is almost as though the world was living again in the days of ancient Greece, when Philip of Macedon first used the phalanx as a sort of thousand-legged tank to crush all opposition. Before the free people of the time could recover from the shock of that new military invention, Alexander the Great had turned it against the Persians and was the conqueror of all he surveyed.

The Persians, it seems, were a little slow in recognizing the phalanx as a threat to their own security. We, too, have had forced upon us with dizzying speed the need for comprehending the threat of the A-bomb and the H-bomb in alien hands.

These rapid new developments are not easy to accept and absorb. We resent the mental effort they entail, and are inclined to complain with Aeschines, the Greek orator of Alexander's day, "What is there in the list of strange and unexpected events that has not occurred in our time? Our lives have transcended the limits of humanity. We are born to serve as a theme of incredible tales to posterity."

Already the people of Hiroshima have served as the theme for such tales, and the people of Nagasaki as well. It is possible—it is very, very possible—that the people of Pittsburgh or Portland or Boston or Baton Rouge may serve as such a theme in the future. That is why we have civil defense. Quite simply, it is the aim of our national civil defense program to insure that the tale shall have a different ending here in the United States of America.

The task is not hopeless. Nothing we are asked to do by way of civil defense is beyond the capability of the average housewife and mother. I am convinced, as a woman in a top policy-making position in our nation's overall defense program, that the incredible tale of our time can have a more fortunate outcome for many more American families than seemed possible at first glance. I believe it will have such an outcome, in fact—but only if all of us learn the measures we must take for our own self-protection and begin putting them into practice immediately—at home, at work, and at school.

The only alternative for most of us, either in an H-bomb attack or in a mass assault with A-bombs and other terror weapons, is to do nothing for our own salvation and take the calculated risk that we, individually, will be out of range if something happens. Our problem is one of individual responsibility. The choice—everyone's choice, if "choice" is the word—is starkly limited. Either we must get ready to protect ourselves, our families and our homes, or we must take a chance on being somewhere else when and if disaster strikes. And since there really aren't many places to hide and still be within reach of our jobs, our homes and our schools, we'd better be ready, just in case.

Now how do we get ready for an attack on whole populations; an attack aimed not at uniformed men in the field, but at unarmed civilians in our great production centers and on our farms?

Obviously, the first step is to study the enemy's attack capabilities. Since 1952, the Federal Civil Defense Administration has assumed, on the basis of intelligence reports and the conclusions of our military leaders, that the Soviet Union has the capability of striking any target in the United States. The main attack presumably would.be delivered by air, and would consist principally of atomic weapons detonated above ground during normal working hours when congestion in our cities is heaviest. Additional weapons might be used simultaneously, such as high explosive and incendiary bombs, biological and chemical weapons, sabotage, and psychological warfare to induce panic.

The initial airborne attack would be pressed home on us by some 400 bombers carrying enough atomic and other bombs to strike all our major metropolitan and industrial areas. This assumption is within the accepted capability of the Soviets, and at least 70 percent of those bombers would get through our military defenses. The objective of the initial attack would be to drive us to our knees with a single knock-out blow. If it failed, subsequent attacks probably would be less heavy.

Bombs used would be at least two and a half times more powerful than the Hiroshima bombs, and warning time for the civilian population might be very short—perhaps as little as 15 minutes. The most likely targets would be the 80 critical target areas listed in a recent and public civil defense news release. Those critical target areas include about two-thirds of our population, most of our skilled workmen, and the bulk of our productive defense plants and equipment.

For each bomb dropped successfully, it is calculated that casualties would total 110,000 killed and wounded. Of the wounded, 73,000 would survive the first day, and 55,000 eventually would recover. On the basis of a perfectly possible distribution pattern of 100 bombs on our principal cities total casualties might amount to 11,000,000 men, women, and children lost in a matter of hours.

To meet a disaster of this magnitude, civil defense must concern itself with readiness in two areas. There must be a readiness in things, such as medical supplies and rescue equipment. And there also must be a readiness of people. Not only must doctors and nurses and first aid people, and auxiliary policemen, and firemen, and utility workers be ready—but plain ordinary people must be ready, too; people whose chances of escaping with a whole skin or, at worst, minor injuries can be doubled if they know what to do when the warning signal sounds.

Getting ready the things we need for civil defense is comparatively simple. It requires mostly money—though Congress has not always shown an awareness of that fact. However, since such things as burn dressings and surgical equipment and fire trucks and bulldozers and spare water pipe need to be stored only once, we are gradually accumulating some semblance of a readiness in things, as represented by our emergency civil defense stockpiles throughout the country.

We do not have adequate supplies of many things still, and in some types of medical supplies we have only enough for a very few days of post-disaster need. But we are making progress in assembling things as fast as Congressional appropriations will allow.

I am happier—very much happier—about our gains in the readiness of people. For us in the Federal Civil Defense Administration, as for your own State and local civil defense directors, the problem of an alert and prepared people divides itself into three parts. We need first of all, of course, a hard core of skilled professionals in the many and complex crafts that enable our modern civilization to function.

If you will ask around a bit in your own communities, I think you will find that your electric light and power people, and your gas man, and your sewage and water plant employees, and many of your local contractors and their crews, have had civil defense briefing. So have your bus and cab drivers, and your communications workers, and your policemen and your firemen. They have taken part in test rehearsals. They know what would be expected of them if an emergency occurred. And they are ready, as always, to do their duty to the last man and woman,

These invaluable specialists had to be enlisted first because civil defense is—first of all—an extension of the regular protective services upon which you depend for the safety of your home. You will find, in fact, that a sizeable proportion of the more than four million civil defense workers on our books today is made up of this same hard core of specialists plus other government and municipal employees and industrial workers, and we can thank our lucky stars for their diligence and sincerity.

The next group of people that concerns us is that blessed band of volunteers upon whom every community must depend for hard unselfish service toward the common good. I include here the block wardens and the rescue crews and the first aid trainees who have given so much of their time and effort to the learning and practicing of their responsibilities.

I include also the doctors and nurses who have sacrificed what little spare time they have to the study of health services and special weapons defense against radioactivity, nerve gas, and other modern threats to our civilian population. In many states and cities this sort of readiness on the part of skilled and willing people has produced gratifying civil defense results.

In others—and perhaps your community is among them—civil defense progress has been agonizingly slow. To be quite frank about it, that may be in part your fault. The Civil Defense Act of 1950 declared it to be the intent of Congress to vest the operating responsibility for civil defense in the states and their political subdivisions; meaning the counties, the cities, and those most irreducible of all political subdivisions—yourselves. According to law, it is up to you and other responsible citizens to prod your local civil defense organizations into action if results are not already evident.

Admittedly, we need a closer gearing of local civil defense performance to national plan. But as the law now reads, that sort of gearing cannot and must not be master-minded from Washington. It is a hometown responsibility. The only appeal from that responsibility is to your own conscience, your own sense of civic duty.

Your Federal Civil Defense Administration can install, and has installed, emergency control centers for operating in close coordination with the states and cities under attack conditions. I was the first woman to view some of these secret installations. They are marvels of efficiency, but they will do your communities no good if you do not have adequate local civil defense organizations, which can respond to official directions in time of attack.

Your Federal Civil Defense Administration can and has set up a nationwide attack warning system capable of alerting all our critical target cities in less than two minutes. I was the first woman to see some of this equipment, too. It is wonderfully fast and effective. But an attack warning relayed to your home cities will do you little good if you cannot hear your local sirens, or if you have too few sirens, or none.

Your Federal Civil Defense Administration can and has set up a countrywide emergency broadcasting system by which all official civil defense information will be transmitted to you by your local broadcasting stations during attack periods, on Channels 640 and 1240 of your standard radios only. This information cannot reach you if you and other people fail to mark your radio dials, or if you have not been told to turn to the proper channels promptly in time of disaster.

Your Federal Civil Defense Administration can make available matching funds to help your community buy the many kinds of emergency supplies and equipment it would require to save your homes and families. That money is of no use to your community if your town council or state legislature refuses to appropriate its half share of the necessary funds.

Your Federal Civil Defense Administration can and does sponsor studies of your local civil defense needs under attack conditions. Those studies are not of much value if the forms on which they depend are left to lie in a desk drawer somewhere. Your local situation must be studied on the spot, and studied carefully, so that you know what emergency resources are lacking in your community and what you need to do to improve them.

Your Federal Civil Defense Administration can and does produce public education booklets, home shelter manuals, family action exercises, educational films, radio scripts and television shows. But even they will be wasted if too few people read, watch or listen—and learn how to protect themselves.

And so you see that any report on the progress of civil defense on the security of your homes—always must come back to what you are doing, personally and organization-wise, in your own communities.

I think you will find, if you live in a critical target area, that much has been done and is being done. But I know you will find, too, that a great deal remains to be done toward adequate local civil defense organization, not by the Federal Government, but by the people who live in the area.

Your home cities need your help and that of your members, and they need it badly. The attack assumptions I mentioned earlier were based on A-bombs two and a half times as powerful as the Hiroshima type. The H-bomb, which now confronts us, is many, many times more powerful.

In other words, the attack threat mounts with each passing hour and with every new development in weapons. We can easily seem to make progress in civil defense, yet still lose ground. And, in a sense, that is pretty much what is happening in many of your communities right now.

Thus everything in civil defense boils down, in the end, to the readiness of the individual and the family to withstand attack. In case of a mass assault upon your community, there would be only two kinds of people left afterward—those who needed help, and those who could help.

The difference between the two might very well lie in the amount of civil defense information, training, organization and practice your community has had. And those are things that cannot be imposed upon your home neighborhoods from without. They must spring from within; from sober, adult realization of the security problems we face, and from intellectual and moral conviction that we must do something about those problems—personally and collectively.

Such conviction is not uncommon in this land of the free. It comes even more easily to women, I think, than to men—at least when community welfare is at stake. Our churches are built on conviction; and so are our schools and hospitals and charities. If these great institutions are worthy of preservation—and our hearts tell us that they are—then our homes must be vastly more worthy still, and our country most worthy of all.

Maxwell Anderson, in his great play called "Valley Forge," had General Washington say to his despairing officers, "This Liberty will seem an easy thing, when no one any longer needs to die for it."

Yet how much harder it is for us sometimes to live for the freedoms we cherish. Civil defense is a way to live calmly and courageously in a troubled world, and to keep on living. It is a way to work—and work hard—for the things we Americans believe in, and to win acceptance for those beliefs. But it is not an easy way, because there is no easy way to security. That is why our local civil defense organizations must have the active participation and support of women everywhere.

I know they will get that support in increasing measure from the organizations represented in this room. Indeed, I know many of you are giving civil defense your full support right now. For the interest and leadership you are furnishing to a great cause, your country is sincerely grateful. I am sure your communities will be equally grateful in days to come. And, finally, as Deputy Administrator of the Federal Civil Defense program, I am grateful, too, for your help and counsel.

In my official capacity, I have sat in on the secret meetings of our defense planners in the Pentagon, with other civil defense officials. After one such meeting, I turned to the Book of Proverbs, where so many sound precepts have been distilled from the long human struggle to bring serenity and order to a troubled world. There I found the words of comfort and advice that seemed best suited to our problems today. "Wisdom is the principal thing," Solomon set down for us many centuries ago, "therefore get wisdom, and with all thy getting get understanding."

We are seeking to follow that precept today in our civil defense planning. All planners try to be wise, of course, but I think most of us realize that mere human wisdom is not enough in this air-atomic age in which we live. We need understanding, too; very great understanding on the part of our people and their leaders at every level of government. And I think we are beginning to get it.

Indeed, I am confident that our American understanding of the new age of peril will be added to increasingly, and in greater measure, by the ablest voices in our land. In the future, we should all be able not only to plan against disaster, but to build to the plan, strong in the informed faith and confident courage of our neighbors and families and friends.

And that, I think, is Civil Defense at its best.

Thank you.

Part III
Organized Support

7. MEMBERS IN GOOD STANDING

> Women's organizations throughout the nation number many thousands. They have experience, committees, programs, and facilities. This vast reservoir of organized human power and competence, existing in every community, must be enlisted to provide leadership in planning, organizing, recruiting, and training for this civil defense task.—*Texans on the Alert for Civil Defense and Disaster Relief*[1]

From its very beginning, the FCDA acknowledged that "the importance of women in civil defense can scarcely be overstated," even though, admittedly, the government viewed women's contribution to civil defense largely within the context of their so-called traditional skill set as wife, mother, and homemaker.[2] What's significant, however, is that the FCDA not only acknowledged women's importance; it also moved quickly to enlist women's support, offering them new opportunities for leadership roles in the nation's homefront defense. And it did so in what it deemed the most effective way: by working closely with national, state, and local women's organizations, which, in turn, promoted civil defense to their millions of members. The Ohio Civil Defense Department, for example, published a pamphlet emphasizing that the mobilization of these organizations would help to attract the 17 million volunteers considered essential for the nation's civil defense. It then continued:

> Women's organizations also can contribute to the recruitment of Civil Defense volunteers by asking their members to register as ready and willing to participate. The jobs open to women in Civil Defense cover practically every phase of operation.... Before women will volunteer for these jobs, however, they must appreciate the need for Civil Defense and understand how it works. Women's organizations can help by familiarizing their members with the various aspects of Civil Defense. The organization members, once they become informed, can use their knowledge to interest friends and neighbors who may not be club members. This knowledge will also help them to know which Civil Defense service they might qualify for with training.[3]

Members of women's organizations were encouraged to work for the appointment of a civil defense chairman and committee. Once the organization formed a civil defense committee, the pamphlet recommended it adopt a resolution pledging the organization's active cooperation with the local civil defense office; register committee members as volunteers; provide updates on civil defense to the organization's members; and participate in local civil defense meetings and activities. In addition, the committee should promote civil defense activities through forums, speeches, skits, the press, radio, television, motion pictures, direct mail, exhibits and individual contacts. Perhaps most important, the committee needed to establish a training program for the organization in cooperation with the local civil defense office.[4]

The FCDA, in fact, initiated efforts to involve women's organizations in civil defense shortly after beginning its operations in 1951. Its first step was to provide these organizations with civil defense information and materials; offer counseling on ways to get involved in civil defense activities; make civil defense exhibits available; and provide speakers for meetings and conventions. In addition, the FCDA named assistant regional directors for women's affairs as a way to attract women's groups at the regional and local levels.

The following year, the FCDA made another proactive move by creating the National Advisory Committee on Women's Participation, which assumed the primary responsibility of working directly with the leaders of women's organizations and encouraging women to volunteer for civil defense services, including transportation, communications, nursing, fire, police, and warden services. The committee's success is evident by the fact that 36 national women's organizations participated in the 1952 FCDA voluntary registration campaign, with numerous states naming women to serve in civil defense executive positions and local civil defense organizations adding women to their staffs and committees.[5] Many states also formed women's advisory committees, with some forming African American women's committees.[6] As part of the campaign, the FCDA had distributed its *Civil Defense Volunteer Registration Guide* to 55,000 women. *Women in Civil Defense*, a 24-page booklet published that year, urged women's organizations to become involved in civil defense, as well. It pointed out that most women's organizations have national, state, or local programs and publications, which should be used so "millions of American women can learn something about self-protection for themselves and their families and about civil defense generally." The booklet also emphasized that women's opportunities covered all phases of civil defense, but the first step was making them appreciate and understand the concept of civil defense. It then recommended specific actions for members of women's organizations to take:

1. Adopt a resolution pledging the organization's active cooperation with the local civil defense office.

2. Contact local civil defense authorities and offer the organization's support and cooperation.
3. Register all members as potential civil defense volunteers, in cooperation with local civil defense officials.
4. Promote civil defense activities through forums, speeches, the press, radio, television, motion pictures, direct mail, exhibits, and individual contacts. These activities should be coordinated with the operations of the local civil defense office.
5. Schedule at least five minutes at every organization meeting in which to spotlight official civil defense activities.
6. Report progress regularly to the organization's members.
7. Set up a training program in cooperation with the local civil defense office.
8. Publicize all club civil defense activities.
9. Launch your civil defense participation program at a public gathering attended by representatives of the local civil defense office.[7]

With these objectives in mind, the National Women's Advisory Committee, the new name of the National Advisory Committee on Women's Participation, held its first conference in 1953 at FCDA headquarters and the National Defense Training Center in Olney, Maryland. For its second annual convention, held in October 1954 in Battle Creek, Michigan, the FCDA's new home, the committee invited President Dwight Eisenhower to give the opening presentation. Expressing his views toward women in civil defense, he told attendees that women in the atomic age had nearly the same duties in war as any man, continuing:

> [T]he strength of the United States is represented ... first of all in the spirit that you women show, not only in your comprehension of what this thing is about, and what you must do, but your readiness to do it—another attribute of free nations—volunteering to do these things. That in itself makes us stronger. I assure you, if war ever comes, the value of your work will be so overwhelming, so incalculable, that it couldn't possibly be gauged in any mere words or by any comparison. It could well mean the difference between victory—or put it this way: between defeat and averting defeat. Because I really doubt whether, in modern times, in global war, there is any victory.[8]

Eisenhower delivered a similar message earlier that year to a group of 173 mayors and city managers. In rather blunt language, the president told the group, "The city has moved from a position of support in the rear. It has moved out in a very distinct way into the front line."[9] Despite Eisenhower's rhetoric, however, the national civil defense program had an ongoing struggle in obtaining funding from Congress and an even bigger battle overcoming public apathy toward national civil defense.

Ironically, though, this battle against apathy actually enhanced women's importance because many held the belief that women possessed the ability to persuade others to become more appreciative of civil defense objectives. The first step, therefore, was to convince women to become involved in their local community. The FCDA's strategy was to connect protecting the nation to protecting the community and, ultimately, to protecting the family. Reflecting this strategy was Mrs. Walter Ewing, director of Weber County (Utah) Women in Civil Defense, who explained at a 1952 meeting in Ogden, Utah: "The whole idea of civil defense is to help you protect yourself and your family to make the best use of your special skills in an emergency as a part of the local civil defense program. Our aim is 100 per cent registration and training in civil defense."[10]

The important point here is not that women's contribution to civil defense was confined to traditional gender roles; rather, the important point is the women seized their opportunity to expand these roles, contribute significantly to the civil defense program, and, in the process, gain recognition and the respect of their families, their peers, their communities, their organizations, and the nation.

One of the early success stories in terms of women's contribution to civil defense occurred in 1952 when 70 national women's organizations—including the American Association of University Women, National Council of Negro Women, Congress of Women's Auxiliaries of the CIO, National Home Demonstration Council, American Home Economics Association, and National Federation of Business and Professional Women's Clubs, to name a few—worked with the FCDA to promote its "Pledge for Home Defense" campaign. The campaign, featured in the leaflet, *What You Can Do Now*, had a twofold goal: mass public education in self-protection and family survival; and mass registration for future enrollment, training, and duty with active civil defense services. The FCDA's public information efforts for the campaign centered on a 10-point family civil defense program, beginning with the distribution of information kits and materials to civil defense officials throughout the nation. The agency also published a series of posters illustrating the need for and benefits from civil defense; distributed the film, *Survival Under Atomic Attack*, and a recruiting trailer to movie theaters; and gave civil defense slides to 86 television stations to broadcast to the public.[11]

With the help of more than 100 national and state organizations, including women's organizations, the campaign resulted in several governors and hundreds of mayors issuing home defense proclamations, plus extensive media coverage in newspapers as well as on radio and television stations. The FCDA also reported the distribution of more than three million pamphlets and booklets as a result of the campaign. To focus public attention on civil defense as a "copartner" with the Armed Services in the nation's defense, the FCDA created "Operation Main Street," a program promoting civil defense groups to join the military in observing Armistice Day. According to the FCDA's 1952 annual report, Operation Main Street met with substantial success throughout the nation and served as a tribute by civil defense workers to "the men and women in the armed services, as well as emphasizing the concept that civilian and military preparedness must move forward together."[12]

In 1953, the FCDA introduced the Home Defense Action Program, which focused on home-protection exercises designed to give "each citizen the opportunity to participate directly in civil defense" and to encourage "every citizen to cooperate with the neighborhood civil defense groups."[13] As part of the program, the FCDA provided a "Home Preparedness Workshop Kit" with information and educational materials for use by supporting organizations and clubs. The materials included sample press releases, radio and television spot announcements and scripts, speeches, promotional ideas, lesson plans for wardens, and a booklet on self-protection home exercises. The booklet, titled *Home Protection Exercises*, covered seven family-action exercises: Preparing Your Shelter; What to Do When the Alert Sounds; Home Fire Protection; Home Fire Fighting; Emergency Action to Save Lives; What to Do If Someone Is Trapped; and Safe Food and Water in Emergencies.[14]

While many women's organizations around the country adopted the Home Protection Program as one of its activities, the National Home Demonstration Council, representing women primarily in rural areas, actively promoted the program as making the home self-sufficient during an emergency. The council, founded in 1936, joined with other rural women's clubs during the 1930s to offer practical demonstrations in agricultural techniques and home economics; however, home demonstrations actually began more than 20 years earlier with passage of the Smith-Lever Act of 1914, which promoted cooperative extension services connected to the nation's land-grant universities. Moreover, the act, passed at the onset of World War I, allowed for expansion of home demonstration clubs from rural areas to cities as a means to educate urban women and their families. Florence Ward, agriculturist for the Office of Cooperative Extension Work, wrote in 1924,

> The enormous consumption of food in cities, the crowded conditions, and the mixed population made the enforcement of war regulations dependent on education. An effort was made to place an agent where possible in cities that had a population of more than 40,000. Salaries were paid by the Federal Government from emergency funds and by such local organizations as were interested. Agents cooperated with existing organizations and created new ones when necessary for the efficiency of the work. At the end of the fiscal year 1918 there were 117 home demonstration agents in 96 cities in 25 states. Through the help of volunteer leaders trained by city agents, thousands of organized groups were thus reached.[15]

By the 1950s, Home Demonstration Clubs, sponsored by both land-grant universities and the United States Department of Agriculture, were active in states across the nation and in both urban and rural areas. Although their main purpose was to teach homemaking practices and to serve as a clearing house for women to express and share their common interests and problems, the clubs were among the first organizations to work with the federal government in disseminating civil defense information through publications and meetings. Some 2,500 women attending the annual meeting of the National Home Demonstration Club in August 1951, for example, heard Mrs. John Whitehurst, the FCDA's assistant director, speak on the importance of civil defense, which complemented the meeting's theme, "Democracy: The Torch We Hold."[16] The Home Demonstration Club of Montgomery County (Alabama) made civil defense one of its top priorities in 1952. Clubs in Colorado and South Dakota developed plans for accepting evacuees in case of an atomic attack, which encompassed studying mass feeding techniques, cooking without electricity or gas, and purifying water. In Deaf Smith County, Texas, Mrs. Paul Rudd of the Westway Home Demonstration Club was named chair of the county's 12 civil defense councils, which, in turn, each named a civil defense chair. An important part of their civil defense activities was obtaining certification in Red Cross home nursing, something accomplished by 53 women and 4H girls.[17]

A 1953 meeting of the home demonstration council in Paris, Texas, focused on ways to enhance their commitment to civil defense. As one step, the council agreed to distribute "billfold cards" to encourage families to register for civil defense. The card contained such information as name, address, physician's name and address, blood type, and any medical condition.[18] A 1953 newsletter, published by the North Carolina Federation of Home Demonstration Clubs, urged readers to study the recommendations for civil defense by the National Home Demonstration Council. These recommendations included continuing to urge women to "assume their responsibilities as informed and active citizens," to encourage states to train leaders in citizenship, and for home demonstration clubs around the nation to work with existing civil defense organizations. Katherine Howard, FCDA deputy administrator, was also quoted as saying, "We must learn to discriminate between rumored danger and real danger. There are too many signs calling for patriotic action to permit the luxury of lethargy or inertia." The newsletter then listed Howard's 10 steps that women, and all Americans, should take:

1. Learn more about the potential of modern warfare.
2. Teach family members how to protect themselves.
3. Keep a three-day supply of food on hand at all times.

4. Have a first-aid kit.
5. Prepare a home shelter or shelter area.
6. Get rid of all trash.
7. Take first-aid courses.
8. Take home nursing courses.
9. Watch for signs of biological warfare.
10. Promote the importance of civil defense to club members.[19]

Howard's recommendations had been heard before, and women throughout the nation had been taking them since the national civil defense program got under way in 1951. Writing in the September 1951 issue of the *Journal of Home Economics*, Arthur Adams, president of the American Council on Education, set the tone for women's commitment to their communities and to civil defense. "In the critical years of what I choose to call the Decade of Decision," Adams wrote, "women, especially those in home economics work, have a highly important role to play, for in these times, when every citizen must have responsibilities in the cause of freedom, the personal and professional resources of each of us must be available for that cause."[20]

Women's involvement in civil defense is readily apparent when examining newspaper articles from around the country. Hundreds of gatherings, if not thousands, took place during the 1950s and into the 1960s, from small towns and rural areas, to suburbs and major cities. These meetings and conventions included representatives of local, state, and national women's organizations, with speakers often from the FCDA or state civil defense department. Although the number of women actively participating in civil defense is difficult to quantify, newspaper coverage from this era confirms beyond a doubt that many women not only were interested in civil defense; they also became active participants in civil defense at all levels and in all capacities.

At its 1950 annual meeting, before the FCDA even began, the National Council of Jewish Women adopted plans to encourage its 93,000 members to participate in civil defense.[21] In January 1951, the first month of operation for the FCDA, the Philadelphia Association of Hospital Auxiliaries, representing hospital auxiliaries in Philadelphia and surrounding counties, pledged its support to the local civil defense organization. Plans were made to name a civil defense chairman for the association, who, in turn, would work with the chairmen from the various auxiliaries.[22] Also in January, Major General Leo Kreber, state director of civil defense in Ohio, delivered a presentation to an audience of homemakers, women teachers, businesswomen, and professional women in Washington Court House, Ohio. Titled "The Role of Women in Civil Defense," Kreber's presentation played off women's role as homemaker, suggesting that the state's forthcoming bulletin would be "the recipe book for women in civil defense."[23] But when women's organizations subsequently met, the message was not hindered by stereotypes. The following month across the state in Pittsburgh, for example, a committee representing 26 area women's organizations agreed to conduct training classes for women volunteering as civil defense speakers, then to schedule them for meetings and events throughout Allegheny County. The committee's goal was to have 100 trained women speakers addressing civil defense topics to a thousand audiences over a four-month period.[24] Also in February, the Woman's Division of the County Civil Defense program was formed in West Palm Beach, Florida, with the first duty of the newly named chairman to register women volunteers for civil defense work.[25]

That April in Tustin, California, the Orange County Nurses Association pledged its support for civil defense, with both registered nurses and inactive nurses organizing for civil defense assignments through the association's Committee on Nursing Resources to Meet Civil and Military Needs. Mildred Croddy, association president, addressed the need to overcome apathy, issuing a statement that read, "The awareness and energy of the nursing profession in perfecting their program to meet civil defense needs should be an inspiration to the general public, which in some communities is displaying apathy which could bring tragic results."[26] At a December 1951 meeting in Phoenix, Arizona, Ressie Croxdale, assistant regional director of the FCDA, spoke on the importance of women first learning self-protection in the home; and, once this was accomplished, volunteering for community civil defense services, such as wardens, communications, and transportation. "Civil defense provides the greatest opportunity yet for the people of this country to unite for their own protection and welfare in any emergency," Croxdale told the women in attendance.[27]

Dorothy Mann, coordinator of women's activities for the Michigan Office of Civil Defense, delivered a similar message at a May 1952 meeting in Detroit. "The whole idea of civil defense is to help you protect yourself and your family if trouble comes," she told women members of the Fruit Belt Auxiliary 1137. "Ask yourself this question: Are you the kind of a person who can think and act clearly when the pressure is on? If so, there's a job for you in civil defense. Whatever talents or experiences you have—put them to use." Mann then outlined the various areas where women were needed, including welfare services, emergency lodging, clothing and child care, emergency medical services, transportation, police services, and wardens.[28] The 300 attendees at the annual convention of the Utah Federation of Women's Clubs in Salt Lake City listened to several speakers address the importance of civil defense involvement. Mrs. W. C. Ewing, who had recently attended a civil defense training school, told the women, who represented 6,000 members, that civil defense "is a bold, challenging program" that needed 15 million volunteers for training. She continued by connecting civil defense to the home—a message often heard at these types of meetings: "Civil defense can make staying in your own city safer than trying to get out of it in case of emergency. Self-defense, that's what civil defense is. It calls for all of us to protect ourselves, our families, and our homes." Apparently, Ewing's comments had some impact because later that year, the state formed the Utah Council of Women in Civil Defense.[29]

The same month, 32 women chairmen representing 17 local women's organizations completed a three-day training course on basic civil defense procedures in Tucson, Arizona. As a result of the training, a more advanced Red Cross-sponsored first-aid course was introduced for the chairmen, who then established first-aid classes for their respective organizations. In addition, the women chairmen agreed to encourage the local Parent-Teachers Association to promote civil defense in public schools and to name a civil defense chairman for every PTA branch. The Tucson civil defense chairman also asked the women to encourage volunteers in community civil defense programs.[30]

Representatives of 24 women's organizations in Lincoln, Nebraska, met in July 1952 to begin the process of forming a statewide civil defense organization. Governor Val Peterson, who would become FCDA in 1953, named the committee, whose immediate plan was to have members of the various women's organizations register for specific civil defense duties. Attendees at the meeting also were encouraged to register for home nursing courses being offered by the University of Nebraska.[31] In Louisiana the same year, Mrs. Marion Porch, director of women's activities for the Louisiana Office of Civil Defense, reported that "hundreds" of women were both willing and qualified for civil defense positions, and that the state office would support the appointment of women deputy directors at the local level.[32] Pennsylvania also became active in recruiting women by conducting the first "All-Women" school for civil defense in October 1952. The two-day course, held at the Civil Defense Training Center at Ogontz, just north of Philadelphia, trained women to be warden instructors, able to return to their respective communities and organizations to teach other women.[33]

A shift in the nation's defense strategy occurred in June 1953, when President Eisenhower announced his New Look defense strategy, which called for more reliance on the nation's nuclear arsenal for deterrence rather than military personnel. As part of this new strategy, he announced $2.5 billion in cuts in the defense budget, which also affected what paltry funding was allocated toward civil defense, and immediately came under attack from members of Congress and others. Among his critics was former President Harry Truman, who said, "Increasing the risk of World War III means increasing the risk of atom bombs on our own home."[34] Also that month, Gordon Dean resigned as head of the Atomic Energy Commission. Adding his final analysis of the world situation, Dean commented, "I think it vital that the policymakers of our government, including our diplomats, congressmen, and heads of agencies, as well as every citizen, should have as clear a picture as possible of our defense capability vis-à-vis the Russians. We have said many times that we are ahead of the Russians, but that is not enough. It does us no good to reach the point where we would be able to wipe out an enemy 20 times over if he reaches the point where he can wipe us out just once."[35]

Despite the president's New Look strategy, or because of it, many saw an increased need for home-front civil defense. The same month as Eisenhower's announcement, the Southern California Women's Conference on Civil Defense, sponsored by the Women's Civil Defense Advisory Committee, was held at Pepperdine University in Los Angeles. Attendees listened as Major General W. M. Robertson, Ret., director of the state's civil defense department, called for 1.5 million volunteers and 5,000 trained personnel for civil defense. The conference also featured the standard array of demonstrations conducted at most civil defense events: fire prevention and control methods, radiological safety programs, plans for the Ground Observer Corps, first aid, home nursing, food preservation, and rescue.[36]

The Georgia Civil Defense Department took the initiative to enlist the aid of women's organizations by publishing *Georgia Women in Civil Defense* in 1954. The pamphlet credited these organizations with commanding "the skills and energies of thousands of women." Moreover, women's organizations possessed a "vast reservoir of power and organizational know-how" in their committees, facilities, and experience that could be applied in organizing and maintaining a civil defense program. Many also published newsletters and other publications, which served as an excellent means of disseminating civil defense information. "Through these organizations," read the pamphlet, "millions of women can learn about self-protection for themselves and their families and about Civil Defense generally." The pamphlet went on to urge women's organizations to set up classes in home protection, and to request representatives from the police and fire departments, health department, and Red Cross to make presentations to their members.

Other suggestions included pledging 100 percent cooperation with state or local civil defense programs, and promoting this cooperation through newspapers, radio, and television. Each organization should establish an educational and registration program; appoint a civil defense chair and a committee to assist her; and integrate civil defense into all of the organization's departments, such as public affairs, welfare, education, and citizenship. In addition, women's groups were encouraged to obtain civil defense literature, and work with area libraries to set up a "Civil Defense Corner," where the public could access these materials easily. In addition, they should create a speakers bureau to inform the community about civil defense, as well as sponsor discussion programs and forums on civil defense. They should promote these activities through the press, individual contact, radio, television, motion pictures and exhibits. Every meeting should have at least five minutes dedicated to updates on civil defense, with regular program reports on member activities and civil defense accomplishments by the parent organization.[37]

In October of that year, the Long Island Federation of Women's Clubs held an all-day conference on civil defense. The speakers were Ruth Roper, Nassau County coordinator of the Civil Defense Welfare Service; Mrs. Norman Hosler, Nassau Red Cross director of nutrition, who spoke on mass feeding; Mrs. James Thornton, who addressed the warden service; and Mrs. Walter Pfizenmayer, medical administrative officer of the Nassau civil defense organization, who talked about women's role in the medical service.[38] In Gettysburg, Pennsylvania, William Weaver, the county director of civil defense, addressed a March 1955 meeting of farm women representing the Adams County Farmers Association. Weaver urged the women to take part in welfare services and the Ground Observer Corps, commenting, "There is a great part to be played in welfare work, in the mass care centers that will be established in churches and schools throughout the country in the event of an emergency. There is also a tremendous need for volunteers to man the spotter posts."[39]

Members of the Pleasant Grove (Utah) Women's Civil Defense organization participated in the Regional Civil Defense Conference, held in Salt Lake City, Utah, in January 1955, which included representatives from seven states. Director of the town's civil defense group joined a panel discussion titled "The Women in Civil Defense," speaking on women as wardens. The Pleasant Grove contingent then performed a skit of their actual experiences in carrying out the organization's educational program—specifically, the methods used to arouse interest in civil defense. The skit also featured the town's civil defense wardens demonstrating how they had gone into homes and showed families procedures for home protection.[40] The following month, Mrs. Victor Bird, Utah County director of women's civil defense activities, outlined the necessary steps to prepare homes and families for an atomic attack. Echoing the statements heard at these types of meetings, Bird emphasized the importance of designating an area of the home as an air-raid shelter, preparing an emergency first-aid kit, having a three-day food supply on hand, and taking a Red Cross first-aid or home nursing course.[41] Also in February, Jean Wood Fuller, director of women's activities for the FCDA, told women attendees at a regional women's conference in Denton, Texas, that Americans "must increase our awareness of civil defense planning." Fuller emphasized the same primary objectives for women as most speakers during this period: to take home nursing courses and to learn first-aid. In addition, she called for more training opportunities for women and for public schools to expand their civil defense training for students. The conference included women representatives from Texas, Louisiana, Oklahoma, Arkansas, and New Mexico. Among the associations in attendance were the Texas Federation of Women's Clubs, the Parent-Teachers Association, the Quota Club, and several home demonstration clubs.[42]

Representatives of some 95 women's organizations gathered in Anderson, Indiana, in January 1958 to form—and to become active participants in—the Madison County Women's Civil Defense Council. According to the newspaper account, "In reaching nearly 100 women, the Women's Civil Defense Council, in reality, reaches nearly 100 women's organizations and, by indirection, literally thousands of Madison County homes."[43] The Civil Defense Women's Advisory Council held its first meeting in November 1958 at the Reno, Nevada, Filter Center, part of the Ground Observer Corps' network. The meeting's purpose was to update attendees on the latest civil defense information. Among the organizations represented were the American Legion Auxiliary, Veterans of Foreign Wars Auxiliary, Parent-Teachers Association, National Federation of Business and Professional Women's Clubs, American Red Cross, and Nevada Federation of Women's Clubs. In addition, civil defense coordinators from various Nevada counties attended. The ongoing struggle to overcome the public's apathy was again a topic, as Mrs. Helmer Hancock, council president, stressed the importance for those in attendance to continue to fight against apathy, confusion, disinterest, and ignorance.[44] Across the country in East Liverpool, Ohio, members of the local Women's Civil Defense Council were meeting the same month to hear from members who had completed two courses in home preparedness. Also on the agenda was a report on civil defense programs recently introduced in the schools, which planned to conduct "duck and cover" drills the following month in observation of Civil Defense Day, and the announcement that the Parent-Teachers Association had purchased identification "dog" tags to be given to school-age children.[45]

The FCDA's Katherine Howard, the highlight of the "Stepping Stones to Survival" series sponsored by Utah Civil Defense, told a receptive audience in June 1956 that just as the nation was adjusting to the Atomic Age, it "entered the Thermo-Nuclear or Hydrogen Age." After pointing out that both the United States and the Soviet Union had long-range bombers that traveled at the speed of sound, she continued, "We may not like to think of this, but we must in order to survive. The more we are prepared in civil defense, the more the possibility of war shrinks." Howard's presentation was part of Leadership

Week held in Provo, Utah. Attendees of the event included state and county civil defense officials, Provo city officials and mayors from the surrounding area, business leaders, and members of various civic organizations. Two civil defenses classes were held each day during the week, with an emphasis on home and family protection. Also on the agenda were demonstrations of Red Cross first-aid procedures and preparations for home emergencies, as well as a review of civil defense progress in the state, a discussion of evacuation plans, the showing of civil defense films, and a look at the work of the Ground Observer Corps.[46] At a meeting in March 1958, the board of the Salina (Kansas) County Women's Civil Defense Council discussed evacuation plans for the local schools and youth involvement in civil defense. More pressing, however, was soliciting persons to open their homes to women attending the upcoming civil defense staff training program.[47]

Home preparedness remained the primary topic at such meetings, as in one held in January 1960 in Klamath Falls, Oregon. Women in attendance heard the county director of civil defense say, "Home preparedness is the very basis of civil defense and the key to our survival is public acceptance of the role civilians must play."[48] The launch of a home preparedness award program was announced at a conference for women and rural residents held the same month in Sioux Falls, South Dakota. The award was designed to recognize more than 100 women who had completed the home preparedness workshop. Addressing the conference, Audrey Smith, FCDA's regional director of women's civil defense, expressed the same message often heard at such gatherings: "Women are the key to civil defense. The national plan for civil defense and defense mobilization points out the responsibility of the individual for caring and planning for their own survival."[49]

In July 1961, the Mesa City, Arizona, council chamber was "filled to capacity," according to the newspaper report, with women interested in learning more about civil defense home preparedness and first aid. There were enough women interested to have eight first-aid classes. The meeting, sponsored by the Women's Volunteer Civil Defense Co-ordinating Council, also covered the city's four-year-old civil defense plan and upcoming program to teach home preparedness.[50] On a much larger scale, the OCDM reported that some 60 million of the nation's estimated 64 million women were represented by attendees at its last conference held in 1961.[51]

Women in Orick, California, formed a civil defense council in April 1962 to be a liaison group between civil defense officials and area women's organizations. The council's main mission was to distribute "survival information and plans" and to coordinate local civil defense plans and programs.[52] More than 400 women attended the California Women's Civil Defense Conference in October 1962. The theme of the three-day conference, which was held in Anaheim, was "Disaster Preparedness Is Everyone's Job," with speakers addressing a wide range of civil defense topics. Sessions covered California's Emergency Medical and Health Program; NORAD (North American Air Defense); school civil defense programs; the national shelter program; and civil defense in the Soviet Union.[53]

As the 1960s unfolded, with new concerns about civil rights, the war in Vietnam, and the coming-of-age Baby Boom generation, the nation's civil defense against the nuclear threat remained a concern. At the fifth annual Women's Civil Defense Day Conference at the University of Delaware, held in April 1965, Lieutenant Colonel J. Arnold Sullivan, director of Delaware's civil defense department, told the women in attendance, "The burden of family survival rests with you." Lois Sprigg Hazell of Chevy Chase, Maryland, who had worked in civil defense programs for twenty years, then addressed the need for women and mothers to protect their teenage sons and daughters. "Contrary to the often heard claims that 'no one cares,'" she said, "I know a large and important group that cares very much and is keenly interested in protection. It is the young teenager. He doesn't want to answer disaster by giving up and dying. He wants every possible chance to survive, no matter what happens. He has no past, only his future, and he wants it."[54]

Whether helping teenagers or adults, family members or the community, women across America became involved with civil defense in the 1950s and 1960s. A representative example of the type of woman involved in civil defense is Mrs. William Kurtz, a wife and mother to two daughters. She became the women's civil defense coordinator for Gardena, California, in 1961, with her first assignment being to start a first-aid class at Gardena Community College—a cooperative project of the American Red Cross and the AMVETS. She later applied for the position of civil defense coordinator for the state, a paid position. She studied, took the exam, and won the position over 44 men and women. Kurtz not only served in this capacity; she also served as state president of the AMVETS Auxiliary, president of the Gardena American Legion Auxiliary, and president of the Wednesday Progressive Club. Her message to women was quite simple: "Women should have the training to meet emergency situations." Then there is Ellen Bryan Moore, a member of the National Women' Advisory Council for Civil Defense in 1965. A former public school teacher in Louisiana, Moore earned her master's degree from Louisiana State University and served as a captain in the U.S. Army during World War II. She also served as a director of Camp Fire Girls and Girl Scouts.[55] Although these two women represent anecdotal corroboration of women in civil defense during the early Cold War, they also reflect the women who assumed leadership roles in civil defense and set examples for others who volunteered to protect the nation.

8. "Pledge for Home Defense"

The Federal Civil Defense Administration launched one of its more successful campaigns in 1952: "Pledge for Home Defense." The campaign had two goals: first, to make the public aware of the importance of self-protection and family survival; and, second, to register volunteers, primarily women, for civil defense services. The FCDA's public information efforts focused on a 10-point family civil defense program, beginning with the distribution of information kits and materials to civil defense officials throughout the nation. The agency also published a series of posters illustrating the need for and benefits from civil defense; distributed the film, Survival Under Atomic Attack, *and a recruiting trailer to movie theaters; and gave civil defense slides to 86 television stations. The following is an excerpt from the FCDA's 1952 annual report listing public activities in support of the "Pledge for Home Defense" program and a list of some of the women's organizations that pledged their support.*

Among the Results of the Public Education Activity Were:

1. Issuance of home defense proclamations by a number of governors and hundreds of mayors, which were widely publicized;
2. Speeches by national executives of participating organizations and articles on civil defense in organization newsletters, newspapers, and magazines;
3. Wide coverage by newspapers, radio, and TV stations, both locally and nationally. Many of the country's leading dailies devoted editorials to the campaign;
4. "Pledge for Home Defense" stories in leading national magazines;
5. Thousands of showings of civil defense films during the campaign period by 150 commercial theatres in 78 cities;
6. Store window displays, outdoor advertising, and poster promotion sponsored by industry;
7. Distribution of over 3,000,000 copies of civil defense pamphlets and booklets;

ACT NOW ON YOUR PATRIOTIC
HOME DEFENSE PLEDGE

REMEMBER THAT A TRAINED,
alert AMERICA
IS A MIGHTY FORCE FOR PEACE

8. Many special events such as dropping of leaflets by Air Force planes over several cities and, in one instance, an entire State, with the message: "This could have been a bomb—Pledge for Home Defense—Register Today."

Women's Organizations Supporting the "Pledge for Home Defense" Program

Amalgamated Clothing Workers of America, CIO
American Association of University Women
American Federation of Women's Auxiliaries of Labor, AFL
America Federation of Hosiery Workers, AFL
American Federation of Teachers, AFL
American Home Economics Association
American Jewish Congress, Women's Division
American Legion Auxiliary
American Women's Voluntary Services, Inc.
AMVETS Auxiliary
Association of the Junior Leagues of America, Inc.
Bakery and Confectionery Workers International Union of America, AFL
Barber and Beauty Culturists Union of America, CIO
Camp Fire Girls, Inc.
Congress of Women's Auxiliaries of the CIO
General Federation of Women's Clubs
Girl Scouts of the United States of America
Ladies Auxiliary to the Veterans of Foreign Wars
National Association of Negro Business and Professional Women's Clubs
National Congress of Colored Parents and Teachers
National Congress of Parents and Teachers
National Council of Catholic Women
National Council of Jewish Women, Inc.
National Council of Negro Women
National Federation of Business and Professional Women's Clubs, Inc.
National Home Demonstration Council
National Ladies Auxiliary, Jewish War Veterans of the United States
National League of American Pen Women, Inc.
National Society of the Colonial Dames of America

National Society, Daughters of the American Revolution
United Daughters of the Confederacy
WAC VETS
Women's Auxiliary to the American Medical Association
Young Women's Christian Association of the United States of America

9. "Texans on the Alert for Civil Defense and Disaster Relief"

> *In 1956, the Texas Division of Defense and Disaster Relief joined the efforts of other states by publishing* Texans on the Alert for Civil Defense and Disaster Relief, *a pamphlet containing recommendations on how women's organizations could become involved in civil defense, as well as a description of the various opportunities for women. Here is an excerpt.*

Women's organizations throughout the nation number many thousands. They have experience, committees, programs and facilities. This vast reservoir of organized human power and competence, existing in every community, must be enlisted to provide leadership in planning, organizing, recruiting and training for this civil defense task.

What Your Organization Can Do Now

- Individually and collectively, assist in developing a strong local and State program for civil defense.
- Participate in organizational meets of overall local civil defense planning groups.
- Appoint a civil defense chairman to represent your organization and function with others coordinating work of all active groups.
- Plan programs by which all members may become familiar with official defense plans of your local community and state.
- Prepare an action plan for your organization that will contribute to the local community civil defense program.
- Invite local civil defense representatives to describe civil defense plans and to help determine how your organizations can best organize and function with the overall local and State program.
- Keep members of your community informed and prepared. Study available civil defense and disaster relief materials. Prepare helpful information for distribution.

TEXANS ON THE ALERT
FOR CIVIL DEFENSE AND DISASTER RELIEF

ACTION PLAN FOR LOCAL GROUPS
A FAMILY PROTECTION PLAN
A PLAN FOR EMERGENCY MASS CARE

THE STATE OF TEXAS
Allan Shivers, Governor

Executive Department
Division of Defense and Disaster Relief

1956

 AMARILLO — POTTER COUNTY
CIVIL DEFENSE OFFICE
Pho. DR 2-5203 — P. O. Box 1623
AMARILLO, TEXAS

- Encourage individuals to volunteer for service and training.
- Increase public interest in a self—and family—protection program, and in volunteering services.

Civil defense is a district and international project of Quota Club International, Inc. Training for members includes first aid, home nursing, mass feeding and canteen. Members learn CONELRAD stations and the New Civil Defense Public Action Signals, and keep their automobile gasoline tanks half full at all times for transportation readiness. Many have battery or A.M. radios.

All Quotarians have first aid and emergency food supplies in their homes. Some have their automobiles packed with Survival Kits, food supplies, water and sanitation tools. A civil defense news bulletin, published monthly, suggests "What we can do now." Civil Defense Public Action Signals cards are printed and distributed to members.

Opportunities for Women Volunteers

Over 17 million hard-working, well-trained volunteers are needed to assume some of the responsibilities of civil defense and disaster relief. At least 60 percent of these volunteers must be women serving in specialized jobs. Your community needs volunteers now and for years to come. Many of the jobs can be filled by YOU and YOUR FRIENDS right now, with only a little training.

[Here are] services in which women are needed in a community civil defense and disaster relief plan:

I. Welfare Services
    A. Mass Feeding
       Nutritionists—Women experienced in providing meals for large groups
    B. Emergency lodging—Women to make survey of accommodations and equipment for homeless people
    C. Women to compile statistics on quantities of clothing (old and new) available
       Women to staff a clothing center during the emergency

II. Emergency individual assistance
    A. Child care
    B. Care of the aged

III. To man information and evacuation centers

IV. Emergency medical services
    Emergency hospital services

V. Women—Ground Observer Corps
VI. Public information services
   A. To receive, record and maintain file
   B. Radio announcer
VII. Auxiliary Police—Traffic Officers
VIII. Warden Service—women wardens—women instructors
IX. Training services

Warden Service—Warden Service is the key to the Civil Defense organized self-protection program. The Warden Service works directly with persons, families, and neighborhoods and employee groups. It is the connecting link between organized civil defense operations and the public. Wardens train people in self-protection, disseminate civil defense information, make rosters of neighborhood residents, and inventory buildings and equipment within their posts. Assistant neighborhood or block wardens train families in individual self-protection, and organize neighborhood self-protection teams such as neighborhood fire fighting, rescue, first-aid, communications and welfare.

Women, particularly homemakers, should play an important part in the Warden's Service. Women are highly qualified for this type of responsibility, as they are generally present in residential neighborhoods at all times. Husband-wife teams are particularly recommended. Wardens must (a) become acquainted with [the] neighborhood and families in the assigned area; (b) train families in self-preservation and for tasks in areas; (c) keep records of essential information and equipment; and (d) assist with communications and transportation.

First Aid and Home Nursing—There is an urgent need for instructors in first aid and home nursing. As part of civil defense, the Red Cross is ready to train volunteers who in turn may train others. Homemakers, at least one adult member of every family, should register now with the Red Cross and take the home nursing course. Another member should take first aid. See your civil defense neighborhood warden or your local director about training courses.

Registration—A system for registration, information and communications is the very heart and nerve center of important operations in any emergency or disaster. These services must plan for effective performance if the masses are to receive direction. Of utmost importance first is to determine what services already have been organized that can be used or coordinated with the function of this phase of defense and relief. All efforts must be to further any adequate program, rather than to duplicate services already established and ready for immediate and effective action.

A training program for volunteer workers might include instructions for registration, filing and cross indexing information on the population of the county. Mobile equipment may be one of the most important items, and special information on the availability of such equipment should be part of the permanent records.

Information Center—The success of a registration program will depend largely on the location of the information center. A central location will permit it to be found easily. All information should clear through this center.

Identification—Identification tags are an effective way in which to extend the program, with the blood type and factor listed on the tag.

Warning Systems—Communities must be made aware of the urgent necessity to provide adequate warning systems. Once provided, it is necessary to educate the public as to how it will operate in each locale.

Stress the importance of CONELRAD—Radio stations 640 and 1240—which can be heard only on a battery or A.M. radio. These stations will be the only source of official Civil Defense information, since CONELRAD will be activated by the Air Defense Command in a national emergency. The radio organizations such as MARS, CAP and the Mobile Amateur Radio Association, better known as "Ham Operators," working together, will provide a most valuable and important supplement to the State and local governmental systems.

Ground Observer Corps—The Ground Observer Corps is an organization sponsored by the Department of the Air Force, to provide military air defense agencies with continuous low altitude visual target areas. It complements and augments the Air Defense Command's radar installations and is composed of civilian volunteers trained by the Air Force. Volunteers give their time to aid the Air Defense in observing, plotting and reporting movements of unidentified aircraft. Some volunteers serve at observation posts, others at central report points, known as filter centers. Volunteers spend two hours per month in the service of the GOC, and are entitled to wear the corps' distinctive silver wings and are given identification cards. Volunteers in filter centers will receive the aircraft reports from observation posts—approximately 100 miles in circumference—which are in direct telephone communication at all times with the filter centers. The Air Defense Command is in charge of training and volunteers may register NOW with their local Civil Defense agency.

Messenger Service—In time of disaster, all types of communications will be required. For ground communications, use messengers, including members of youth organizations, as runners. If possible, provide them with crepe soled shoes. Following the Texas City disaster, numerous workers suffered serious burns to the soles of their feet because they did not have the proper soles.

Health and Emergency Medical Services—Responsibility for the administration of Health and Emergency Medical Services in Defense and Disaster Relief in each instance is vested in a Medical Director (physician) who is designated by the appropriate government authority. This is true whether national, state or local programs are involved. All operation of this Branch necessitates the services of professional personnel but in all instances non-technical volunteers are needed as well.

Training for volunteer services in the areas of possible need is essential and should be sought in the local community in which the volunteer lives. Among the services which are under the primary jurisdiction of Health and Emergency Medical Services are: Casualty Aid Stations, Hospitals, Public Health Programs, and Care of Ill Patients at Home.

The Health and Emergency Medical Services Branch also participates in Evacuation Operation and Emergency Lodgings.

Properly trained women would be of great assistance in these services.

Part IV
On Guard

10. Serving the Community

> Without volunteer workers of the right kinds in the right places and the right numbers there can be no effective civil defense. The great damage that can be inflicted on this country makes it necessary to recruit and train approximately 17½ million volunteer civil defense workers. This is the largest mass mobilization of our human resources that has ever challenged this country.—*Federal Civil Defense Administration*[1]

Women in the early Cold War era could not escape the constant reminders about their responsibility for protecting their families and communities. Government agencies at all levels repeatedly emphasized that the success of civil defense—and thus the safety of the nation—depended upon their commitment. As early as 1950, the National Security Resources Board, precursor to the Federal Civil Defense Administration, indicated that "women, and particularly housewives, should play an important role in the warden service. Experience has proved that women are particularly qualified for this type of responsibility."[2] The following year, the FCDA concluded in its annual report that "the importance of women in civil defense can scarcely be overstated."[3] Fifteen years later, a civil defense pamphlet offered a similar message: "It is up to you, as a responsible American woman, to recognize the urgency of the job of acquiring knowledge that every individual should have—the minimal, personal knowledge that may help save lives and possessions when natural and man-made disasters strike." This responsibility applied to homemakers and to women in the workforce. The government encouraged—even mandated—that all women not only protect their homes, but also become active participants in national, state, and local civil defense activities.[4]

Women answered the call to duty by serving in a wide range of capacities. They joined the FCDA's civil defense service areas—warning and communications, shelter, health and special weapons defense, emergency welfare, fire, police, engineering, rescue, transportation, facilities self-protection, supply, and warden—and helped organize and implement mass feeding operations. They also volunteered for the Ground Observer Corps, re-formed in 1950, to "watch the skies" for enemy bombers; and they performed until January 1959 when the GOC ended. In Arizona, for example, women constituted a major component of the state's GOC operation; and Iowa had an official Women's Ground Observer Corps. In Redwood City, California, members of several women's social and service organizations launched a recruitment effort for GOC volunteers in the spring of 1953. In New Haven, Connecticut, 98 percent of GOC volunteers were women. Women throughout the country and with varied backgrounds joined the GOC. Just two examples are Mrs. Donald Fischer, the mother of three and part-time employee in a bicycle shop in Wisconsin Rapids, Wisconsin; and Maxine Olson of Klamath Falls, Oregon, a mother of one and president of a local social group. Fischer served as the local chief observer, logging some 7,000 hours of air spotting as of 1953. Olson volunteered for two-hour watches per week in 1954, with a goal of reaching a total of 250 hours to receive the GOC's Merit Award medal.[5]

Arguably, however, their most significant contribution was in the warden service, deemed by the FCDA as the most critical civil defense service because wardens had to know first aid, firefighting, and rescue techniques, as well as

Women volunteers in the Ground Observer Corps learn about the Air Force grid at the Spokane, Washington, civil defense filter center in 1950 (photograph by United States Navy).

have the leadership and organizational skills to coordinate overall civil defense assistance in an emergency situation. The warden service had a complex hierarchal structure, beginning with chief warden at the top, followed by deputy warden, zone warden, sector warden, post warden, and block warden. Moreover, there were fire wardens, rescue wardens, communications wardens, first-aid wardens, and evacuation wardens.[6] The most visible warden, however, was the block warden, who was "commander of the neighborhood under conditions of emergency" that "everybody knew and trusted," writes historian Andrew Grossman.[7] One newspaper described the warden service this way:

> Wardens have a far greater role in today's civil defense program than had the air-raid wardens of World War II. Today they will serve as the basis of our civil defense organization and operation.... As planned, the new warden service will be the largest in the civil defense organization and will affect every family, neighborhood, and community. It will need a great number of men and women organized by neighborhoods and blocks. Women will be heavily relied upon to staff the warden service and in many communities half the wardens will be women. Wardens will be the first civil defense workers to meet emergency situations on the spot. They will substitute for the professional and skilled civil defense personnel who may not be immediately available in necessary numbers.[8]

The duties of the block warden were divided into four components: pre-attack, alert, post-attack, and restoration periods. Pre-attack duties included selecting, equipping, and training assistants; ensuring that everyone in the assigned "block" had been instructed on civil defense procedures; making a map of the warden's responsible area; and taking inventory of requisite supplies. Block wardens had to organize neighborhood firefighting, rescue, first aid, communications, and welfare self-protection teams. Once an alert sounded, the warden had to notify persons in her block about the proper procedures to follow, such as finding the nearest shelter. After an attack, the warden was charged with surveying the block and reporting the level of destruction and casualties, and assisting families as necessary. Finally, wardens had primary responsibility for coordinating the restoration of water, electricity, and other essential services.[9] As the FCDA stated it: "[Wardens] must know what to do when an attack comes, and they must be able to show others what to do. They are the link between the civil defense organization and the people."[10]

To facilitate warden training, the government opened the National Civil Defense Training Center at Olney, Maryland, in 1952. The center served as the technical training school for basic and advanced rescue training for wardens, firefighters, and rescue squads. Trainees learned rescue methods and performed actual rescue operations in buildings designed to duplicate conditions that might result from an enemy attack. Also that year, FCDA distributed lesson plans and audio-visual aids to civil defense instructors, and introduced a training program specifically for local warden instructors.[11]

The FCDA set an ambitious goal of four million wardens, with more than 50 percent being women; and although it did not reach its overall goal, it correctly assessed that women would play a significant role in the warden service. In January 1951, Dr. William Warner, Ohio's director of civil defense, announced that the state immediately needed 100,000 air raid wardens, although some thought his estimate was not high enough. As reported in *The Evening Independent* in Massillon, Ohio, "Civil defense officials plan to have two air raid wardens in each city block in Ohio. That will mean in excess of 100,000, many of them women. In all cases, the second warden for the block will be a woman and many of the head block wardens will be women."[12] Brigadier General Clyde Dougherty, Detroit's civil defense director, also stressed women's role in his city's warden service, particularly for daytime service—a reflection that more men than women held full-time jobs and that men were needed for the military and more physically demanding civil defense responsibilities. Nonetheless, Dougherty called for 20,000 wardens and stressed that thousands of the city's women had performed exceptionally well during World War II.[13] His estimates were clearly lofty, and it is unclear how close Dougherty came to his goal. Civil defense officials in Delaware issued their own significant, although less ambitious, goal of 6,300 block wardens, consisting of men and women volunteers. In planning for a statewide air raid alert in February 1951, M. duPont Lee, Wilmington's civil defense director, announced that the state would be divided into four sections, with each sector having four districts; these districts would then be broken down into 10 posts. Each post consisted of 10 blocks, with block wardens playing an essential role.[14]

By 1952, the FCDA reported that the warden service had enrolled and trained some 550,000 persons—a 206 percent increase between December 31, 1951, and August 31, 1952. It also reported the development of state and local warden service programs, as well as the introduction of state training programs based on FCDA's guidelines as covered in its two publications, *The Warden Service* and *The Warden Handbook*. The FCDA also announced plans for a 1953 series of seminars designed to improve these state programs, as well as to achieve national standardization for warden training.[15] An important element in this standardization was the development of 12 training bulletins to be used by state and local civil defense organizations for the training of volunteers. The bulletins, each with accompanying color filmstrip and sound recording, included the following:

1. *Map Making for Wardens*: Instructions on how to prepare a block map.
2. *The Block Census*: Techniques for taking a block census.

3. *The Role of the Warden Service*: Basic rescue techniques for wardens.
4. *The Role of the Warden in Fire*: A description of a warden's firefighting duties.
5. *Conducting a Neighborhood Civil Defense Meeting*: A review of the techniques used to organize and conduct a civil defense meeting.
6. *Reconnaissance Functions of the Block Warden*: Instructions on how to take a survey of a damaged area.
7. *Facilities and the Block Warden Organization*: A description of existing small facilities and people that can be used during an emergency.
8. *The Warden's Responsibility for Emergency Sanitation Measures*: Emergency sanitation techniques.
9. *The Role of the Warden in Receiving and Billeting* Evacuees: A description of how to manage evacuees.
10. *The Role of the Warden in Moving Disaster Victims to Welfare Assembly Area*: Techniques in the movement of disaster victims to assembly areas.
11. *The Warden Post Message Center*: Basic communication techniques to train wardens and auxiliaries in the field of communication.
12. *Organizing a Neighborhood for Survival*: An overview of a warden's neighborhood responsibilities.[16]

The first course for women air raid wardens in Pennsylvania was held in October 1952 at the state's Civil Defense Training Center at Ogontz. The 14-hour course was the first of a series to train women wardens who would serve throughout the state. According to a statement from the training center, "[I]f the chips are down, women will be called upon to carry up to 75 percent of the load of home defense." The course covered advanced firefighting; light rescue work; working in smoke and gas; organizing blocks and buildings to minimize panic; and handling thousands of homeless persons in a post-attack scenario.[17] In New Jersey, the state's Division of Civil Defense enrolled more than 56,000 persons in the state's warden service, many of them women, by the end of 1952. The District of Columbia achieved 100 percent in warden appointments, 99 percent in shelter identification, 95 percent in warning activities, and 90 percent in total personnel assignments.[18] In Syracuse, New York, Mrs. Milton Lamb, Mrs. Milner Noble, and Mrs. Ralph Brown became the first area wardens to organize their respective warden groups for a survey of the city's housing and residents. The women then directed survey operations in three, 10-block areas.[19]

10. Serving the Community

This photograph depicts women staff at Maine's First Civil Defense Staff College working with a 20 by 40 foot map of Baltimore used to locate assembly areas and evacuation routes (National Archives).

The next year, 20 women were admitted to the New York State Civil Defense Rescue Training School in Albany for the first time. The women, who had completed warden and first-aid training, were selected from the state's major target cities. Lt. Gen. C. R. Huebner, the state civil defense director, also announced that New York State now had 900,000 civil defense volunteers,

CIVIL DEFENSE PERSONNEL ENROLLED AND CURRENTLY ASSIGNED TO CD DUTIES [1]

SERVICE OR PROGRAM	PERSONS ENROLLED AND ASSIGNED
ADMINISTRATIVE AND STAFF	58,563
EMERGENCY WELFARE	275,691
ENGINEERING	323,763
FIRE	333,723
HEALTH AND SPECIAL WEAPONS DEFENSE	653,248
POLICE	320,993
PUBLIC AFFAIRS	9,694
RESCUE	42,850
SUPPLY	12,565
TRAINING AND EDUCATION	65,186
TRANSPORTATION	290,358
VOLUNTEER RECRUITMENT	37,926
WARDEN	549,314
WARNING AND COMMUNICATIONS	147,962
GROUND OBSERVER CORPS	147,152
MISCELLANEOUS [2]	717,698
TOTAL	3,986,686

[1] Partial data based on reports from 48 States, the District of Columbia, and 5 territories and possessions as of August 31, 1952.
[2] Personnel not classified by services or program such as clergy, school, plant protection, etc., plus 544,130 personnel in New Hampshire, New Jersey, and Pennsylvania for whom no service assignment data has been received.

The Federal Civil Defense Administration's 1952 annual report included this chart on the number of persons enrolled in the national civil defense program, including nearly 550,000 in the warden services.

allowing the state to "move with confidence from the planning into the operational state."[20] The four-day training program covered such topics as the effects of an atomic bomb on buildings and other structures; lifting techniques; handling and moving casualties; and firefighting. Upon completion of the program, the women were expected to return to their communities and train other women in rescue techniques for an emergency situation. *The Journal News* in White Plains, New York, reported that "the state rescue training school has been filled to capacity for many months, but because of the large proportion of women enrolled in warden duties, it was felt they should have the basic rescue training and become local instructors to other women in their organizations."[21] Expanding on the decision to admit women to the rescue training school, Adelaide Healy, chief of the warden service for the New York State Civil Defense Commission, issued this statement:

> Women will be called upon in [an] actual emergency to perform a great number of jobs, and they form the backbone of the entire state warden service. They are the ones most likely to be at home and able to go into instant action in their respective neighborhoods immediately after an attack, and before the other elements of civil defense are able to move into action. Before the fire apparatus, ambulances, and other equipment and personnel are able to reach a stricken area, the wardens, many of them women, will have had to take control of the immediate situation. To do this properly, they must have certain basic training such as they will receive in the special rescue course, in addition to their first aid and own basic warden training.[22]

In Williamsport, Pennsylvania, sector wardens began a recruiting campaign to enroll block wardens. While farther west, Pleasant Grove, Utah, became the state's first town to switch from men to women wardens, as recommended by the Utah Civil Defense department. The reasoning behind this move reflected gender stereotypes (i.e., men worked during the day); however, the result was greater empowerment for the 100 women wardens, whose first assignment was visiting every home in their blocks and inviting them to a community-wide fire demonstration.[23] The main topic at the 1953 fall meeting of Allegheny County Federation of Women's Clubs, held in Pittsburgh, was leadership training, deemed critical for the warden service.[24]

Wisconsin Governor Walter Kohler called a special conference in November to reappraise the state's vulnerability to an atomic attack, and to review how best to use the state's resources if such an event were to occur. Speaking at the conference was Val Peterson, FCDA director, who expressed the need to be prepared not only for an atomic attack but also for a bacteriological one, saying, "We must confess that little progress has been made to cope with such a possibility." Governor Kohler added that it "is no exaggeration to say that the civil defense conference might conceivably be the most important business any of us have ever engaged in."[25] In Cincinnati, the Emergency Medical

Service of the Cincinnati-Hamilton County Civil Defense organization hosted the fourth annual Target Areas Medical Civil Defense Conference, which was closed to the public. In attendance were 100 representatives from various medical societies and city or county health divisions from cities likely to be prime targets in an atomic attack.[26]

The FCDA continued to promote training during 1953 by sending representatives to meet with state civil defense departments and civil defense officials in target cities. The main goal was to introduce its warden training kit and home protection kit, and to conduct civil defense demonstrations. In Flint, Michigan, for example, approximately 250 volunteers demonstrated police, fire, rescue, engineering, communications, welfare, and first-aid services. In February, the FCDA held a national training conference of state and local personnel interested in warden programs, and then hosted a Warden Operations Conference in November. Its new Warden Instructors' Course was made available to states through the agency's regional offices. Moreover, the FCDA's Western Technical Training School in St. Mary's, California, graduated hundreds of men and women from its Warden Staff Advanced Training Course before permanently closing in September. Yet despite these efforts, the FCDA reported that the 700,000 persons enrolled and trained in the warden service constituted only 23 percent of its goal of 2.9 million wardens.[27]

By 1954, civil defense strategies had shifted from taking shelter against an atomic attack to evacuating the city as quickly as possible because of the devastatingly destructive power of a hydrogen bomb. For wardens, this meant new responsibilities because they now had to educate people about proper evacuation procedures and oversee the handling of evacuees in reception areas; for the FCDA, it meant revising its warden training. As part of this process, the FCDA held three warden training conferences in Olney, Maryland, with warden service personnel from more than 100 communities in the Northeast attending. In addition, three similar regional conferences were held, each focusing on new evacuation duties.[28] Several women's organizations attended a conference held in Albany, New York, where new training guidelines were presented. Members of the Women's Civil Defense Rescue Squad of Speigletown, New York, conducted rescue demonstrations in conjunction with the conference. The squad demonstrated rescue from a bombed building, a second story building, and a bomb shelter buried in debris.[29] The University of Arizona provided the setting for the revised training program under the new guidelines. The program encompassed 29 hours of civil defense training, covering organization and operational control, emergency duties and responsibilities, high-explosive missiles, firefighting, basic rescue, atomic warfare, and practical field problems. In addition, trainees had to take 22 hours of first-aid work. Wardens who completed the course qualified to teach the program to others.[30]

The FCDA tested the readiness of wardens and the entire civil defense program on June 14, 1954, with Operation Alert, a fictional atomic attack on the United States that would be repeated annually through 1961. Hypothetically, atomic bombs hit 42 U.S. cities and eight cities in Canada, resulting in nine million deaths, four million injured, and some seven million homeless. Public exercises and public drills took place in 233 cities, representing 62 million Americans. The national exercise, which received extensive press, radio, and television coverage, revealed numerous shortcomings in the nation's civil defense program. Two hundred police officers and civil defense wardens cleared 3,000 people from Times Square in New York City in just 70 seconds, but workers in Chicago rushed to their office windows to watch police and civil defense workers direct traffic below. In Philadelphia, crowds gathered on the streets rather than taking shelter, and half the populace, according to newspaper reports, failed to lower their window shades as instructed. The FCDA's Val Peterson commented, "Today's nationwide civil defense test has thus far proved effectively what we had assumed—that the nation's civil defense team still has a long way to go in the field of operational readiness.... We believe that the impact of this national civil defense exercise will serve both as a grim and reassuring alert to the American people."[31]

Despite the mixed reactions to Operation Alert, women wardens performed their duties. Beginning in February, Bert Lowe, director of Otsego County (New York) Civil Defense, initiated efforts for 150 men and women wardens to be ready for the June exercise. Five hundred members of the Women's Warden Corps of Springfield Township in Montgomery County, Pennsylvania, took their positions during the Operation Alert as instructed. The women wardens, who were each responsible for six homes, had been trained in first aid and firefighting, as well as control-center operations and light rescue procedures. One member commented, "The urge to protect home and family is a natural with us gals. All the Women's Warden Corps does is to supplement that urge with efficiency and know-how through organization and training." Similarly, 110 women wardens in Orem, Utah, took their positions during Operation Alert, working with the telephone company, other civil defense units, and auxiliary police and firemen to expedite proper civil defense procedures.[32] One of the positive aspects of national testing was to bring more awareness to civil defense, and thus encourage people to volunteer. That fall, for example, the Park Forest (Illinois) Woman's Club hosted a meeting for the purpose of creating a local women's warden service. Seventeen area women's groups supported the effort.[33]

The FCDA again revised the warden service in 1955, focusing more on the effects of radioactive fallout in addition to guidelines for evacuation and shelter operational tactics. The agency introduced several new training courses, including an eight-hour warden training course covering warden duties, warden assistance to other services, how to organize neighborhood survival plans, how to train warden volunteers, and how to instruct neighborhood residents in civil defense. At the recommendation of the Women's National Advisory Committee, the agency created a training course expressly for women wardens. The course contained 20 hours of group instruction on preparing families for evacuation; the care of children, the aged, ill, handicapped, and other dependents in an evacuation situation; emergency family feeding and sanitation; and personal and home decontamination. The FCDA also revised the home defense action program, introduced in 1953 to assist cities in organizing warden units, to reflect the need for shelter from radioactive fallout and an understanding of evacuation.[34]

In another move, the FCDA introduced a warden program to help prepare rural and nonurban residents for the possibility of receiving people from other areas. Fourteen national rural leaders, including Mrs. Frank Haucke, head of the Women's Civil Defense Committee, met in Battle Creek, Michigan, in February 1956 to form the National Advisory Council for Rural Civil Defense.[35] The primary purpose of the council was to formulate a five-point approach: the protection of rural families and their property; the continuation of food production; delivering food where needed; managing and caring for evacuees; and assisting in rescue and rehabilitation efforts in targeted cities. In an article titled, "Rural C.D. Can Save America," *The Fairmount News* in Fairmount, Indiana, described the new realities of a possible nuclear attack:

> If America should be threatened by attack, more than a third of the nation's population, evacuated from cities, would become dependent upon rural help and resources. These estimated 70 million persons fleeing potential target areas would bring with them only enough food for a short time. They would be without shelter. Care of these people would be a rural civil defense job.... Rural civil defense, made up of rural residents, would be responsible for and direct such vital work as reception, registration, feeding, and billeting of evacuees. Rural officials would be in charge of these operations. Rural people would form the basic teams to get the work started.[36]

Shortly after the creation of the rural civil defense program, the FCDA launched the "Putting Civil Defense Awareness to Work" campaign based on a grassroots warden program called STEP (Survival Through Emergency Preparedness). Under STEP, which applied to both rural and urban areas, civil defense directors worked with block wardens to promote neighborhood survival planning. At a two-day meeting at FCDA headquarters to launch the program, attendees included representatives of the National Council of Catholic Women, National Council of Negro Women, Association of Junior

Leagues of America, and women's auxiliaries of the American Legion, Veterans of Foreign Wars, and Catholic War Veterans, among others. Gertrude Baker, a block warden from Standale, Michigan, received a citation in recognition of her outstanding service.[37]

Through such programs as STEP and rural civil defense, women continued to lend their time, energy, and experience to the warden service, as well as other civil defense services. In Salina, Kansas, the local Women's Civil Defense Board launched a new effort to enlist women chief, district, and block wardens in the fall of 1956. One hundred members of the Battle Creek, Michigan, branch of the American Association of University Women convened in January 1957 to tour FCDA headquarters and learn more about how to become involved in civil defense. The civil defense director in Janesville, Wisconsin, issued a call in May 1957 for 200 wardens and 100 women to work at civil defense control posts. The annual women's conference on civil defense in Edinburg, Indiana, was held that September. The conference presented the latest civil defense guidelines and, more specifically, a discussion of the changing role of women in civil defense. Sessions included Education to Meet Disaster, Red Cross and Civil Defense Cooperation in the Community, and Civil Defense in the Schools.[38]

In 1958, President Dwight Eisenhower created the Office of Civil Defense and Mobilization, consolidating the functions of the Office of Defense Mobilization and FCDA. Despite this change at the national level, though, state and local civil defense organizations continued their activities with little change. At a January 1958 meeting in Anderson, Indiana, Dolaras Johnson, Indiana's assistant state director of the Women's Civil Defense Advisory Committee, reminded some 100 representatives of women's organizations that Anderson was considered a target area, making it critically important to urge their members to volunteer for civil defense. According to the local newspaper, it was the largest civil defense meeting since 1945. That same month in Black River Falls, Wisconsin, Mary McDonald, head of the city's civil defense program, told a meeting of the Jackson County Federated Clubwomen that the biggest enemy of civil defense was ignorance about what to do in an emergency. "Women have many skills that will be needed in an emergency, such as nursing, first aid, blood bank, food handling, driving, and registration," said McDonald, "if only they would devote some time now in trying to learn how they can best help." The Women's Council for Civil Defense in Burlington, Vermont, invited specialists in housing, feeding, transportation, fire, and warden services to speak at its April meeting, where the council also introduced a women's training course.[39]

The National Women's Advisory Committee held its 1958 annual meeting in Battle Creek, Wisconsin. Among the decisions made by the national committee was approval of the Eisenhower Administration's new National Policy on Shelters.[40] The following month, members of the committee provided updates on local meetings around the country. For example, 30 representatives of area women's groups in Alton, Illinois, attended a meeting of the Women's Council for Civil Defense to hear a report on the national meeting's actions, including details of the Shelter Plan, which had five major objectives:

1. To inform all Americans about the dangers of fallout and steps they and their governments can take to minimize it.
2. To conduct pilot fallout-shelter surveys to determine the current status of shelter awareness and shelter facilities.
3. To expedite research on shelter design and radiological defense.
4. To implement plans for the construction of 100 prototype fallout shelters.
5. To require all federal departments and agencies, including the OCDM, to include fallout shelter design and construction costs in their budget estimates.[41]

On April 17, 1959, the government tested people's level of preparedness during the civil defense alert phase of its annual Operation Alert (with four additional phases held throughout the year). As foretold in the teleplay, "Atomic Attack," New York City and cities throughout the state were hit with multiple fictitious hydrogen bombs. Philip Benjamin of *The New York Times* reported that despite some persons in New York City who objected to the exercise and were arrested, the drill went smoothly. "The role of the public was confined to a ten-minute period between 1:30 and 1:40 p.m.," Benjamin wrote. "During that time people in public places took shelter at the direction of Civil Defense workers and policeman…. The public took shelter quickly and traffic halted on cue." Of note was the role of wardens assigned to the city's public places, including its department stores. At Macy's, for example, the warden on duty, Louise Mahler, directed shoppers to safe shelter areas.[42]

Women's civil defense groups held programs and conducted training courses well into the 1960s, even as the OCDM gave way to the Office of Civil Defense, established by President John Kennedy. For example, Pleasant Grove, Utah, continued to hold its annual civil defense school for local residents, with more than 100 women wardens distributing invitations to individual families in 1960 to encourage them to sign up. Women wardens in Steuben County, Indiana, also called on individual households, in this instance to update their information for civil defense purposes. This information included the number of family members; the location of shut-off points for water, gas, and electricity; kinds of firefighting equipment available; and other pertinent information of possible importance in an emergency.[43]

10. Serving the Community

Louise Mahler, a civil defense warden on duty at New York City's Macy's department store, surveys the silent main floor during the nation's annual Operation Alert drill in April 1959 (Carl Gossett/*The New York Times*/Redux).

The next year, in July 1961, A. E. Snyder, director of El Paso (Texas) Civil Defense, announced plans to form a Women's Division of Civil Defense with its primary responsibility to encourage home and family preparedness in case of war. More urgently, however, after acknowledging that El Paso residents were "swamping his office with calls about civil defense plans," Snyder launched a drive to recruit more men and women as block wardens and assistants, and his actions were not isolated. Americans who had been apathetic about civil defense suddenly realized its importance during the Berlin Crisis, in which Soviet Premier Nikita Khrushchev threatened action if the Western Allies did not leave Berlin. On July 25, President Kennedy addressed the nation on television, describing the threat of nuclear war and stressing the critical necessity for civil defense. He reminded the American people that they had a "sober responsibility" to know what to do and where to go if a nuclear war were to occur. To aid in this effort, which had begun a decade earlier, President Kennedy announced that he would request new funds be approved by Congress to identify and mark space in existing public and private structures capable of serving as fallout shelters, and to stock those shelters with food, water, first-aid kits, and other minimum essentials. In addition, the funds were to be used to create new fallout shelters, improve air-raid warning and fallout detection systems, and take additional measures that would help save lives in case of attack. "We owe that kind of insurance to our families, and to our country," the president said.[44]

Ben Fowler, director of Iowa Civil Defense, responding to Kennedy's remarks, said, "President Kennedy's civil defense message on July 25 has had a phenomenal impact. It's a real inspiration to see how people are accepting the responsibility of survival; it's something we haven't had in the past 10 years." Women's civil defense groups in Kentucky held a series of meetings in August to compare the civil defense programs in the United States with those of the Soviet Union in an attempt to enlist more women. And the state of Virginia, in a joint announcement with the State Department of Education and State Office of Civil Defense, issued a manual outlining the responsibilities of school personnel, primarily teachers, in the warden service. Following Kennedy's speech, the Galveston (Texas) civil defense department announced the need for more than 100 additional wardens to ensure the city was prepared. "The need to complete our program is immediate," said Milton Scales, the city's director of civil defense. "That it is also urgent is evident from the rapidly changing picture of world conditions."[45]

Khrushchev backed down in 1961 and again in October 1962 in the Cuban Missile Crisis. With these nuclear "stand downs" by the Soviet Union, the threat of nuclear war eased somewhat, although the civil defense program continued under President Lyndon Johnson. Throughout the early 1960s, states and cities held civil defense meeting and conferences, such as one called by Nebraska Governor Frank Morrison in February 1965 with the theme, "Operation Defense Self-Help." Women also continued to play an essential role, such as Frances Jones Mills, a member of the Federation of Women's Clubs, the Medical Auxiliary, and the Business and Professional Women's Club, who was named community relations officer for the Kentucky Division of Civil Defense in 1965.[46]

The connection between women contributing to the community and safeguarding the family was an oft-repeated refrain during the early Cold War. Addressing this relationship, Percy Maxim Lee, president of the League of Women Voters, told attendees of the 1952 annual meeting of the American Home Economics Association,

> I believe every family benefits—as does the nation—when a woman ... becomes a useful member of her community and assumes her community responsibility. In the first place, this sort of activity helps develop a social conscience within the family—an essential quality if this nation is to flourish. Secondly, it promotes an intellectual curiosity without which we will become static. A woman who is constructively involved in the affairs of her community invariably builds a better family for America.[47]

An FCDA pamphlet delivered a more forceful message: "If your community does not have an active civil defense organization, much of the blame must fall on you and your neighbors. Unless you, as a responsible American woman, take action you are gambling with the safety of your family, your friends, your community, and your country."[48] Although most people remained apathetic to civil defense during this era, millions of women did heed the nation's call by becoming proactive contributors in all facets of civil defense at the national, regional, state, and local levels. As evidenced here, the warden service, in particular, provided women with an opportunity to cross the line into such male stereotypes as leader, organizer, and protector. As block wardens, women represented more than just voices in their communities; they were action figures—first responders in today's terminology.

11. "This Is Civil Defense"

The Federal Civil Defense Administration distributed 54 million copies of nine pamphlets in 1951, its first year of operation. One of these pamphlets was This Is Civil Defense, *which answered typical questions assumed being asked by American citizens. In addition, the pamphlet provided a brief description of the various civil defense services, pointing out which ones should be of special interest to women. These included warden, health, welfare, staff, transportation, and communication services. Here is an excerpt.*

Who Is Responsible for Civil Defense?

You are.

Civil defense is set up by Federal and State law. But no law in the world will work unless you back it up by your own actions. That's why, in the end, responsibility for civil defense is yours.

The thing to remember is this: If the bombs from enemy planes ever fell on your city, they would not fall on a plan, or an organization, or a system of government. They would fall on you and your family and friends.

If you were a soldier, you would be trained to take care of yourself and keep on fighting. As a defender of the home front, you must learn to protect yourself and keep on working. Despite every precaution, a solder might be killed. So might you. But the more you know, and the better trained you are, the better your chances for survival.

The whole idea of civil defense is to help you protect yourself, and to make the best use of your own special ability and skill in an emergency. Then you will be able to save yourself and others if trouble comes.

What Does Civil Defense Do Before an Attack?

Civil defense gets you ready to meet an attack. It gives you information on such things as how to safeguard your home, how to fight fires, and what steps to take against atomic, biological, and chemical warfare.

THIS IS CIVIL DEFENSE

THE OFFICIAL U. S. GOVERNMENT BOOKLET

Civil defense arranges for shelters in your city, and operates the warning system that would tell you when to go to those shelters.

Civil defense is getting medical supplies and special equipment ready. It also is training technical services needed to restore a stricken area. Finally, civil defense is organizing mutual aid and mobile support.

If You Don't Live in a City, Should You Take Part in Civil Defense?

Yes. Civil defense is your business no matter where you live.

If you're a farmer, if you raise livestock or crops, you're on the high priority list for some kind of biological warfare attack.

If you're not a farmer, but a resident of a small town, you still have a special kind of civil defense job—helping and sheltering bombed-out people.

Let's make it clear that the people of the big cities are not going to take to the hills. Nevertheless, in case of enemy attack, some people might have to be moved out of the city because their homes had been gutted by fire or otherwise made unlivable.

Young children, expectant mothers, invalids, and older people would have to be cared for. Your locality might be named as an evacuation area for this purpose. If you are anywhere within reach of a major city, hospital facilities in your community would be tagged as reception areas for casualties.

To sum it up, if you live in a large city, you will have a critical civil defense job to do. You will serve both as part of the civil defense team and as a member of a family which must make every effort to take care of itself. If you do not live in a large city, you have a civil defense job that is very vital.

Should You Volunteer for a Civil Defense Job?

Yes—right away.

Every good American will want to volunteer for civil defense. Every thinking citizen knows there is no other way to recruit the millions of workers who will be needed.

Being a civil defense worker is not a job for those who can't face facts or who aren't willing to work. It is a job for real Americans with courage. If we are attacked (and remember that we can be attacked), the hard, terrible task of getting our cities back on their feet will fall mainly on civil defense volunteers.

No one can do the civil defense job but the American people themselves. The Armed Forces have another job to do. There are not enough people in Federal, State, or local government agencies to do the job for you. One local civil defense organization has adopted the slogan, "Service means Survival." That about sums it up. A good, tough, determined civil defense program can mean survival for the American people.

How Do You Volunteer for Civil Defense?

Your newspapers, radio or television stations will be glad to tell you. Also, you can watch for announcements from your local civil defense director. Or you can phone or visit your local civil defense headquarters.

Right now your Red Cross chapter is ready to train you in first aid. This training will be required of all civil defense volunteers. But whether or not you are able to volunteer, you should take the latest Red Cross first-aid course. Home nursing and nurses' aide courses are given by the Red Cross, too. These courses may save a life in your family someday, war or no war.

In addition, the Red Cross needs blood donors. Thousands of pints of blood and plasma would be needed after an enemy attack. The Red Cross is in charge of this part of the civil defense program.

What Services Can You Join?

There are 10 major volunteer services, all of them vital.

For the sake of national uniformity, the Federal Civil Defense Administration has the following basic services set up: Warden, Fire, Police, Health, Welfare, Engineering, Rescue, Communications, Transportation, and Staff. Some 15,000,000 trained volunteers will be needed to man the various services.

The Warden Service

The warden service is the backbone of civil defense. It is the source of neighborhood civil defense leadership before, during, and after an attack. It is the warden's job to save lives first and property next.

Before an emergency, the warden's main duty is that of helping people to prepare. During an emergency, he conducts people to safety. After the emergency, he helps restore order.

Wardens must be volunteers, well-known, and respected in the community, whose leadership will be accepted by their neighbors or fellow workers. As a general rule, each warden post will be responsible for a residential block or factory area where about 500 people live or work. Several wardens may be assigned to such a post.

Wardens teach people how to protect themselves, instruct them in civil defense regulations, and distribute civil defense information. They will keep lists of the people in their charge and gather information about buildings and equipment in their neighborhoods.

Wardens' records will include the home address, age, and physical condition of all persons in their charge. Wardens also should know which people need special care and how to get in touch with their relatives and friends.

If a warning sounded, wardens would conduct workers or the occupants of buildings to safe areas. It would be their job to help prevent panic, render first aid, and perform light rescue duties. If needed they also would help other services to fight fires and clear debris.

Immediately after attack, the warden would take a roll call of all people in his area. If anyone was missing, or needed nursing or medical attention, the warden would report the facts at once to the control center. The warden service also would help restore the orderly life of the community after an attack.

The warden service works directly with individuals, families, neighborhoods, and employee groups. The warden is the link between the specialized civil defense services and the people. Outstanding men and women who can assume responsibility are urged to volunteer for the warden service.

Woman, and especially housewives, play an important part in the warden service. Most women are at their home posts day and night. Usually they know their own neighborhoods better than men can ever know them. Women should interest themselves in the warden service as a first step in the organizations of civil defense for their neighborhoods.

The Health Service

The health service needs all persons with experience in work that has to do with health of medicine. It also needs volunteers who can be trained in special weapons defense—which means defense against atomic, biological, and chemical warfare. Finally, it needs non-professional volunteers who can do manual and clerical work. Thousands of such volunteers will be needed for the big job of protecting the health of a city after an attack, and caring for the injured.

Professional people of the health fields will be a part of civil defense, and will be contacted by their local civil defense organizations. In addition, however, willing hands are needed to do many kinds of work under professional direction. If you have had any related technical training—or even if you haven't—the health service can find a useful job for you.

Thousands of first-aid workers will be needed. This does not mean merely people who have had first-aid training. It means people who can be organized for definite jobs at first-aid stations. The health service also must have thousands of women volunteers who have taken home nursing and nurses' aide courses.

Men are asked to volunteer as litter-bearers, ambulance personnel, hospital orderlies and attendants, supply handlers, and maintenance workers. Extra sanitation workers and food inspectors will be needed for our defense against disease and gas warfare, and against radiological contamination.

The radiological monitoring teams will need teachers, or advanced students of physics and other related sciences, as team leaders. High-school graduates who have taken physics courses will be needed as members of such teams. So will some radio repairmen.

Many thousands of clerical workers will be recruited by the health service. In the event of enemy attack, records must be kept of ill or injured persons, and the dead. There will be room for many volunteers who can be taught to help in laboratory work. The blood service under the charge of the American National Red Cross needs people who can help in the procurement of blood.

Women especially are urged to interest themselves in the health service as part of the civil defense program. Even if your only skill is the ability to wash laboratory glassware or mop floors, the health service will have a place for you in its vitally important work of saving lives.

The Welfare Service

In case of disaster many families might find themselves homeless and without food, clothing, or money. The emergency welfare service would provide these things, in addition to locating missing persons and caring for infants, the aged, and the infirm.

If an attack comes, the welfare services will gather and pass on news of people who are separated from their families, and register those who must receive individual care. Welfare workers will contact relatives in other cities, and refer families to places where they can get special help.

Many volunteers will be needed in this field, and you can be one of them.

If you live near a large city, it may be possible for you to offer room in your home to bombed-out persons. You may be called upon to help feed large numbers of persons who have been evacuated. You may be needed to help distribute clothing. Or you may be asked to care for homeless children.

All these are welfare service activities. Training courses will be available in the various branches of welfare work, under experienced instructors. Women particularly should interest themselves in this end of the civil defense program. By background and experience, women are especially good at caring for others in time of need.

The Transportation Service

In case of enemy attack, a lot of people and equipment would need moving from one place to another in a hurry. The injured would need transport to hospitals. Emergency food and medical supplies would have to be rushed into the stricken area. Thousands of training workers would be required for the transportation service.

If you are a skilled driver, there may be a place for you in the transportation service. It will teach people to drive in organized fleets under emergency conditions. Where necessary, it will also teach simple repair and maintenance work. Assembly points will be set up and a mission will be assigned to every volunteer and every official vehicle.

Women can be very useful to the transportation service. In the last war, many women acted as drivers for the military and the Red Cross.

The Staff Service

Local civil defense headquarters will need a lot of administrative people for staff work. Records must be kept. Letters must be written. Telephones must be answered. If you have had any experience in typing, filing, or running a switchboard, there may be a volunteer job for you in the staff service.

If you have experience in any technical phase of civil defense, you may end up with a supervisory job of your own. You would need a thorough knowledge of your special subject. You would be expected to know how to train or direct other people in that field.

Staff jobs in civil defense are positions of great responsibility. If you have a real background in any of the technical skills, vocational training experience, or administrative ability, you should offer your services as a staff worker.

The Communications Service

The communications service is the nerve center of civil defense.

In handling a disaster of any kind, everything depends upon good communications. That is doubly true of civil defense operations in the face of enemy attack.

Control centers must keep in touch with one another. Air raid warnings must be relayed promptly. There must be some reliable means for directing fire, police, rescue, warden, medical, and engineering services. Unless headquarters knows what is happening, and where it is happening, it cannot get the situation under control.

Thousands of volunteers will be needed to man the communications network for civil defense. If you have any technical training in radio, television, telegraph, or telephone work, you will be needed in this service. Women volunteers can be especially useful in answering phones and in operating message centers.

What Does All This Add Up To?

Civil defense adds up to just one thing—your help is needed.... Find out where you can serve best. Then—volunteer for work you can do.

Millions of Americans must be trained in civil defense before our country can call itself ready for enemy attack. Meanwhile, that attack might come at any time. We have not a moment to lose in preparing ourselves. Your home, your job, your family, your own life may be at stake.

Make no mistake about it—civil defense is here to stay. It may be a part of our lives for years to come.

The outcome of modern war is not necessarily decided by armies in the field. Wars today can be won or lost on the home front. The home front cannot be hidden, and it cannot retreat—not if we are to survive as a free people. That puts the problem squarely up to you.

Learn—and live. Get into civil defense right now. Your Nation needs your help.

12. "The Warden's Handbook"

> *Among the various service areas for civil defense, the warden service was unquestionably the most important. The FCDA wasted little time in outlining the importance of the warden service and the requirements for volunteers by publishing* The Warden's Handbook *in its first year of operation. The following excerpt offers suggestions for recruiting, training, and equipping block wardens.*

You, Your Neighbors, and Civil Defense

Since pioneer days, Americans have joined together to combat common dangers of warfare and natural disasters. Again we are faced with a serious threat—a threat that an enemy attack may destroy our homes, kill our people, and paralyze the productive power of our cities. You, the block warden, have joined other civil defense volunteers to meet this threat. Progress in civil defense recruiting, equipping, and training is being made throughout the country. If this progress continues and we become strong enough, an enemy will think twice before he attacks.

A strong, effective civil defense depends on a strong, effective warden service. The results of an all-out enemy attack will be manageable only through assistance the warden service will give the other civil defense specialized services. The warden service is the most familiar civil defense service to the average person, primarily because the block warden himself is the direct link between the police and the local civil defense organization. He has frequent and personal contact with the residents of his block. To many of them he *is* civil defense.

The Local Warden Service

Locally, the chief warden should serve on the staff of the civil defense director. The chief warden develops a warden organization pattern based on such factors as the municipality's population density, geographic features, and transportation facilities. He is responsible for organizing the warden service into zones, districts, and blocks in conformity with the general target area pattern for other civil defense services.

The size of the typical warden district is about 1 square mile in area. Under direction of the zone warden, the district warden divides his area into "blocks" of approximately 500 people who reside, assemble, or work there. These "blocks" may be of various shapes and sizes determined by local civil defense authorities, and are not necessarily related to city blocks.

In some cities terms other than zone, district, and block are already in use. However, it is recommended that for the sake of uniformity these terms should be standardized.

The Block Warden Unit

The basic operating group of the warden service is the block warden unit. Before an attack it will:

(a) Record and maintain essential information concerning residents, available protective equipment, and physical features of the block.
(b) Organize and train block residents and neighborhood groups for their individual and common protection against enemy attack.

After an attack it will:

(a) Mobilize the resources of the block to give first aid, fight small fires, and do light rescue work.
(b) Report casualties, damage, and general conditions.
(c) Call for assistance from civil defense technical services when necessary, and assist them at the scene of the disaster.
(d) Direct people to reception centers and emergency welfare centers for desired information, food, clothing, temporary lodging, and materials or tools for minor home repairs.

In your block, there may be commercial buildings, schools, stores, and other establishments. Some of these institutions and establishments may organize their own protective services under a facilities self-protection program. If they do, you should arrange for mutual assistance in case of emergency. If not, they will depend upon you and your assistants for organization, leadership, and training in self-protection. Whatever the situation, know your assigned area, buildings, and people.

The block warden unit should consist of a block warden, warden assistants, and neighborhood protection groups as required. Although warden assistants and their protective groups may be given special titles and assignments, such as first aid and rescue, they should be able to perform all general warden duties. They should take direction from the block warden or higher authority.

Block wardens and warden assistants should designate one of their staff to succeed them if they should be unavailable or disabled. The organization should be sufficient to provide round-the-clock operation.

Selecting and Recruiting

You, as block warden, should select warden assistants on the basis of experience and leadership ability. For example, a retired fireman may be considered a good candidate for either fire warden or rescue warden. Don't overlook anyone in your block. Women are particularly important for the warden unit since many are available during daytime hours. In addition, many are highly trained specialists who have had valuable professional and technical experience. You will also find older teen-agers who can be of valuable assistance. Likewise, some older people and persons with limited physical disability could perform such duties as telephone operator, evacuation registrar, or clerk. Don't overlook persons who speak more than one language. They are especially needed where some block residents do not speak English.

Making a Block Census

In many cases, a block warden census would be given citywide publicity by the local civil defense organization, and conducted simultaneously in all warden blocks at the direction of the chief warden. Contact your district warden for advice and material assistance such as block warden census forms.

To accomplish the census, divide the block among a few selected assistants. Women are particularly suited to this job. Householders should be assured that the census information will be kept confidential and is for official use only. A tactful approach is important to avoid antagonizing many persons by the careless handling of a few.

In many cases, your census assistants will provide your neighbors with their first civil defense information. Thus, your unit will be informing the residents as well as taking census. This is a good opportunity to tell them where they may volunteer, what courses they make take, and how they may participate in the warden unit.

If you must make up your own block warden census forms, the following information should be included:

(a) Name, street, and telephone number. (If apartment, give apartment number.)
(b) Occupants
    1. Name.
    2. Age (if over 65 or under 16).
    3. Sex.
    4. Occupation, sleeping quarters, and evacuation classification.
(c) Business addresses and telephone numbers.
(d) Incapacitated persons.
    1. Nature of incapacity.
    2. Special care required.
    3. Persons responsible—day, night.
(e) Person to be notified in case of emergency.
    1. Name, address, phone number of relative and close neighborhood friend.
    2. Name and phone number of family doctor.
    3. Name, address, phone number of clergyman (optional).
(f) Type of shelter available—its location.
(g) Facilities for emergency billeting.

The warden census taker should also ask if residents have any of the following equipment and where it is located.

Ladder (give length)	Buckets (water, sand)
Rope	First-aid supplies
Chains	Blankets
Jacks (give capacity)	Lanterns
Shovels	Fire extinguishers
Axes	Wrecking bars—crowbars
Mattocks	Wheelbarrows
Picks	Garden hose
Other hand tools	

Those who express a willingness for their equipment to be used for community self-protection during emergencies should mark each item to aid in its return.

The warden census should include locations and availability of vehicles and whether or not owners would supply operators. Smaller vehicles may be required for messenger service. This information is especially important to transportation officials.

Census information should be filed by street and house number.

Part V
Aid and Comfort

13. JOINING THE RANKS

> It will take all of us to do the jobs that must be done ... in our civil defense organizations.... This is not just a man's job. It is a woman's job, too. There is great work to be done by the women in this country in every part of our national effort.—*President Harry Truman*[1]

Although the Federal Civil Defense Administration emphasized the importance of women in the warden service, it encouraged women to become involved in all service areas, particularly the police service and the nursing service—both deemed critical in a post-attack situation. To address the need for additional police personnel in case of atomic attack, the FCDA published *United States Civil Defense Police Services* in 1951 outlining the scope of the program, open to men and women, and detailing the training and certification requirements to be followed by states and cities. The following year, the agency published *Women in Civil Defense*, which reinforced the point that "women trained in police methods and techniques can be of great help to the police services."[2] The FCDA also turned its attention to nurses in 1952, publishing *The Nurse in Civil Defense*, which focused on the planning and operations of state and local nursing services; and *Civil Defense Nursing Needs*, which presented a program for increasing nursing services to meet the anticipated needs in a post-attack environment. As with the warden service, women across the nation soon stepped forward to contribute to these two civil defense programs.[3]

United States Civil Defense Police Services stated the same refrain as other civil defense publications: "Modern warfare is not limited to military men. Every city, village, and farm can be involved; and every man, woman, and child is a possible casualty." This stark reality, the result of the Soviet Union's entrance into the atomic age two years earlier, necessitated the need for new services to augment and support present ones. The pamphlet stressed that the police must fulfill their responsibility of protecting the public and preserving order, while the civil defense, or auxiliary, police must handle duties required in emergency situations.[4]

A case could be made that women who volunteered and actively participated

Federal Civil Defense Association posters issued during the Korean War have a more somber tone than later ones.

in the FCDA's civil defense police service helped, albeit indirectly, regular women police officers gain more acceptance and increased responsibilities during the 1950s. Women, in fact, represented only one percent of the nation's publicly employed police officers in 1950—approximately 2,600—and just two percent—or 5,617—by 1960.[5] Moreover, many of the cities with women officers adhered to "the California style" or "California professionalism" promoted by O.W. Wilson, author of *Police Administration*, considered at the time as the "bible" of law enforcement. Wilson argued that women police officers should be restricted to the areas of juvenile delinquency, morality crimes, and administrative work—all areas acceptable to traditional gender roles. While acknowledging merit in women's work with juveniles, though, Wilson adamantly stressed that women were not qualified to head even juvenile units.[6]

This changed as the decade progressed. Historian Dorothy Moses Schulz has argued that by the mid-1950s—at the same time civil defense became more pronounced with the Soviet Union's development of a hydrogen bomb and intercontinental ballistic missiles—women police officers began demanding and obtaining changes in their roles. "The idea that uniform patrol on an equal basis with male officers was a viable use of female police personnel was part of a progression that began in the 1950s toward greater integration of women in the police environment," Schulz has written. "A large measure of this integration was fostered by the diminishing importance of the concept of 'women's sphere' in many areas of society."[7]

This same pattern existed in the government's civil defense police service, where initial calls for volunteers focused primarily on men. A good example of this is the announcement by Mayor William O'Dwyer of New York City in 1950 that the city needed 40,000 auxiliary police volunteers, of which 500 would be women.[8] Men's lack of interest, however, opened the door for women to serve in the FCDA's program. In fact, many state and local officials soon changed their strategies and began recruiting women, who were deemed more interested and more available during daytime hours than men. William Kent, New York City's chief of auxiliary police, reported in June 1951 that only 16,000 persons had joined his service, well below his call for 40,000 volunteers. In Delaware, only 300 men volunteered for the auxiliary police service, far short of the state's quota of 1,000. This led Colonel Harry Shaw, superintendent of the Delaware State Police, to comment, "Lack of interest shown by men in the state has made it necessary to augment their numbers by women…. Any woman over 21 years of age, married or unmarried, may volunteer for the service."[9]

Even though women in the auxiliary police did encounter gender bias, they trained for—and were expected to perform—a wide range of duties. In the event of an atomic attack, for example, men and women in the civil defense police service assumed responsibility for preventing and controlling "panic, disorder, hysteria, and mob action," as well as the following duties:

1. Coordinate mutual aid and mobile support operations.
2. Assist in the care and direction of displaced persons.
3. Route traffic for emergency evacuations.
4. Direct people to shelters and manage shelter activities, if needed.
5. Provide first aid.
6. Patrol contaminated and special danger areas.
7. Guard against looting.
8. Use protective measures in connection with unexploded bombs and contaminated areas.
9. Enforce civil defense regulations.
10. Identify the dead and injured.[10]

In December 1950, Colonel Lawrence Wilkinson, acting chairman of the New York Civil Defense Commission, sent a special directive to 104 county and city civil defense directors calling for the recruitment of housewives for part-time service. The following month, New York City published twenty major categories for civil defense, including the qualifications for each category. Under Auxiliary Police Corps, the qualifications read: "Requirements: Physically strong men and women responsive to discipline, capable of commanding respect. Duties: General police work supplementing the regular force; anti-looting, anti-sabotage guard; assistance to other services in air raids." William P. O'Brien, the city's police commissioner, added, "These men and women will be trained for emergency police work, and will, as the name implies, serve as auxiliaries in time of emergency. They must be men and women of excellent reputation and in good physical condition and be prepared willingly and voluntarily to face any danger that may arise in the future." Among the duties for auxiliary women police were assisting at public gatherings, rest centers, shelters, and evacuation points, as well as providing protection of life and property.[11]

New York was among the first states to set its quota for auxiliary police. But by the end of 1951, twenty states had determined their needs. Moreover, the International Association of Chiefs of Police, the National Sheriffs' Association, and state police and sheriffs' organizations had endorsed the civil defense police services. The following year, the FCDA published two more publications promoting auxiliary services: *Aids for Police Service Training Officers* and *Handbook for Auxiliary Police*. In its annual report, the FCDA stated its position on these services:

In order that police forces in necessary numbers can be concentrated where needed, plans have been made for mutual aid between communities within the target areas, and

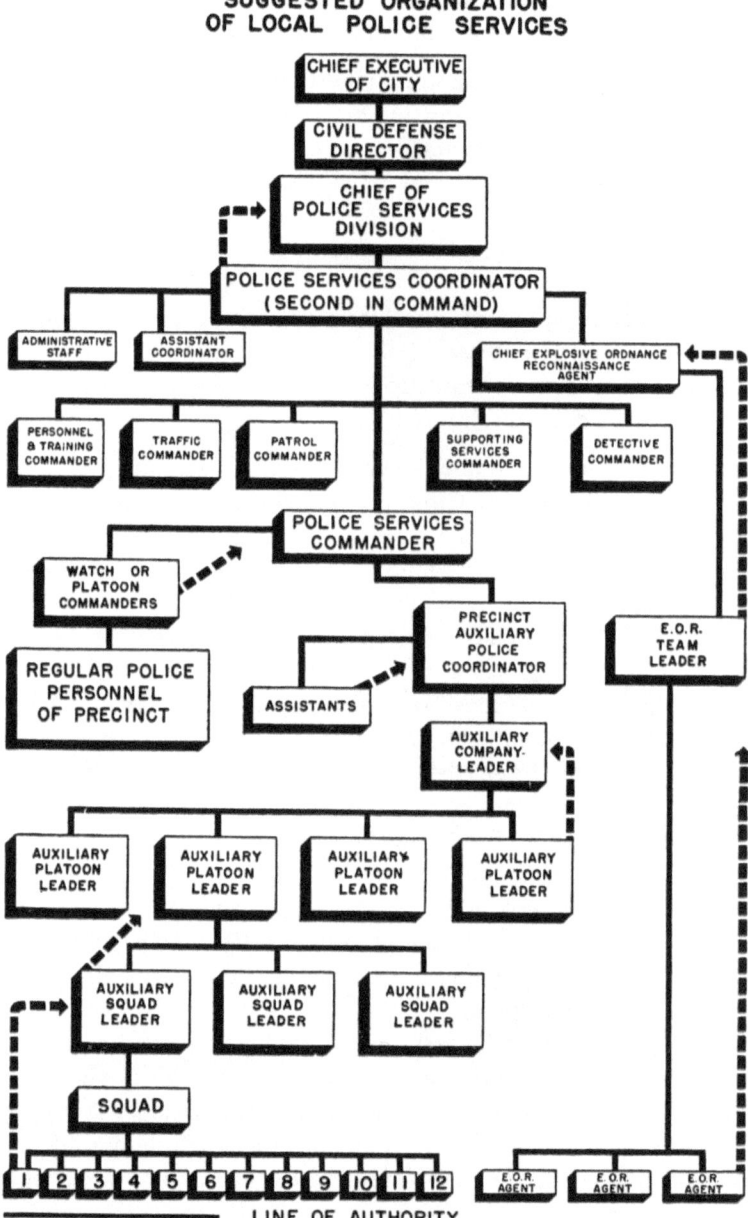

The Federal Civil Defense Administration developed this organizational chart on how the civil defense, or auxillary, police service would be organized within a city. Note that everyone ultimately reports to the civil defense director, who reports directly to the mayor or the city's chief executive.

for mobile police support to be sent into those areas from more distant points. In addition, auxiliary police are being recruited and trained in communities all over the country. These auxiliaries will be used not only to augment the normal police force within an area which is attacked, but in support areas will take the place of the regular police dispatched to aid stricken communities.[12]

The News Journal in Wilmington, Delaware, reported in February 1951 that some 1,500 men and women had entered training for the state's auxiliary police, with 250 representing Wilmington. The training program consisted of twenty weekly sessions. Major D. Preston Lee, state director of civil defense, announced that the auxiliary police division was the state's first division to meet its quota. Lee's goal was to recruit ten volunteers in the auxiliary police for every one regular police officer.[13] Similar stories appeared in cities across the country that year.

Oakland, California—the first city in the state to open the auxiliary police to women—announced in August 1951 that twenty women had volunteered, with one exclaiming, "It is going to be fun to have the same kind of civil defense duties as our husbands." Among their duties were assisting at casualty stations, emergency housing centers for women and children, administrative centers, and registration stations. They also would serve as radio operators and be part of anti-sabotage squads, according to Lester Divine, the city's police chief, who described the women auxiliary police as "Petticoat Police," reflecting his obvious view toward women police officers.[14]

In Hartford, Connecticut, Police Chief Michael Godfrey reported in January 1951 that 103 women had volunteered for the civil defense police service, joining 378 male volunteers. Godfrey earlier had announced that if enough women volunteered, he would form a Women's Police Auxiliary Corps. In another announcement, made in October 1951, William Schatzman, Connecticut's chief civil defense security officer, announced the graduation of 130 men and women from an extensive 40-week course in police work. The next step for the graduates was a period of field training with regular police officers, followed by assignments for specific duties during a disaster. In Greenwich, Connecticut, the local civil defense organization sent requests to 14,000 families seeking volunteers for civil defense, including auxiliary police, with a goal of 1,500 participants.[15]

More than 320,000 men and women joined the civil defense police services in 1952, the same year the FCDA introduced the Emergency Traffic Control Training Course. The course, conducted at the Northwestern University Traffic Institute in Evanston, Illinois, focused on the coordination of traffic control by police, traffic, engineering, and transportation officials. The next year, the FCDA presented the course, which had been modified to encompass a new approach to tactical population dispersal in urban areas, in each of its seven regions. Also in 1952, the FCDA sponsored a regional police institute for 175 persons concerned with police duties, and presented a program on police problems in civil defense emergencies to 11,000 police officers, both regular and auxiliary, through closed-circuit television. The program was shown in ten cities: Boston, New York, Baltimore, Philadelphia, Pittsburgh, Cleveland, Detroit, Chicago, Milwaukee and Toledo, Ohio. By 1953, civil defense police training courses were being offered in Lincoln, Springfield, Joliet, and East Peoria, Illinois; Sioux City, Iowa; Evansville, Fort Wayne, Indianapolis, and South Bend, Indiana; Chicago; Milwaukee; and other cities.[16]

In March 1952, the American Legion and the St. Louis (Missouri) Police Department introduced a cooperative program to recruit auxiliary police for civil defense. According to Joseph Netteler of the American Legion, the goal was to recruit 1,000 volunteers in sixty days.[17] In December, pointing out the shortage of "man power" during daytime hours, Spencer Patterson, director of civil defense in Eatontown, New Jersey, called for the recruitment of women for the auxiliary police force. Even though the city had men in the auxiliary police, Patterson declared that the community would be without emergency protection during the day because many of the men volunteers worked outside the town. Adding women, he pointed out, would ensure "round the clock" protection.[18]

The following February, the newly formed Women's Police Auxiliary in Carneys Point, New Jersey, demonstrated its members' capabilities during a mock enemy attack, while in June 700 men and women enrolled in the Minneapolis, Minnesota, training program for the city's civil defense auxiliary police reserve. The Parent-Teachers Association in Kingsport, Tennessee, introduced a plan in August 1953 to recruit a women's auxiliary police force for civil defense emergencies, as well as to assist regular police officers at school crossings. Members of the women's police auxiliary in Iowa held a statewide convention in September. In December, 50 new members of the Indianapolis civil defense police began a fourteen-week training program, as 115 volunteers graduated, which brought the total number of auxiliary police volunteers to 1,400. Thirteen women began their training for the Athens, Pennsylvania, Auxiliary Police Unit the following March. At the end of the training, the women received radio dispatcher licenses.[19]

The FCDA's 1954 annual report reiterated the overall objectives for its civil defense police services, emphasizing the importance of conducting research on the requisite police functions resulting from a large-scale emergency, such as an atomic attack, and providing this research to the nation's regular police departments. This included developing plans for evacuating people prior to an attack, and moving emergency vehicles and equipment in a post-attack scenario. It also emphasized the role of civil defense police in ensuring the maximum utilization of police resources to "cope with the abnormal problems and expanded requirements which would be created by an enemy attack." To realize its objectives, the FCDA worked with the Civil Defense Committee of the International Association of Chiefs of Police, whose members included police executives from around the country. Among the joint efforts of the FCDA and IACP was the development of a program of police participation in civil defense and natural disasters, which represented 20 percent of the entire program at the association's annual conference in New Orleans in September 1954.[20]

Other activities that year included providing technical advice and assistance to "police institutes" for the purpose of promoting civil defense readiness and offering an opportunity for national, regional, state, and local civil defense police personnel to share knowledge and experience. States conducting these institutes included Connecticut, Georgia, Alabama, North Carolina, Arizona, Delaware, and Maryland. The FCDA also sponsored conferences for regional and state civil defense authorities to discuss and develop an inventory system for police resources and a means to determine potential requirements for these resources. Additional activities included developing outlines and criteria for auxiliary police training courses; creating matching fund programs for conducting these training courses, as well as a program for "expanding existing police communications systems to meet civil defense requirements and to tie them in with civil defense control centers"; and studying emergency traffic operations and providing technical guidance to states and cities related to evacuation planning.[21]

By the mid–1950s, women's participation in the FCDA's police services was well established nationwide. In Indianapolis, men and women completed a seven-week training course in police work and seven weeks of intensive first-aid training. The women's auxiliary police unit had been trained to handle disaster situations and relieve male auxiliaries where necessary. Major William Plummer, coordinator of the Monroe County (Pennsylvania) Civil Defense Auxiliary, endorsed the value of women, saying, "Women auxiliary police are a very valuable asset to any civil defense organization, for when men are detained or cannot operate because of work conditions, women can take their places." Floyd Allen, police chief in Johnson City, New York, issued a similar message in his announcement of a new women's auxiliary police unit. Allen noted that following their training program, the unit would be capable of handling disaster situations and relieving male auxiliary police. In Uniontown, Pennsylvania, the Redstone Township Women's Auxiliary Police conducted a public panel discussion on civil defense needs and objectives.[22]

As the 1950s gave way to a new decade, women's auxiliary police continued to garner attention. In 1959, the Mission, Kansas, civil defense police unit formed a women's police and civil defense auxiliary to assist the men's unit in times of emergency or natural disaster. Training for the new women's auxiliary included courses in first aid, police communications, and civil defense procedures. Members of the Women's Service, Naugatuck (Pennsylvania) Civil Defense, undertook an extensive ten-hour course in basic civil defense in April 1960. *The Morning News* in Wilmington, Delaware, reported in June 1964 that fifteen women had joined the women's auxiliary police, and had begun an eight-week course in medical self-help, shelter management, and basic police work. The Office of Civil and Defense Mobilization stated in its 1960 annual report that the auxiliary police that year counted some 350,000 men and women.[23] Although the exact number of women serving in the civil defense police cannot be verified, it is evident that women represented a significant percentage.

The number of women in the FCDA's nursing service also is difficult to quantify; however, it is clear from historical records that throughout the early Cold War hundreds of thousands of nurses contributed to the nation's civil defense program—either actively involved in the FCDA's nursing service or completing training courses and attending workshops in civil defense procedures. In 1952 alone, the American Red Cross trained 255,191 home nursing students and approximately 5,000 volunteer nurse's aides, while thirteen states provided courses on nursing aspects of atomic warfare to some 100,000 active nurses, 10,000 inactive nurses, and 6,200 auxiliary personnel.

As early as 1950, the American Red Cross had made a commitment to support civil defense by allotting $35,000 to assist the government's efforts to train one million people in home nursing. The first step was training nursing instructors in rural areas. *The Burlington Free Press* summarized the government's objective:

> This is part of the program of teaching people how to protect themselves in the event of an atomic attack. A nation well-prepared for such an event will suffer far less than one which is not prepared.... Besides the lack of trained persons in rural areas, there is another reason for putting emphasis on training rural persons first. If cities are bombed, refugees will move from the urban into the rural areas. But few nurses would move with them if still able to work. They would be very busy in the bombed areas. It would be important to have persons trained for practical nursing in the rural areas to meet the need of the refugees, perhaps to set up temporary hospital units.[24]

The crucial role of home nurses was expressed in a 1951 pamphlet published by the American Red Cross: "Immediately following a bomb attack, you may be sharing your house with strangers or you may be one of many people in a shelter where only the necessities are available.... Those who have had a home nursing course or a volunteer nurse's aide course will assume important roles as assistants to professional nurses in the event of a major catastrophe." By 1951, in fact, numerous states and cities had introduced civil defense training programs for nurses. According to the FCDA, 77,000 persons completed training in the nursing aspects of atomic warfare and more than 270,000 took home nursing courses that year. In March, for example, Alexandria Central Louisiana State Hospital offered one of the government's training courses titled "Nursing Aspects of Atomic Warfare," which was designed to train nurses as civil defense instructors. According to the local newspaper, "The purpose of the course is to give instructions to the nurses so that they can provide the maximum amount of skilled nursing care to the greatest number of civilian casualties in case of atomic warfare." Elsewhere, the Wisconsin State Nurses Association held a statewide enrollment for civil defense of all active and inactive nurses, practical nurses, and Red Cross volunteer nurses. The association then encouraged nurses to attend the "Nursing Aspects of Atomic Warfare" course, while offering training workshops to inactive nurses in order to bring them up-to-date on nursing techniques. The Warren County (Pennsylvania) Nurses' Association made a roster of active and inactive nurses for its civil defense program; the Indiana Nurses' Association sponsored a "Nursing in Civil Defense" program; and the Allegany County (Maryland) Civil Defense organization organized a nurses unit and reported that the unit could draw from more than 300 registered nurses in the county. The next year, the Minnesota Nurses Association offered a course in civil defense nursing in modern warfare. The instructor, Myrtle Coe, president of the association and associate professor of nursing at the University of Minnesota, emphasized the need for nursing instructors to train lay people in home nursing skills, which would be critical following an atomic attack.[25]

The same stories continued as the decade progressed. Six nurses in Baytown, Texas, traveled to Houston in 1954 for civil defense training. Also in 1954, nurses in Muncie, Indiana, participated in a civil defense program presented by the Central East Indiana District Nurses Association, with the area director of the American Red Cross disaster unit speaking on the role of the nurse in emergency situations; nurses in Newington, Connecticut, formed a civil defense group and recruited additional members at local hospitals; and 29 graduate (or newly trained) nurses in Pittston, Pennsylvania, formed a Nurse Corps for civil defense.[26]

Writing in the *American Journal of Nursing* in 1956, Margaret Schafer, chief nurse in the FCDA's health office, called nursing services "essential in any disaster" and pointed out that nurses "must be organized and prepared to meet the total nursing needs in enemy-caused disaster." In the same issue, Ann Magnussen, national director of nursing services for the American Red Cross, agreed with Schafer, writing that nurses had to be prepared for any emergency situation and "the better organized they are, the better will be the quality of care that is given to the disaster victims in the early stages following a disaster."[27]

To ensure that nurses were well trained and organized, the American National Red Cross strengthened its cooperation with the FCDA by developing new courses on home care of the sick and injured. It also created the position of assistant to the president on civil defense affairs; placed a full-time liaison officer at FCDA headquarters in Battle Creek, Michigan; and provided representatives for liaison and program planning in each of the FCDA's seven regions. Other associations strengthened their commitment to the nurse service as well. The American Legion Auxiliary conducted its annual training course in home protection at the FCDA Staff College in Olney, Maryland, while the women's auxiliary of the American Medical Association presented a special program on civil defense during its annual convention, held in Atlantic City, New Jersey. The Future Homemakers of America added a roundtable discussion on civil defense at its annual meeting in Chicago.[28]

State nursing associations also continued their training programs. In 1957, the Montana State Nurses' Association sponsored a series of courses on civil defense for active and inactive nurses. The first program featured a lecture titled "Emotional Shock in Disaster"; subsequent courses covered emergency treatment of injured persons in war and civilian disasters. The Oklahoma State Nurses Association and Oklahoma League of Nurses jointly sponsored a two-day program on civil defense in June 1957, with speakers including both civil defense officials and medical experts. The following year, the New Jersey Division of Civil Defense and Disaster Control offered a light-duty civil defense rescue course for nurses. The twelve-hour course included instruction in how to use a rescue truck and its tools, knot tying, stretcher handling, casualty handling, first aid, firefighting, and rescue reconnaissance. In Wellsville, New York, interest in a civil defense course for nurses in May 1958 had such a good response that the county's civil defense organization arranged a second class. In November 1960, the Idaho State Nurses Association sponsored a civil defense workshop in Pocatello, Idaho, that offered the public an opportunity to learn more about medical needs in a disaster.[29]

As the 1960s began, tensions between the United States and the Soviet Union intensified, particularly during the Berlin Crisis in 1961 and the Cuban Missile Crisis in 1962. In June 1961, the first of seven state civil defense conferences was held at the United States Army Reserve Training Armory in Lansing, Michigan. The two-day conference, sponsored by the Michigan Office of Civil Defense, the Michigan State Nurses Association, and the Michigan League for Nursing, provided registered nurses and other nursing personnel with an opportunity to learn more about emergency hospital operations. Registered nurses gained instruction in operating a 200-bed emergency hospital on the first day; the second day gave licensed practical nurses the same opportunity. The Michigan Office of Civil Defense provided the hospital for demonstration purposes, and had 70 pre-positioned hospitals around the state with equipment ready to be set up in case of an enemy attack.[30]

In Magee, Mississippi, members of the District Eleven Nurses' Association attending a civil defense meeting in 1962 listened as a local doctor explained that as many as 95 percent of the area's population would be affected by radiation in a nuclear attack. Nurses in Troy, New York, took a ten-week civil defense course titled "Emergency Medical Services for Nurses" in 1964. According to a newspaper report, "The purpose of the course is to provide nurses with first-hand experience in setting up and operating an aid station and improvised hospital, and stressing the medical skills and treatments nurses would be expected to perform following a nuclear attack." The next year, the Leominster (Massachusetts) Civil Defense Office, in cooperation with the local hospital, sponsored "Operation Mercy 1965," a training exercise involving civil defense and hospital personnel, including doctors and nurses, responding to a disaster situation.[31]

From these newspaper articles spanning the country during the early Cold War, it is evident that nurses understood their civil defense role in a post-attack situation. As with women serving in the warden service, Ground Observer Corps, and other civil defense services, the nurses—registered, practical, student, and auxiliary—taking instructional workshops and training courses to be prepared for an emergency scenario did so with a sense of purpose.

"[T]he role of the nurse in the event of enemy attack," wrote Catherine Sullivan, R.N., in a 1959 article titled "The Civil Defense Role of Nurses," "will be to adapt comprehensive nursing care to the situation where the numbers of patients needing care and treatment will greatly exceed the number of professional people available and where supplies, equipment, physical facilities, and utilities will be limited. In such a situation, the civil defense nursing service mission is to provide nursing care to the sick and injured and to prevent and minimize illness and injury to the surviving population."[32]

Sullivan's comments concerned nurses, yet they also apply to women in the auxiliary police and all women participating in the nation's civil defense program during the early Cold War. "Civil defense is nonmilitary defense," Sullivan wrote. "It is everyone's business and is a way of life and will be for some time to come."[33]

14. "Police Services"

> *The FCDA's police services represented a major component of the government's civil defense program—both for its role prior to an atomic attack and especially its role in a post-attack scenario. While regular police would be expected to perform their normal duties following an attack, the civil defense, or auxiliary, police would be needed for a wide range of emergency duties, including routing traffic for evacuations, coordinating support operations, and directing people to shelter areas. In 1951, the FCDA published* United States Civil Defense Police Services *outlining the policies, responsibilities, and objectives of the service. This is an excerpt.*

Modern warfare is not limited to military men. Every city, village, and farm can be involved; and every man, woman, and child is a possible casualty. New services must be organized, and existing services must be expanded. As existing organizations, the police services must continue to perform their regular activities of protecting the public and preserving order. In addition, they should train regular and auxiliary police for special civil defense duties. This administrative guide suggests methods and techniques for assisting police officials responsible for organizing or directing police civil defense services.

State Civil Defense Organization

Because of differences in the organization of State governments and, also, geographical variations among States, the exact composition of the State civil defense organization is a matter for each State to determine.

The larger and more populous States should be divided into civil defense sections to provide flexible operation and efficient coordination.

Where State sections are established they should be headed by sectional directors, who would be deputies to the State civil defense director.

The staff at the sectional level will vary according to needs, governed by the scope of civil defense activities assigned to sectional civil defense offices. In general, the sectional director will be assisted, if necessary, by an administrative staff and will rely on the State office for professional assistance.

UNITED STATES CIVIL DEFENSE

POLICE SERVICES

FEDERAL CIVIL DEFENSE ADMINISTRATION

UNITED STATES GOVERNMENT PRINTING OFFICE : MAY 1951

For sale by the Superintendent of Documents, U. S. Government Printing Office
Washington 25, D. C. - Price 20 cents

Metropolitan Area Civil Defense Organization

In planning for civil defense, the terms "metropolitan area," "mutual aid area," and "critical target area" are frequently used and in general are synonymous. These terms refer to an area in which the resources of the political units involved should be pooled and integrated to insure maximum use of personnel, equipment, and facilities for civil defense purposes. These areas may embrace any number of contiguous political units forming a logical group. The units may be either municipalities or counties or any combination of them and may include portions of more than one State.

This arrangement does not prevent each component municipality or county from having its own civil defense organization. However, it is recommended, for the sake of efficiency and economy, that these units agree to establish an over-all civil defense organization. A civil defense coordinating council with representation from all the participating units should be organized. The members of this council, who might well be the mayors, county chairmen, or other chief governing officials, should appoint a director or coordinator of civil defense for the area as a whole. The coordinator should have charge of all civil defense activities and be responsible to the council.

In some instances, at the option of the Governor, certain metropolitan areas would have status equal to the State civil defense sections. At such times, it would simplify and improve liaison with the State organization if the director or coordinator is a representative of the State as well as a locality.

Plans, and agreements involving an area organization must not be in conflict with State and local laws. Interstate compacts must be in accord with provisions of the Federal Civil Defense Act of 1950.

Civil Defense Police Services

Civil defense police services are built on existing organizations. For this reason, they escape some of the problems of other civil defense services which must be established independently. Through years of law enforcement America's police departments have developed and used methods and procedures for handling emergencies of all types. Police problems encountered in civil defense are closely related to those of peacetime operations and are multiplied under emergency conditions in direct proportion to the extent of the emergency.

Therefore, knowledge and experience gained previously are of great value.

The many independent police agencies which participate in America's law-enforcement program must be ready to mobilize for civil defense emergencies, and to work together as one functioning organization. To this end, the civil defense policies, administration, operation, and training of police services should be uniform.

This manual recommends model police organization and activities, which if followed in principle will assure uniformity of State and local police services. The manual is designed particularly to help those States and communities that have not yet organized a civil defense police service. It supplements the general civil defense program described in United States Civil Defense, which covers in brief form all civil defense services, including the police services. As conditions change and civil defense experience broadens, this manual may be amended or superseded by future editions.

Police Services In The State Civil Defense Organization

1.1. Each State civil defense director should establish a police service division and a State coordinator of police. The head of the State police or highway patrol might hold this position along with his regular assignment. Or if a full-time coordinator is required, an experienced police administrator should be appointed. The State coordinator of police should have a staff to assist him in coordinating the functions and operations of the various civil defense police service sections.

1.2 When the State coordinator of police is not serving also as head of the State police force, the latter should serve in an advisory capacity to both the State civil defense director and the coordinator. Close liaison should be maintained between the State civil defense director and the head of the State police.

1.3 A police services advisory committee composed of outstanding law-enforcement experts should be appointed by the Governor to advise him and the State civil defense director on police matters.

1.4 A sectional coordinator of police should be appointed for each general civil defense section and serve on the staff of the sectional civil defense director. An experienced police administrator from the State police force or from a large urban community should be selected for this position. Some sections may require a full-time coordinator without other responsibilities, while in less critical sections the coordinator may serve only part time.

1.5 The State police services civil defense advisory committee advises police agencies on ways of maintaining personnel strength under wartime emergency conditions. It recommends procedures for civil defense police service operations and develops methods for maintaining morale and interest of regular and auxiliary police under stress of increased work and longer hours of duty. The committee also advises on matters of authority, assignment of auxiliary police, equipment, insignia, terminology, and titles.

1.6 Through the directors of civil defense at all levels, the State coordinator of police supervises the various sectional coordinators, and through them he extends plans and operations, personnel and training, and procurement and supply arrangements throughout the State. He transmits instructional and informational material from Federal and State civil defense offices to local civil defense police services. He directs the taking of inventory and maintains master inventory records of all police facilities, personnel, and equipment within the State.

He develops plans for State-directed police mobile support, including the command of intrastate and interstate police resources. He stimulates the organization of regular and auxiliary police training throughout the State and advises on the development of training materials, training aids, and texts through the training division of his State civil defense organization and the vocational training unit of the State education department.

1.7 The sectional coordinator organizes and directs the State civil defense program for police in his section. This includes the planning for State-directed police mobile support from his section. He coordinates and integrates the civil defense police functions with the functions of other civil defense services and assists and advises in developing mutual aid compacts between police agencies operating in the section. This also includes the sectional units of the State police force.

The sectional coordinator is responsible for making or obtaining, and keeping current, an inventory of police resources of the section and transmitting the inventory data to the State coordinator. The sectional coordinator assists and advises in developing and improving police communication systems at all levels. He assists in procurement and distribution of police equipment and supplies and, finally, he plays an important part in the training of police. He is responsible for stimulating civil defense training for regular police and for promoting basic police training for auxiliary police within the section.

1.8 When a metropolitan area coordinator or director of civil defense is established, there should be a coordinator of police on his staff.

He should coordinate with those of other civil defense services; implement police planning for civil defense operations, including mutual aid agreements; obtain, and keep current, an inventory of police personnel, equipment, and facilities in the area; and transmit the inventory data through channels to the State coordinator of police. He assists in developing and improving police communication networks within the area and should play an important part in stimulating the organization and training of auxiliary police, as well as special training of regular police in civil defense functions. This position requires an experienced police administrator, whose opinions, advice, and instructions will command the respect of police executives within the area. He may be a full-time administrator or the chief of one of the larger police organizations involved.

Basic Policy Statements

1.9 The basic policies set forth below should be followed in planning and developing the civil defense police services program:

(a) The regular staffs of all police agencies within the State should be augmented by trained auxiliary police. Additional personnel are required to replace regular personnel lost to the Armed Forces before the emergency; to meet the increase in police duties and responsibilities during a national emergency; to replace casualties at the time of the emergency; and to aid other communities under mutual aid or mobile support agreements.

(b) Auxiliary police should be carefully selected and properly trained.

(c) Police should be given uniform police authority throughout the State so that there will be no conflict in the coordination of forces and activities at the scene of emergency, when auxiliaries are assigned to mutual aid or mobile support operations.

(d) In mutual aid operations, men and equipment should be dispatched only when requested by the responsible director of civil defense through the commander of the police force (or his alternate) in the stricken area.

(e) In mutual aid operations, the head of the local police force in whose jurisdiction the emergency occurs is in command of all police personnel and equipment. However, he directs assisting police forces through their own officers.

(f) In planning for police aid under a mutual aid agreement local police should not be expected to deplete their own personnel and equipment to a point where police operations in their own jurisdictions are endangered.

(g) When requests for mutual aid are received, regular police personnel should be dispatched so far as possible, and trained auxiliary police should be assigned temporarily to take their place.

(h) In mobile support operations the Governor assumes authority over police forces in the State. He may direct them through the head of the police force in whose jurisdiction the emergency occurs, or through the State civil defense director and the State coordinator of police. A proclamation of emergency would ordinarily specify the delegation of command.

(i) The term "auxiliary police" is used in this manual to distinguish volunteer police from regular police. However, it is not intended for use on a Nation-wide basis as an official title, since many police agencies have designated volunteers as "reserve police officers" and the organization as "Police Reserve." Several States have recommended that this designation be used on a State-wide basis.

Summary of State Organization Objectives

1.10 The organization and operation of civil defense police services in a State are based upon the following fundamental objectives:

(a) To stimulate and review police planning and operations in communities.

(b) To coordinate State and local police services planning and operations with planning and operations of all other civil defense services.

(c) To initiate and maintain a continuing inventory of all police resources within the State.

(d) Under the authority of the Governor, to coordinate police mobile support with local police operations and to direct such support in specific emergencies.

(e) To coordinate training programs for regular and auxiliary police with the general civil defense training program.

(f) To transmit through proper channels information and instructional material from Federal and State civil defense offices to all civil defense police services in the State.

Police Services in the Local Civil Defense Organization

5.1 The chief of police, or the sheriff where there is no chief of police, should be the chief of the police services division in the local civil defense organization. The size of his staff and the number of commanders and supervisors will depend on the size of the community and the scope of its police operation. The planning and organization of police civil defense operations should be based upon existing organization and operational procedures. Additional civil defense duties, responsibilities, and functions should be integrated with the regular functions and follow the same operational pattern.

5.2 In the small community the chief of police services will designate officers from his regular staff to succeed him if he should be incapacitated or unavailable. The same arrangement should be made for all supervisory personnel in his command. The designation of alternates and the succession of command should be made known to all personnel, both regular and auxiliary.

5.3 In larger cities the chief will find it advisable, because of the pressure of his regular duties, to appoint his administrative assistant or another executive as the civil defense police service coordinator.

5.4 When the local police force has no assistant chief, the commander of the regular patrol force should be designated as coordinator. The uniformed patrol force, with its reinforcement of auxiliary police, is the most active component of the civil defense police services. Its commander, therefore, is in a good position to coordinate the civil defense police program.

5.5 The police service coordinator will require a staff of assistants and clerical personnel. One or more alternate police service coordinators should be designated and should become thoroughly familiar with local civil defense police functions.

5.6 At the precinct level the commanding officer should be designated as the police service commander. After conference with the police service coordinator, the police service commander should designate the following: Alternates to provide a succession to his command; a full-time precinct auxiliary police coordinator; an assistant or assistants to the precinct auxiliary police coordinator. The assistants should also serve as alternates to the precinct auxiliary police coordinator.

5.7 The following plan is recommended for those communities now in the process of organizing police auxiliaries and those desiring to reorganize their auxiliaries. Local conditions must, of course, be taken into consideration.

5.8 The auxiliary police should be organized into squads, platoons, and companies. This arrangement is advantageous for drills, simulated emergency tests, crowd-control training and operations, and some types of emergency operations.

5.9 Police experience has shown that an efficient organization is 12 men to the squad, 3 squads to the platoon, and 4 platoons to the company. There should be leaders and assistant leaders for each of these units. To avoid confusion and misunderstanding on the part of the other civil defense services working with the police during tests and emergencies, supervisors of auxiliary police should be designated as squad leaders, platoon leaders, and company leaders rather than by the titles of regular police officers.

5.10 Auxiliary supervisors normally would be assigned only on the precinct level, where very few regular police (usually not more than three for the largest precinct) are available to supervise auxiliaries. Large precincts may possibly have as many as three or four companies of auxiliary police and may require numerous supervisors.

15. "The Nurse in Civil Defense"

The Nurse in Civil Defense, *published by the Federal Civil Defense Administration in 1952, outlined the critical need for health professionals and volunteers "to care for the overwhelming number of casualties resulting from enemy attack." The FCDA's nursing service sought registered nurses, practical nurses, Red Cross volunteer nurses, home nurses, graduate (or newly trained) nurses, nurse's aides, and even inactive and retired nurses for its civil defense program. The booklet also covered the need for specialized training, first-aid stations, emergency hospitals, and emergency lodgings. Here is an excerpt.*

Civil Defense Nursing Service

1.1 Existing health services, as their part in the Nation's civil defense, must prepare in peacetime to care for the overwhelming number of casualties resulting from enemy attack. In an emergency, all professional and technical health personnel and facilities would be needed to function under civil defense rules and regulations as civil defense health services. Their primary responsibilities then would be to relieve suffering, apply emergency lifesaving measures, and preserve or restore normal health services.

Pattern for Civil Defense

1.2 Under the Federal Civil Defense Act of 1950 the Federal Civil Defense Administration was established as an independent agency within the executive branch of the Government. FCDA is organized to coordinate and guide essential services in an emergency. These include technical operations, training and education, health and welfare, and public information.

1.3 The Federal government establishes principles, standards and guides in national civil defense planning and operation. The States, as key operating units, provide leadership and supervision in civil defense planning within their boundaries and direct supporting operations in an emergency. Com-

**UNITED STATES
CIVIL DEFENSE**

THE NURSE IN CIVIL DEFENSE

TM-11-7

FEDERAL CIVIL DEFENSE ADMINISTRATION

munities make and implement plans to meet their own crises and supervise local civil defense operations in time of disaster.

Federal Organization

1.4 The health and welfare office, a major component of FCDA, has two divisions: Emergency welfare services division and health and special weapons defense division. The emergency welfare services division plans for emergency lodging, mass feeding, emergency clothing, evacuation, temporary rehabilitation, registration and information, and related services. The health and special weapons defense division plans for civil defense health services relating directly to care of casualties and restoration and maintenance of public health facilities. This division is composed of representatives of the professional services who share the responsibility for planning and operating programs for safeguarding health and caring for casualties.

1.5 The nurse consultant in the health and special weapons defense division is a member of the casualty services branch and is responsible for:

(a) Planning modifications of usual nursing methods and techniques and developing new procedures and techniques necessary to complement plans for medical care.
(b) Coordinating nursing care on a mass basis under conditions of attack.
(c) Developing educational programs for professional and nonprofessional nursing groups, and assisting in proper dissemination of information to the general public on nursing care of casualties.
(d) Promoting instruction of volunteer nurse's aides and home nurses in coordination with the American National Red Cross.
(e) Coordinating and integrating civil defense nursing plans.
(f) Establishing liaison and program coordination with other Federal nursing services, the Red Cross, professional nurses' associations, and auxiliary groups.
(g) Advising and consulting within FCDA and with other Federal agencies, State and local governments, and professional societies.

State Organization

1.6 The head of the State health department usually serves as State director of civil defense health services under the State civil defense director. It is recommended that he have a health advisory committee of physicians, dentists, nurses, hospital administrators, veterinarians, pharmacists, sanitary engineers, and allied specialists.

1.7 In most instances the State director of public health nursing service, or her designated delegate, now serves as appointed head of the State civil defense nursing service, under the guidance of the civil defense health services director. She is responsible for initiation and development of civil defense nursing service plans and programs within the State. She should have a nursing service advisory committee appointed from such groups as State nurses' association, State league of nursing education, State industrial nurses' organization, American National Red Cross, State board of nurse examiners, State organizations for public health nursing, practical nurses, school nurses, voluntary nursing service agencies, and volunteer lay groups interested in nursing.

Local Organization

1.8 Generally the local civil defense health service organization follows the State pattern. Under supervision of the local director of civil defense health services, the local nursing service director plans, administers, and coordinates nursing services. She also consults with representatives of local nursing groups who serve as an advisory committee.

Basic Casualty Service Pattern

1.9 Emergency operations of civil defense health services are aimed at restoring injured, sick, or debilitated persons to normal activity. Some persons trained in first aid or home nursing should be able to care for their own and their neighbors' minor injuries. However, organized civil defense health services should be available to care for all injured.

1.10 Specially trained teams of first-aid workers and litter bearers would provide initial casualty care. These teams, working out of first-aid stations, would enter the damage area, giving on-the-spot first aid to the injured, and work toward the center or ground zero. After emergency treatment, ambulatory casualties would be directed to first-aid stations. Litter cases would be carried to first-aid stations or to litter collecting points for transportation to first-aid stations. As soon as traffic lanes could be cleared, ambulances functioning on a shuttle basis would transport litter casualties to first-aid stations and then to improvised or existing hospitals.

1.11 Existing hospitals should transfer, according to prearranged plans, all but seriously ill patients, to provide space for incoming disaster victims. All transportable patients should be moved to homes or facilities in the immediate vicinity or to hospitals in nearby mutual aid or support areas.

Local Planning

1.13 One of the major difficulties in planning for civil defense nursing service is the severe shortage of nursing personnel. Therefore, the local nursing service director must consider the following factors:

(a) Change in the primary responsibility of the professional nurse.—Professional nurses should be used only for highly skilled care and for supervision of non-professional auxiliary workers (known as auxiliaries). These auxiliaries include practical nurses, trained nurse's aides, first aiders, first-aid technicians, medical corpsmen, home nurses, and people with little or no first-aid or nursing training. Some of the functions, normally the responsibility of nurses, must be delegated to these auxiliaries. This need is illustrated by the amount of time that would be consumed taking pulse and respiration rates every four hours or measuring fluid intake and output for 30,000 patients. To provide minimal care for the large numbers of anticipated casualties and conserve medical personnel, professional nurses, as well as dentists and veterinarians, will have to assume certain functions normally the responsibility of physicians. These functions might include patient screening, administration of intravenous injections, removal of foreign bodies from eyes or wounds, and emergency repair of minor lacerations.

(b) Expansion of nursing service personnel through the wide use of auxiliaries.—Thousands of auxiliaries must be trained to assist in providing:
   1. Simultaneous nursing care to living casualties resulting from enemy attack.
   2. Replacements for anticipated casualties among nurses.

1.14 The local civil defense nursing service director should consider adjustment of nursing procedures to possible shortages of essential facilities, equipment, and supplies needed for mass treatment and care of casualties. As part of the civil defense program, nurses should be trained in improvising acceptable substitutes consistent with the application of principles of medical asepsis. Resourcefulness of nurses during the first few hours of an emergency will greatly increase chances of survival for many casualties.

Coordination With Related Services

1.15 Nursing service, to be most effective, must be fully coordinated with other civil defense health and welfare services. Key nursing personnel should understand the organization, functions, and responsibilities of these services and participate in joint planning for efficient distribution and use of nursing service. For example, nurses are needed now to help educate the public on atomic, biological, and chemical warfare; and to teach nurse's aide and home nursing courses. Following attack, they will be needed in first-aid stations, existing and improvised hospitals, emergency lodgings, and other installations where large groups of people present health problems.

Nursing Service Personnel

1.16 Professional nurses—active, inactive, and retired—should be conserved for duties auxiliaries cannot perform. Therefore, the local nursing service director should seek cooperation of State, county, and local professional nurse organizations and assign specific civil defense nursing responsibilities to their key personnel.

1.17 Practical nurses should be assigned duties which make full use of their training. They should have continuing experience in working with professional nurses as teams.

1.18 Red Cross volunteer nurse's aides form a significant group since they will carry a major share of nursing service during a national disaster. They should be assigned to nursing service teams for practice. This will strengthen peacetime nursing service as well as prepare for a national emergency.

1.19 Red Cross home nurses should be used to perform many of the less technical duties needed in caring for casualties.

Training Program

1.20 Training for nurses in local communities should be provided by civil defense or the existing health agency through staff and nursing organization meetings and special groups assembled for this purpose. Courses for nurses should include:

(a) Nursing aspects of atomic, biological, and chemical warfare.
(b) General nursing care of casualties.
(c) Organization and operation of first-aid, rescue, ambulance, and improvised hospital services.
(d) General civil defense administrative and organizational problems.
(e) First aid.
(f) Nurse leadership or supervision training.
(g) Red Cross disaster conferences.

1.21 Training courses on "Nursing Aspects of Atomic Warfare" were conducted on a national scale between November 1950 and February 1951 to provide instructors for the States. The courses were completed by 372 nurses from 46 States, Territories, and Canada. The National Security Resources Board, Atomic Energy Commission, and the U.S. Public Health Service sponsored the courses.

1.22 The American National Red Cross had agreed to conduct the training program for nurse's aides and home nurses. Courses for home nurses will be about 14 hours, and for nurse's aides, 80 hours. Nurses should volunteer their services as instructors for nurse's aide courses and as instructor trainers for home nursing. The Red Cross method of teaching simple nursing skills in home nursing will prove useful should nurses have to train auxiliaries in the first few hours after an attack.

1.23 Refresher courses on nursing procedures in medicine, surgery, medications, and first aid should be given to inactive nurses.

Part VI
Be Prepared

16. Home Protection and Preparedness

> To fashion from simple everyday materials a house of comfort and cheer; to create through tolerance and wholesome interests a home of peace and pleasure; to inspire respect for the lowly duties of daily life; and to kindle love and understanding of people and all expressions of beauty—this I would do.—*Homemakers Creed, Delaware Home Demonstration Club*[1]

Practically every community in Michigan knew her name. Her goal was home protection. Her enemy was apathy and lethargy. Dorothy Mann, a native of London now living in Detroit, was the director of women's activities for the Michigan Office of Civil Defense, as well as a member of the National Advisory Council of Women's Activities in Civil Defense. In 1956, Mann trained close to 2,500 organization leaders about home protection. Overall, she had trained some 15,000 women in basic home protection at national, state, regional, district, county, and local conferences and meetings. "When Dorothy accepts an invitation to address a women's organization in a community," wrote the *Lansing State Journal World*, "that community is about to wake up to the need for home protection, to the means for home protection, and to the desire for home protection."[2]

Mann is representative of women throughout the nation dedicated to training others in home protection and preparedness, a major component of civil defense throughout the Cold War era. "Every man, woman, and child in the Nation should know exactly what to do if an attack comes, and every home must be properly prepared," read the Federal Civil Defense Administration's 1952 report. This objective had to be done before an enemy attack to be successful. "When personal and family preparedness is adequately accomplished nationally, along with other fundamental civil defense measures, the country's security experts believe that the resulting national readiness on the home front can be a major deterrent to war."[3] Following the success of its "Pledge for Home Defense" campaign that had, according to the agency, prompted millions of Americans to take action for individual and group preparedness, the FCDA introduced the Home Protection Program and Family Action Program in 1953 to provide women around the nation with information and materials to help them teach what can be labeled "full home preparedness." The FCDA distributed more than 12 million publications in 1953, including *Home Protection Exercises—A Family Action Plan*, a booklet of eight self-protection home exercises: What to Do When the Signals Sound, Preparation of Your Shelter, Home Fire Protection, Home Fire Fighting, Emergency Action to Save Lives, What to Do If Someone Is Trapped, Provision of Safe Food and Water, and Home Nursing. The booklet, which was revised annually, represented part of a home protection kit that also contained sample press releases, radio and television spot announcements and scripts, speeches, and ideas for promoting community activities.[4] For example, Parent-Teacher Associations and the Federation of Women's Clubs, among other organizations, performed the agency's 15-minute script on home protection at their various meetings.[5] One civil defense pamphlet described the importance of the Home Preparedness Program—and women's responsibility—this way:

> A Home Preparedness Program in Civil Defense which offers training and education to alert family members of the dangers to expect and how best to combat them has been developed, as the greatest assurance for the security and the survival of America's home life. Home preparedness is actually "Family Action in Civil Defense"—action by the whole family to protect itself in case of an emergency. It embodies a program of training and teaching which, to be successfully experienced and practiced, will largely depend on the initiative, dedication, and devotion of women.[6]

Historian Laura McEnaney has argued that the aim of the FCDA's booklet *Home Protection Exercises* "was nothing less than to transform families into well-trained paramilitary units that required little or no government assistance." She goes on to suggest that family preparedness "borrowed from and reinforced the traditional social arrangements of the period" and home protection was "a militarized elaboration of postwar domesticity, in which the husband assumed the role of sergeant and the wife acted as second in command."[7] This argument suggests some sort of massive government conspiracy, developed by master manipulators of the human condition; implemented with regimented accuracy; and, ultimately, duping American women, such as Dorothy Mann and millions of others, dedicated to civil defense.

What's important to remember is that the development of atomic bombs had occurred just a few years earlier in 1945, completely changing the concept of war and national defense. No longer could the United States feel safe because of its geographic location. During World War II, men and women had achieved unprecedented productivity on the home front—a home front safe from the battles of war being fought in Europe and the Pacific. But by

1953, long-range bombers could strike any city at any time. Commenting on the new reality, Brigadier General J. Wallace West, director of the Utah Council of Civil Defense, said:

> It has been established by our government that the Soviets have the atomic bomb and also possess long-range bombers capable of dropping such bombs anywhere in the United States. It also has been established that the Soviets are well prepared to launch a germ attack against the United States through any of several methods. Under such circumstances, the sensible course of action is to prepare to survive, if such an emergency should arise, by training and equipping a capable defense force. Such preparation can reduce damage and casualties 50 percent.[8]

Because of this, President Harry S Truman, followed by President Dwight Eisenhower, attempted to address this new threat by establishing a domestic civil defense program. The agencies responsible for this program, the Federal Civil Defense Administration and its successor, the Office of Civil and Defense Mobilization, then experimented, if you will, with various programs, policies, and strategies designed to protect civilians by enlisting them to protect themselves. Although the Home Protection Program undeniably focused on women, their role took on much more significance than a "second in command" home manager. As historian Andrew Grossman has argued, women's management of the home was not merely a domestic role. "It is true that FCDA instructions for 'home exercises' at times addressed women's roles in a 'traditional' fashion.... But these 'traditional' depictions of a woman's role in managing the nuclear crisis were not the central themes in these home exercises, and they were not, by any means, the only kind of jobs that women were expected by the FCDA to do during an emergency."[9]

What is apparent from *Home Protection Exercises* and the FCDA's many other publications is that women—often referred to as the understood "you"—represented an essential element in the nation's civil defense. For example, *Home Protection Exercises*, reads:

> Every person, whether he lives in a possible target or a nontarget area, should be trained to act instantly when a warning signal sounds. This applies especially to the family at home. Every person should know the official instructions for taking action on the receipt of warning. The members of your family may have only a limited time to take protective measures if an attack should come. That is why it is important to plan what to do ahead of time, and to practice doing it. Whether you are told to evacuate your city or to take shelter in your home, your chances of survival will be better if your family knows what to do and is trained to act as a unit.[10]

Anyone reading this statement then, and now, clearly understands that "you" equates to a woman. Moreover, illustrations of the protection exercises depicted women in familial roles, from buying groceries and cleaning the house, to checking the furnace and practicing first aid. Yet these depictions did not deter women from conducting workshops and training courses; nor did they stop women from attending them.

Typical topics in these home protection or preparedness courses included how to prevent home fires and fight fires if necessary; caring for the sick and first-aid basics; food and water stockpiling; locating and preparing a shelter area within the home; and having an emergency radio, flashlight, batteries, and other supplies on hand. Instructors, such as Mann, also encouraged women with special skills to register with the local civil defense agency, and all women to take the 14-hour American Red Cross home nursing course and to volunteer for the Ground Observer Corps. "A very large share of home protection in case of disaster of any sort naturally falls on the shoulders of competent homemakers," Mann was quoted as saying. "If the home is prepared for emergency, there will be more peace of mind for the mother, the father, and the children ... and much less fear and tension."[11]

By 1954, the need for home preparedness had escalated because both the United States and the Soviet Union now wielded hydrogen bombs. Despite this escalation of destructive power, or because of it, Katherine Howard, FCDA's deputy administrator, urged women to maintain "a carry-on spirit in the direst of circumstances." In a newspaper interview, Howard said that women would be better off in "the age of peril" if they accepted the possibility of an H-bomb attack. "Emotionally and psychologically," she said, "it is better than an ostrich-like attitude of not wanting to think about it." She then repeated the FCDA's recommendation that women have their families do home protection exercises; identify a shelter area in their home; and prepare the necessary food, water, and other emergency supplies.[12]

Many states and local civil defense groups, as well as women's organizations, followed Howard's and the FCDA's advice by initiating programs in home protection. In May 1954, civil defense teams throughout Louisiana, plus units of the American Red Cross and staff members from the state's civil defense office, met in Alexandria to demonstrate how women could provide emergency home self-protection. Demonstrations included emergency sanitation, firefighting for householders, emergency lighting, and light rescue. The Red Cross conducted first-aid and home-nursing demonstrations, as well as a simulated emergency registration of workshop participants and canteen service operations.[13] That September, some 200 men and women representing 35 counties and 52 communities from across the state met for a one-day conference on home protection at Michigan State College (now Michigan State University) in East Lansing. Attendees also included city and county civil defense directors and the state leaders of 50 women's organizations. The primary objective was to teach how to conduct local programs based on the FCDA's home protection exercises.[14] The next month in Kansas City, Missouri,

Mrs. Charles Noel addressed a meeting of the Culture Club on the importance of home protection. She stressed the need for a home shelter, plus the need to volunteer for civil defense. And if the community did not have a warden system, Noel told the women to take the lead in creating one.[15]

The FCDA held the first in a series of three-day home protection exercise courses in November 1955. The courses, held at the agency's training facility in Olney, Maryland, were sponsored by the Maryland Federation of Women's Clubs in cooperation with the regional director of women's civil defense activities and the state training officer. The regional director also worked with Girls' Nation and Girls' State, Future Homemakers of America, and the Girl Scouts on similar programs.[16] In Provo, Utah, Mrs. Victor Bird, Utah County director of women's civil defense activities, issued a state-wide announcement in 1955 outlining the steps to take in home preparedness, beginning with building a home shelter or identifying an area of the home that provided the most protection. In line with the FCDA's Home Protection Program, Bird also emphasized the need for an emergency first-aid kit, ensuring that the home was fireproof, and there was an adequate food and water supply. In addition, she recommended that families form neighborhood discussion groups with local civil defense wardens.[17]

Representatives of women's organizations from six counties in West Virginia met in May 1957 to attend a Home Protection Exercise Course. The Raleigh County civil defense director encouraged each organization to send five members so one person could attend each of the five classes being held, including Radioactive Fallout and Preparing Your Shelter; Emergency Sanitation and Safe Food and Water; What to Do When Someone Is Trapped; Emergency Action to Save Lives; and Home Fire Prevention and Home Fire Fighting.[18] In September, events were planned across the country in conjunction with Civil Defense Week. Women from five states—Michigan, Wisconsin, Illinois, Missouri, and Indiana—met in Indianapolis for a civil defense conference with the theme, "Education to Meet Disaster." Top billing, according to a newspaper report, was the role of women in home protection, with a presentation by Mary Ellen Pangle, national assistant director of women's civil defense activities. Members of the Altrusta Club in Alexandria, Louisiana, listened as Andrew Gambordella, director of civil defense for Rapides Parish and the city of Alexandria, encouraged them to become more involved in civil defense. The club responded by adopting a home preparedness program with the goal of 100 percent participation among its members. Each member's home was to be inspected following completion of the program, with an award given to the member with the best home preparedness plan. In Provo, Utah, the Women's Civil Defense Counsel heard George Larsen, director of the Provo City Civil Defense Program, explain the importance of home protection. The council included representatives from area women's organizations, clubs, churches, and schools.[19]

In April 1958, more than 200 women attended a home preparedness workshop in Eugene, Oregon, sponsored by the Lake County civil defense organization and Lake County Chapter of the American Red Cross. The workshop emphasized civil defense in the morning sessions, with demonstrations of first aid and medical procedures for caring for the sick held in the afternoon. The morning program typified how workshops were conducted. The chair of the local women's civil defense committee welcomed attendees. This was followed by a discussion of the importance of home preparedness; a skit on home preparedness; a presentation on the essential medical facts for home care; a review of potential health and sanitation problems; an educational talk on radioactivity; a civil defense film; and, finally, handouts of instructor kits, with attendees encouraged to conduct their own smaller workshops.[20] The next month, the Silver Bow Civil Defense Administration in Butte, Montana, hosted a course on home preparedness presented by Alberta Paxton, a nurse with extensive training experience around the nation. The course's objective was to train instructors, who would then teach others. Topics covered fire prevention, first aid, and home nursing.[21]

More than 100 women in Wilmington, Delaware, enrolled in a 16-hour home-preparedness course in November 1958 offered by the city's Civil Defense Department. The course was designed to teach at least one member of the home about planning and implementing a home survival plan. Topics covered the usual ones: air raid signals, radioactivity fallout and shelters, emergency sanitation, home fire prevention, first-aid training, home nursing, light rescue, and preservation of food and water. Women completing the course then received certificates and civil defense identification cards.[22] Shortly thereafter, the *Palm Beach Post* in West Palm Beach, Florida, reported that 34 women had completed a similar home protection course.[23]

At a meeting in Reno, Nevada, held in January 1959, Evan Peterson, assistant director for Region 7 of the newly formed Office of Civil and Defense Mobilization (OCDM), commented on the public's indifference toward civil defense, telling those in attendance, "The apathetic and complacent attitude toward civil defense which is purportedly assumed by the people of America is entirely due to lack of knowledge. And if civil defense headquarters were expanded so as to make their education possible, civilian defense would become an effective branch of the defenses of our country." He then went on to outline the establishment of home preparedness workshops based on the government's official program.[24] Members of 21 homemakers' clubs in Washington County, Maryland, took a one-day course on home protection that September. The course, organized by the Maryland State Civil Defense Agency, featured specialized trainers in first aid, firefighting, and rescue. Also speaking was Henry Nathan, public information officer with the Maryland Civil Defense Agency, who stressed the importance of learning the warning signals and knowing what they mean, and understanding the use of CONELRAD, the nation's emergency broadcasting system.[25]

A workshop titled "Home Preparedness to Meet Disaster—A Family Action Program," held in McKinney, Texas, in July 1959, attracted representatives from a wide range of organizations. These organizations included home demonstration clubs; civil and service clubs; Parent-Teachers Associations; and the American Red Cross. In addition, state, city, and county police attended, as did teachers and health officials. Grace M. Martin, state consultant for women's civil defense activities and columnist for *Texas Defense Digest*, directed the workshop, which included several presenters who covered the basic topics in home preparedness. In addition, the workshop featured a presentation on "Packing Survival Kit and Extra Equipment Needed for Car," which had become more important as evacuation became a viable means of survival—if there were enough time.[26]

Home preparedness programs did not slow down as the nation entered the 1960s. At a January 1960 civil defense conference in Sioux Falls, South Dakota, Olive Berg, the state director of women's activities for civil defense, addressed the importance of home preparedness workshops, and introduced a new state-wide Home Preparation Award Program based on the OCDM's 20 areas in which a family should be prepared in case of emergency. The program was to be coordinated by the state's county civil defense directors. Audrey Smith, regional women's civil defense director, told attendees that women were the key to civil defense. "The national plan for civil defense mobilization points out the responsibility of the individual for caring and planning for his own survival," she continued. "It also points out the responsibilities of organizations. It is through the 60 million women who belong to different organizations that we expect to reach more than 40 million families." The conference ended with Paul Forsythe, the Denver regional liaison officer, explaining the FCDA's new rural civil defense program and passing out an information kit to attendees.[27]

Women gathered later that year in Yuma, Arizona, to form the Woman's City Council for Civil Defense, whose initial objective was the introduction of a Home Preparedness Award Program.[28] To receive the OCDM's Home Preparedness Award, participants had to achieve the following requirements:

1. Know the warning signals and what they mean.
2. Know my community plan for emergency action.
3. Have selected our family shelter area.

4. Have plans for emergency cooking.
5. Have plans for emergency heating.
6. Have plans for emergency lighting.
7. Know what to do about radioactive fallout.
8. Have a two weeks' supply of food and water.
9. Am prepared to purify unsafe water.
10. Have a radio that does not depend upon a commercial source of power.
11. Know the CONELRAD stations, and am prepared to listen for survival instructions.
12. Have a first-aid kit.
13. Have emergency clothing and blankets.
14. Have recreational and morale supplies.
15. Do fire-preventive housekeeping.
16. Have emergency firefighting plans and equipment.
17. Have made emergency sanitation plans and preparations.
18. Have plans for evacuation in accordance with my community plan.
19. Have a family emergency plan with which all members of my family are familiar.
20. Will maintain preparation current with state and local plans.

Cities and towns around the country offered similar programs. But one of the more ambitious undertakings in 1960 was the Home Preparedness Program sponsored by the Jefferson City (Missouri) Women's Council for Civil Defense, under the leadership of Gay Goddard, who also served on the state's Civil Defense Women's Advisory Committee. The program, aimed at women's organizations, included a chairman's kit and individual home preparedness kits for each member. Goddard stressed the importance of the program because Jefferson City, the state capital, had been identified as one of the state's target cities. The other target cities were St. Louis, Kansas City, Springfield, St. Joseph, and Whiteman Air Force Base near Sedalia. Goddard was even featured in a five-part television series on home preparedness, with interviews focused on a woman's role in preparing her home for an emergency. As a community service, the *Jefferson City Post-Tribune* carried a series once a week in its Sunday newspaper on the program's 20 requirements. The first home recognized as being prepared for emergency was the home of Mr. and Mrs. Rottmann. In May, five months into the program, John Sullivan, the city's civil defense director, presented the Home Preparedness Award to Nancy Rottmann, who had learned of the program through the Women's Advisory Council.[29]

How to earn your

To receive the Office of Civil Defense Mobilization's Home Preparedness Award, participants had to fulfill 20 different requirements, including having a two weeks' supply of food and water and "recreation and morale supplies."

Women in St. Cloud, Minnesota, took a six-week civil defense course in early 1960 for the purpose of instilling five steps that each person should know. These steps included knowledge of warning signals and what they mean; knowledge of the community emergency plan; knowledge of radioactive fallout; knowledge of first aid and home preparedness; and knowledge of CONELRAD. Reporting for the *St. Cloud Times*, Sue Ossanna pointed out that individuals needed to know the warning signals because the city sounded sirens each month in a practice alert drill to make residents stop and think about what they were to do. Moreover, she stressed the importance of taking additional first-aid classes. "Civil defense education is a type of insurance," Ossanna wrote in reference to a teacher's comments. "It is better to be prepared in knowledge and supplies, than to face a catastrophe with blank mind and an empty cupboard."[30]

On January 20, 1961, John Kennedy assumed the presidency and offered this cautionary statement to the American people: "The world is very different now. For man holds in his mortal hands the power to abolish ... all forms of human life.... [T]o those nations who would make themselves our adversary, we offer not a pledge but a request: that both sides begin anew the quest for peace, before the dark powers of destruction unleashed by science engulf all humanity in planned or accidental self-destruction." Wasting little time to make his position known, Kennedy addressed Congress on May 25 about the need for a new and revitalized civil defense program to protect the civilian population of the United States from the hazards of possible nuclear war. Among the major actions in the new civil defense plans were the assignment of the civil defense program to the Secretary of Defense, appropriation of an additional $200 million to civil defense for fiscal year 1962, expansion of civil defense training and educational programs, and renewed emphasis on a nationwide system of public or community fallout shelters. In his message, titled "Urgent National Needs," the president told the members of Congress:

> One major element of the national security which this nation has never squarely faced up to is civil defense. This problem arises not from present trends but from national inaction in which most of us have participated. In the past decade, we have intermittently considered a variety of programs, but we have never adopted a consistent policy. Public considerations have been largely characterized by apathy, indifference, and skepticism; while at the same time, many of the civil defense plans proposed have been so far-reaching or unrealistic that they have not gained essential support.

The next month, Kennedy flexed his muscle during the Berlin Crisis, in which the Soviet Union demanded that the United States and its allies abandon Berlin, located within East Germany. U.S.–Soviet relations remained tense for several months, until the Soviet Union eventually backed down. The following year, however, in October 1962, the nation again ventured to the brink of nuclear war during the Cuban Missile Crisis. What had begun with the promise of "The New Frontier," had given way to a growing sense among many Americans of the urgency—the necessity—of being prepared.

Close to 300 men and women participated in the first of five home preparedness workshops in Butte, Montana, in the summer of 1961 during the Berlin Crisis. The workshop was endorsed by Montana Governor Donald Nutter.[31] Also that summer, women in Nashville, Tennessee, enrolled in a 10-hour home preparedness course. Noted Wayne Whitt, a reporter for *The Tennessean*, "Civil defense activities involve a lot of men. But more women are being exposed to these activities. And one of the important things is that the home preparedness course is something they can use in their everyday family life."[32] The home preparedness coordinator in Scottdale, Pennsylvania, announced a new course to begin in November. James Robbins, the local civil defense director, urged residents, both men and women, to enroll, urging them to "wake up now and become part of the unit. We must get prepared now. We need the cooperation of every citizen to make this a successful civil defense unit. We can't wait until something happens."[33] In November, some 300 women's clubs and social agencies sent representatives to an instructor course in Syracuse, New York. The six-house course covered the fundamentals of home defense against nuclear attack, and provided attendees with the knowledge to teach others in their respective organizations.[34]

At the height of the Cuban Missile Crisis in October 1962, Jim Waesche, a reporter for *The Daily Times* in Salisbury, Maryland, wrote: "The people of the United States are presently faced with a crisis which threatens to bring war uncomfortably close to their own shores. Many people are beginning to think, some for the first time, what they would do if this war, if begun, should spread to the continental United States. Inquiries have been flooding in to local civil defense agencies. 'Are you offering any preparedness courses?' someone asks. 'Do you have any plans for fallout shelters?' another questions anxiously. The agencies do, of course, have both courses and plans available—and have had for some time in the past." The Somerset County Civil Defense Agency, formed the previous year, had moved proactively in many areas, Waesche reported, including the planning of food stockpiles, the study of mass feeding, and the distribution of civil defense materials. In addition, the agency had conducted courses in medical self-help, protecting yourself against radioactivity, and home preparedness—both to individuals and to organizations. In fact, it planned to hold its next home preparedness workshop the following month. Members of the area Homemakers and Somerset Women's Civic Club of Princess Anne who had completed the workshop set their goal to enroll individual homeowners, men and women, who had no previous survival instruction.[35]

Home preparedness courses continued to be held, even though interest in civil defense continued to decline as the 1960s unfolded. With the nation now embroiled in the Vietnam War, protests against the war, and the civil rights movement, the Johnson Administration and Congress turned their attention to the general state of the nation's overall military preparedness. Yet civil defense remained a concern. In fact, shortly after announcing on March 31, 1968, that he would not run for a second term, President Johnson issued a statement on the "Need for Federal, State, and Local Cooperation in Civil Defense and Emergency Preparedness," reminding the nation that the nuclear threat still existed, and Americans had to remain vigilant.

"While we are working for peace, and hope that there never will be an attack upon this country," read the statement, "it has been the long-established policy of our nation to maintain both military and nonmilitary preparedness." The nation's security, moreover, required cooperation among federal, state, and local governments, with the chief executives of these various governmental units discharging "their clear and compelling responsibility for leadership in civil defense and emergency preparedness."[36]

As is evident in Johnson's statement, the Cold War remained on high alert even as the nation dealt with increasingly urgent social, political, and military issues in the mid–1960s. Americans had to be prepared and ready in case of a nuclear attack—as they had been reminded earlier and repeatedly by Presidents Truman, Eisenhower, and Kennedy. More specifically, women had to remain vigilant in their commitment to prepare their homes and protect the home front for a nuclear attack. Although much progress had been accomplished, acknowledged the president, there was no time to rest. "Additional fallout protection for our citizens and complementary preparedness programs will continue to strengthen our strategic defense posture," he stated. "In time of emergency, what matters most is advance preparations."[37]

17. "Women in Civil Defense"

Women had a critical role in civil defense: to make sure the home was well equipped and the family was ready at any moment. Women in Civil Defense, *published in 1952 by the Federal Civil Defense Administration, not only outlined women's importance at home and in the community, but it also made clear their responsibility—their duty—to actively participate in civil defense.*

The home is the basic unit of the community—and the basic unit on which defense of the home front must be built.

Whether you are a housewife, secretary, business executive, or nurse, civil defense looks to you, as a woman, to take an active role in protecting your home. No one else can do that job for you.

Your first duty in civil defense is to act at once to educate your family in self-protection against modern weapons, and to make your home as safe as possible against the dangers of enemy attack.

Your second duty is to participate in your community civil defense organization. There must be a basic civil defense organization in each community in the United States, regardless of size or location. Without fully organized communities, there can be no adequate national civil defense program.

If your community does not have an active civil defense organization, much of the blame must fall on you and your neighbors. Unless you, as a responsible American woman, take action, you are gambling with the safety of your family, your friends, your community, and your country.

You would hardly blame others for failing to provide food, clothing, and shelter for your family. That is your family responsibility. And so is family civil defense. Community civil defense can be effective only if the families of the community are solidly behind it, willing to give time and effort to make it work. National civil defense can be only as effective as the people of the Nation make it.

Civil defense is here to stay. We will need it just as long as we need a strong military force. Without civil defense, no military force can win a major war.

Women

IN CIVIL DEFENSE

FEDERAL CIVIL DEFENSE ADMINISTRATION

This fact was recognized by Secretary of Defense Robert Lovett when he said that "civil defense is a co-equal partner" of the military forces.

In these days of atomic, biological, and chemical weapons carried by bombers, submarines, and agents, no part of America is beyond the reach of an enemy. What's more, we cannot prevent attack. General Vandenberg of the Air Force has said repeatedly that the *best* our anti-aircraft and interceptors will be able to do is to knock down 30 percent of attacking planes. Seven out of ten enemy planes will get through.

If this comes as a surprise, remember that our own air raids on Germany during the last war lost less, on the average, than one out of ten planes. *No enemy ever knocked down as much as 30 percent of our planes in any raid we ever made....*

Furthermore, an enemy would strike at our cities and our people first. This is true because our two greatest strengths are the civilian will to fight and to produce the sinews of war. To win a war, military forces must have a constant pipeline of supplies flowing to the fighting fronts. Civilians produce the things the military forces need. If our people, farms, and factories are destroyed, the military forces will soon have no supplies with which to fight.

And remember that American soldiers, sailors, airmen, and marines are fighting for the people at home. If the home front crumples behind them, they not only have nothing to fight *with*, they have nothing to fight *for*.

That's why civil defense is just as important as a strong military force and why civil defense is important to every community and person in America.

Not every community will be attacked. But those that are attacked cannot hope to take care of themselves without help. The help must come from the organized civil defense forces of communities and States which are not attacked. That's why *all* communities must be organized.

To do the job, over 17 million hard-working, well-trained volunteers are needed. Your community needs volunteers now and for years to come.

The greater percentage of these volunteers will be women like you.

At least 60 percent of civil defense volunteers must be women serving in hundreds of specialized civil defense jobs. Many volunteer jobs can be filled by you and your friends right now, with only a little training.

When you have trained your family and prepared your home, you have more than doubled your chances for survival in an atomic attack.

When you have joined in organizing your community, you have given the community and the Nation a far better chance to survive an enemy attack.

But you will have done more than just prepare in case of war—you will have made a positive contribution to keeping the peace.

An unprepared nation invites attack. A nation without civil defense is unprepared.

A strong civil defense preparedness program, like a strong military preparedness program, is not just a shield but a sword. Adequate civil defense preparedness can actually help hold the enemy at bay. If the enemy knows that he can demoralize us by an all-out attack on the home-front; if he knows that we are not prepared for it; if he knows that our civil defense system is ill-manned, ill-trained, and ill-equipped—this is a direct invitation to launch such an attack on our people and on our cities.

But, if Russia knows that millions of American men and women are well trained and organized and ready to move into action when the attack comes; if Russia knows that we have thousands of trained rescue squads and tens of thousands of wardens and millions of American families trained in first aid and self-protection; if Russia knows that we have this kind of adequate civil defense preparedness which would save at least half the American lives that might otherwise be lost—then Russia, or any other enemy, will think long and hard before launching an attack on this country.

The stronger we are in America in civil defense, the more Russian atomic bombs it will take to do the damage to our cities and people that the enemy must inflict in order to win a war.

Thus, a strong national civil defense program actually cuts down sharply the effectiveness of the enemy's stockpile of atomic bombs and his stockpile of other modern weapons.

Said quite simply, a strong American civil defense program forces Russia to use two atomic bombs instead of one, thus reducing the size and effectiveness of the Russian stockpile.

A strong civil defense stands side by side with our armed forces as a major deterrent to enemy attack on our own country. This makes civil defense a major force in helping keep the peace and in preventing World War III.

There is another value in civil defense which is becoming more apparent by the day—its peacetime use in natural disasters.

There have been many recent instances where the organization and training for civil defense in wartime have paid great dividends in meeting peacetime disasters; most all of the training you get in civil defense is useful in saving lives in peacetime, too.

Getting America prepared on the home front is a responsibility that falls in large part on the shoulders of all American women. It's your job—and you have no time to waste.

Family Civil Defense

Here are the simple steps you should take now to prepare your home and family against enemy attack:

1. Learn the civil defense air-raid alert signals.
2. Equip the most protected place you can find in or near your home for an air-raid shelter.
3. Learn the effects of an atomic explosion and the safety precautions you can take at home or at work to minimize danger and injury.
4. Prepare an emergency first-aid kit for your home.
5. Take a regular Red Cross first-aid or home nursing course as soon as you can.
6. Practice fire-proof housekeeping. Learn to fight fires in the home.
7. Get official civil defense identification tags for yourself and family, if available.
8. Learn the simple safety measures you and your family must take to protect yourself against germ and gas warfare.
9. Maintain a three-day supply of food and adequate water for use in an emergency.

Identification Tags

You should get identification tags for each member of your family from the local civil defense authorities.

Home Drills

Once you and the family have a basic knowledge of self-protection, you should hold air-raid drills and practice fire-fighting techniques. Give each member of the family a task in keeping with age and physical capabilities. Alternate duties as much as possible so that all members of the family are familiar with each air-raid and fire-fighting task. Hold drills frequently so that responses to emergency situations become automatic.

18. "Get Acquainted with the Home Defense Corps"

The core objective of civil defense was ensuring that every American home was prepared for an atomic attack. Cities across the nation conducted programs and activities to achieve this objective. Milwaukee established a special civil defense unit called the Home Defense Corps. Its mission: to visit each home in the city and teach families the basic survival skills and practices, such as identifying a shelter area, making the home fireproof, and stocking an emergency supply of food and water. Here is an excerpt from Get Acquainted with the Home Defense Corps, *a brochure distributed to Milwaukee's residents.*

Survival Training—for Any Emergency!

"The best laid plans" of civil defense officials to meet and defeat disaster in any form—natural or man-made—are useless on paper. They demand the active participation of every man, woman and child in the community to succeed. Public education in basic survival techniques is one of the most important phases of civil defense. The HOME DEFENSE CORPS can provide you with the knowledge to survive any disaster.

The Need: The free world today faces the threat of annihilation. Never before has war come so close to all human beings. Never again will any portion of the earth be safe from the ravages of war. Natural disasters, too, make their mark on all communities. The individual citizens—YOU—are on the front line of battle against the complete extinction of civilization.

Training: Looking at the few pamphlets on the subject will not give you the necessary knowledge to protect your family in time of peril. Ignoring the threat to your way of life will not help when disaster strikes. It takes training in the fundamental techniques of survival—training offered by the HOME DEFENSE CORPS—to make a family confident that they are ready to face disaster. Classes are held periodically in your neighborhood at convenient times and places.

Opportunity: The HOME DEFENSE CORPS offers you an unparalleled

opportunity to serve your community as well as yourself. A prepared community helps your own chances for survival in disaster. You can bring the knowledge learned through training to your neighborhood by becoming a HOME DEFENSE OFFICER or a HOME DEFENSE INSTRUCTOR. You will feel the satisfaction that comes from helping people and experience the satisfaction of being a useful citizen.

CIVIL DEFENSE IS EVERYBODY'S BUSINESS

19. "Individual and Family Preparedness"

In 1959, the Office of Civil and Defense Mobilization (OCDM) published Individual and Family Preparedness, *building on the policies of its predecessor, the Federal Civil Defense Administration, in outlining the responsibilities of every American to be ready for a potential nuclear attack by the Soviet Union. By the late 1950s, both the United States and the Soviet Union had intercontinental ballistic missiles capable of delivering hydrogen bombs, which had enough destructive power to spread radioactive fallout for hundreds of miles. As a result, more emphasis was placed on protection from radioactivity. Here is an excerpt.*

> Civil defense and defense mobilization is the responsibility of every citizen. The individual must be capable of caring for himself in an emergency and contributing to the organized community survival effort. Similarly, the family unit trains and prepares to solve its own emergency problems (including home preparedness) and to assist others in need.—*The National Plan*

Purpose

OCDM recommends that Federal, State, and local governments use all available media to inform the public of the importance of self-help, and to urge that all persons prepare for survival in emergencies....

Planning Basics

A. The protective actions recommended for families and individuals are vital in carrying out the provisions of The National Plan for Civil Defense and Defense Mobilization under which all governments and citizens will operate in the event of enemy attack....

B. In addition to the destruction of target areas by the blast and heat effects of thermonuclear weapons, radioactive fallout contamination could immobilize the citizenry for days or weeks in much of the remaining part of

Appendix 1
(Annex 2-Individual Action)

Individual and Family Preparedness

NP-2-1
National Plan Appendix Series

 Executive Office of the President
OFFICE OF CIVIL AND DEFENSE MOBILIZATION

the Nation. The National Plan therefore states: "Individuals and families will be prepared to exist on personal stocks of survival items in homes and shelter areas for 2 weeks following attack."

Basic Survival Needs

A. Important survival requirements for individuals and families are: Shelter from radioactive fallout, a 2-week supply of food and water, cooking and eating utensils and equipment, fuel, clothing, bedding, first aid supplies, special medicines (if required by chronic illness), sanitation supplies and equipment, and a battery-powered radio.

B. Survival items should be stored in the home shelter, or if not there, in some convenient place where they can be quickly moved to the shelter or where selected items can be easily carried to the car in case of evacuation.

Know the Community Plan for Emergency Action

Know the emergency plans and actions of your local government. Learn how they affect you and how you can cooperate to make them more effective. For example, learn the evacuation routes to reception areas, how radioactive fallout information is disseminated, and what to expect in billeting displaced persons.

Know Where to Get Welfare Assistance

After enemy attack, report to the nearest welfare office as soon as possible when your local authorities report that it is safe to do so. The welfare office will be the source of information concerning survivors and disaster conditions, the means for contacting friends and separated family members, and the place where you can learn how to obtain the specific assistance you may need.

Prepare a Fallout Shelter

1. Prepare a home shelter for protection from radioactive fallout. The major requirement of such a shelter is that the top and sides be covered with enough dense material (e.g., concrete, earth) to shield the occupants from penetrating gamma radiation. Other requirements include proper entrance design, ventilation, adequate space, and sanitation facilities.

2. If you have not already prepared a home shelter before an attack

comes, you will find it difficult to improvise one that will provide sufficient protection—particularly if fallout becomes heavy in your community. An inner hallway of your home would offer some protection. A basement corner would be more effective because the earth around it would provide more shielding. To the extent that time permits (it may take an hour or more for fallout to reach your home) and dense shielding materials are readily available, you can improvise shelter in a selected area of your home. To improvise for fallout protection, stack dense shielding materials (e.g., solid concrete blocks, sandbags, bricks) around your shelter area (e.g., a basement corner), place supports across the top, and cover with dense materials.

3. Lacking a prepared shelter or sufficient warning to improvise one before arrival of fallout, you should seek the best cover available. Away from your home or other buildings, you could obtain substantial protection in tunnels, mines, and some culverts, especially if the openings could be closed to exclude radioactive dust.

4. Be prepared to make a fallout shelter your home for 14 days or longer. In areas of very light fallout, shelter occupancy time may be as little as one day. In areas of heavy fallout, it may be as much as 14 days or more, but occupants probably could spend some time outside the shelter after the first few days.

Increase Home Food Stocks

1. After a thermonuclear attack, a most difficult task of survivors will be that of obtaining food and water without overexposing themselves to fallout radiation. This fact emphasizes the importance of keeping on hand at least a 2-week supply of food and water. This supply can mean the difference between life and death. During emergencies, stored food and water should be used conservatively to prevent wasting them or exhausting them too rapidly. Your hot water heater is a good emergency source of water. If refrigerators or deepfreeze units become inoperable, the food in them should be used first. By opening them only once a day, you can keep remaining food in them from spoiling for a reasonable time. If you do not already keep a 2-week food supply in your home, increase it accordingly at once. Maintain it continuously by one of the following methods:

    a. *Increased current food stock*—This method merely means that you keep a 2-week supply of food on hand. It is no different from the food that you normally use in preparing your daily meals. You just make sure that there is always sufficient food to last for 2 weeks by replacing the food as you use it.

b. *Shelter reserve food supply*—This method means that you always keep a 2-week supply of food stored in your family shelter. Processed foods should be selected for storage that are precooked and can be consumed directly from the package, if necessary, either cold, or warmed if facilities permit.
c. *Food kits and multipurpose foods*—(1) A number of companies are marketing special food kits designed to sustain one or more persons for a given number of days. The kits are readily portable, easily stored, and are advertised to have a shelf-life in excess of the food products normally in commercial channels. (2) Specially prepared dehydrated foods, food concentrates, and multipurpose foods designed for long storage are also available commercially. Generally these products are not designed to serve as complete meals for long periods, but are used as food extenders and fortifiers. Most dehydrated and concentrated products require reconstitution by the addition of hot water.

Be Prepared to Evacuate—
If You Live in a "Target Area"

1. If you have an automobile, keep it in good running order, keep the fuel tank at least half full, and keep the battery fully charged. Your automobile is your best means for evacuating if you are advised to do so; its radio, tuned to CONELRAD (640 or 1240), can bring you survival instructions and fallout warnings; and, with its vents and windows closed, it offers some protection from radioactive fallout while you are driving to better shelter.

2. Take with you essential survival items packed in boxes, suitcases, or other suitable containers. Take as much of the total supply as possible.

Part VII
Out of the Kitchen

20. Feeding Family and the Masses

> Every one of us has a personal duty to help develop and maintain the non-military part of our nation's defense.... Through family and community civil defense preparedness, in such things as first aid, home firefighting, and mass feeding, we will be better able to cope with every kind of emergency....—*President Dwight Eisenhower*[1]

A boy's questioning voice comes on the radio and asks his mother, "What's with the basket ... picnic?"

The mother responds reassuringly, "Nope, this is Grandma's Pantry, modern version."

"Great, Mom," the boy replies. "Only what's it for?"

"Civil defense," the mother says with calm conviction. "And you're the one who brought the idea home from Scout meetings. Here, help me check off the list."

"Yep," the boy says.

Mom: "Powdered milk."

Boy: "Right."

Mom: "Canned meat."

Boy: "Yeah."

The radio announcer then adds:

> Into civil defense comes Grandma's Pantry, the symbol of preparedness. Unexpected company, Grandma always had plenty for everyone. No matter what unexpected disaster, your family should have a seven-day supply of food on hand, kept well protected in jars or tins, and safe in a shelter area. In an emergency or during evacuation in case of enemy attack, it's too late to plan. You'll have to depend on your own resources ... on Grandma's Pantry. Assure the future; know the six steps to survival. Make this year your family's year for civil defense. Civil defense—an American tradition![2]

Civil defense ads, such as this one for Grandma's Pantry, were heard daily on radio stations throughout the 1950s, often read by leading actors and entertainers such as Lucille Ball, Bob Hope, Mitzi Gaynor, Fred MacMurray, and

20. Feeding Family and the Masses

BY, FOR, AND ABOUT Women in Civil Defense

Mrs. Jean Wood Fuller
DIRECTOR OF WOMEN'S ACTIVITIES

GRANDMA'S PANTRY BELONGS IN YOUR KITCHEN

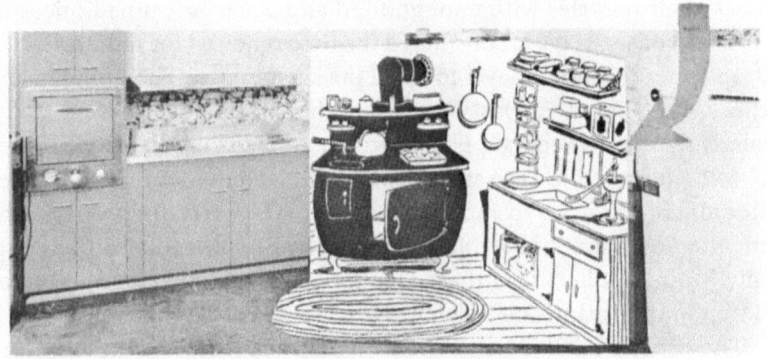

GRANDMA'S PANTRY AND HOW IT GREW

GRANDMA'S PANTRY is creating considerable interest all over the country, thanks to civil defense minded women.

As you probably have learned, GRANDMA'S PANTRY is the catch phrase for the civil defense emergency food storage program.

Borrowing an idea from Grandma's long years of experience in taking care of her family, the theme is: "Grandma's Pantry Was Ready – Is Your Pantry Ready in Event of Emergency?"

FEDERAL CIVIL DEFENSE ADMINISTRATION · BATTLE CREEK, MICHIGAN

The Federal Civil Defense Association's Jean Wood Fuller introduced Grandma's Pantry on a nationwide scale in 1955, although she credited the Maine Civil Defense Agency for the idea of stocking the family pantry in case of atomic attack.

Groucho Marx. In 1955, the year this ad was broadcast, nearly every American home had at least one radio. Parents listened to programs like *The Frank Sinatra Show, The Jack Benny Program, Burns and Allen, This Is Your Life, I Love a Mystery*, and countless other dramas, comedies, variety shows, and news programs. Their younger children followed the exploits of such radio heroes as *Lone Ranger, The Cisco Kid, Sky King*, and *Tom Corbett, Space Cadet*, while the older ones began tuning in to the new sound of rock 'n' roll. Yet the primary target for these civil defense messages, of course, was the homemaker, the person ultimately responsible for protecting her family and ensuring that her home was well prepared to survive the destructive power of a nuclear attack.

The Grandma's Pantry program, introduced in 1955, encouraged women to stock their pantries with enough food and water or canned juices to last a minimum of seven days, considered the time required for radioactive fallout to drop to a safe enough level to leave the shelter area. The homemaker was to check the "pantry" at least once a month, and rotate both food and water regularly. Home-canned supplies were encouraged, and safety precautions were to be followed for the storage of cooking equipment using bottled gas or liquids. In addition to food, the Grandma's Pantry program instructed women to add a first-aid kit, flashlight, and portable radio to their survival supply. Women adhering to these recommendations had taken an important first step in the nation's civil defense preparedness.

The Federal Civil Defense Administration's Jean Wood Fuller credited Inez Wing, the director of women's activities for the Maine Civil Defense Agency, with the idea of Grandma's Pantry. Wing launched the original idea by issuing membership cards and calling for a "Grandma's Pantry Week." Fuller expanded the idea by announcing Grandma's Pantry as a civil defense emergency food storage program in the FCDA's newsletter, *By, For, and About Women in Civil Defense*.[3] Fuller, appointed director of the FCDA's women's programs by President Dwight Eisenhower, worked with the National Grocer's Association, several pharmaceutical companies, and the American National Dietetic Association to develop Grandma's Pantry, which built its message around traditional—and admittedly idyllic—views toward women and the home, as exemplified in the newsletter:

> Borrowing an idea from Grandma's long years of experience in taking care of her family, the theme is: "Grandma's Pantry Was Ready—Is Your Pantry Ready in Event of Emergency?" Remember GRANDMA'S PANTRY with its shelves loaded with food, ready for any emergency, whether it be unexpected company or roads blocked for days by a winter's storm? Today, as a result of the newly-created perils of possible enemy attack, GRANDMA'S PANTRY, or the re-creation of GRANDMA'S PANTRY in a sheltered area of the modern home, is once again a necessity.[4]

The brochure emphasized the need for homemakers to have a three-day food supply at a minimum, with a one-week supply preferred. Canned items headed the list for Grandma's Pantry, including canned milk, canned meats, canned soups, canned fruit, canned vegetables, and canned juices. In addition, every pantry needed such essentials as toilet tissues, pails and buckets, candles, first-aid kits, a can opener, safety matches, and canned heat. Fuller took her message on the road, teaching women around the country not only how to stock their pantries, but how to make simple shelters in their basements by leaning a board against a basement wall.

Grandma's Pantry also took to the road, as the government shifted its emphasis from bomb shelters to evacuation (i.e., moving as far away as possible as quickly as possible to escape the deadly impact of a hydrogen bomb). In 1956, the FCDA published *Grandma's Pantry Goes on Wheels*, which stressed the importance of keeping the car ready for any emergency by making sure it is in good running condition; the gas tank is at least half full; and a three-day supply of food and water, first-aid items, flashlight, blankets, and a portable radio are in the trunk at all times. "Civil defense figures Grandma had the right idea at home and on the westward trail," read a special edition of *By, For, and About Women in Civil Defense*. "That's why Grandma's Pantry, already adopted as a must in home defense preparations, is going on wheels."[5]

States soon began promoting Grandma's Pantry by publishing pamphlets and sponsoring events. A number of state and county fairs featured skits based on *Grandma's Pantry Goes on Wheels*, for example. The New York State Civil Defense Commission was among the states taking the lead on Grandma's Pantry, publishing a pamphlet titled *Grandma's Pantry Was Always Ready—Is Your Pantry Prepared?*[6] The Michigan Office of Civil Defense published a four-page pamphlet titled *Family Food Sheet* that followed Grandma's Pantry's guidelines for stocking the home "shelter area" with food, water, and supplies. Other states sponsored local food fairs and set up "Pantry Booths" at county fairs. Organizations such as the Daughters of the American Revolution and the Veterans of Foreign Wars Auxiliary helped to promote Grandma's Pantry, as well.[7]

Grandma's Pantry was, indeed, a woman-oriented, home-centered program that gained widespread acceptance. Historian Dee Garrison makes a valid point that the FCDA wanted women to focus on such traditional roles as child care and medical care after an attack.[8] Yet it also can be argued that the program elevated women's responsibility in ensuring the nation's civil defense. In other words, Grandma's Pantry stands as an example of the government's mission to "infuse the traditional role of women with new meaning and importance, which would help fortify the home as a place of security amid the cold war," in the words of historian Elaine Tyler May.[9]

WHAT SHOULD YOU PUT INTO A MODERN GRANDMA'S PANTRY?

The following items have been suggested for your GRANDMA'S PANTRY. Remember, a three-day supply is the minimum, a week's supply would be preferable.

Select your own requirements in quantities suitable to your personal or family needs. Check "pantry" at least once a month and rotate regularly. Remember bottled water is important, and it must be changed every six weeks. Items packed in glass or other than tin should be wrapped in paper for protection against breakage or damage. Keep in dry storage. Home canned supplies are good items too. All safety precautions should be taken for storage of cooking equipment using bottled gas or liquids.

CANNED MILK

Evaporated
Instant Non-fat Dry
Condensed

CANNED MEATS

Chicken
Fish
Meat Varieties
Stews
Bacon

CANNED SOUPS

All Varieties
Chowders

CANNED FRUIT

All Varieties

CANNED VEGETABLES

Potatoes
Peas
Baked Beans
String Beans
Corn
Tomatoes
Others

MISCELLANEOUS NEEDS

Flour - Also Prepared Types
Dry Yeast
Sugar
Salt and Pepper
Soap and Powder
Paper Supplies
Toilet Tissues
Safety Matches
Candles
Kitchen Silver, etc.
First Aid Kits
Olive Oil
Can Opener
Baby Foods
Pet Foods
Canned Heat
Shortening
Pails and Buckets
Crackers
Honey
Jam
Spreads
Dry Fruits
Cereals
Brown Bread

CANNED JUICES

Fruit and Vegetable

BEVERAGES

Coffee
Tea
Cocoa

Water, (Jugs)
Soft Drinks

Grandma's Pantry provided a detailed list of all the essential food and beverage items to keep stocked in your pantry—enough for at least three days, and preferably for a week or more.

Fortification of the home did not equate to women's containment in it, however. Despite the government's endorsement of women's traditional gender role in many respects, it repeatedly heralded women's contribution to the nation's survival, as it had done during World War II when women entered the labor force in unprecedented numbers and capacities. The point here is not to dismiss the FCDA's rhetoric, publications, and programs designed to encourage women to stock their pantries and prepare their survival food supply; rather, it is to reassess women's role as food managers and food preparers within the realm of civil defense. This expanded role is much more evident when examining the government's mass feeding program, which the FCDA had discussed from its very beginning and the OCDM and OCD continued into the 1960s. As early as 1952, at a meeting with representatives from nine welfare organizations, including the American Red Cross and the Community Chest, FCDA officials warned that an atomic attack would leave seven million people homeless, and that some ten million people would need emergency welfare services. The officials called for a mass feeding program, in addition to providing emergency clothing, registration at welfare centers, resettlement assistance with relatives or friends, and the issuance of travel funds.[10]

Writing in the September 1952 issue of *Public Health Reports*, Paul Murphy, food consultant, and James Hundley, nutrition consultant, for the FCDA, along with Leonard Trainer, director of the food distribution branch, Production and Marketing Administration, Department of Agriculture, addressed the government's plan for the mass feeding of casualties following an atomic attack. The FCDA was responsible for coordinating the overall plan and obtaining the cooperation of the food industry, while the Department of Agriculture had the responsibility for securing the food supply and distributing it where needed. Among the FCDA's recommendations was the appointment in each state, either by the governor or by the civil defense director, of a civil defense food director, who would ideally be a volunteer from the food industry. At the local level, a food supply advisory committee and a director of emergency feeding were to be appointed by the local civil defense director. Their primary duty was to establish a working relationship with local leaders in charge of emergency feeding, and establishing the food requirements for taking care of the homeless, those in hospitals, and civil defense workers and other organizations assisting in mass feeding efforts. Although not specifically mentioning gender, the authors called for groups of volunteers to be recruited, organized into teams, trained, and assigned to designated feeding centers—many of whom would, in fact, be women. They wrote: "The experiences and 'know how' of dietitians, nutritionists, home economists, commercial chefs, as well as church groups, and such public feeding groups as school lunchroom personnel, should be utilized in training activities."[11]

The FCDA estimated that millions of civil defense workers would be required for an all-out atomic attack. Directors of civil defense emergency welfare services, including mass feeding, had been appointed in almost every state. In addition, several states issued plans and written guides, manuals, bulletins, and training materials on one or more emergency welfare services—all following the FCDA's recommendations and guidance—as well as held regional and state meetings on handling mass emergencies. The director of Emergency Feeding for Great Britain, at the FCDA's invitation, even met with some 6,000 local welfare and mass feeding leaders in nineteen cities to discuss advance planning for target and support areas, and to assist them with specific local problems. Cities conducted public demonstrations of emergency feeding techniques with improvised facilities. According to the FCDA's 1952 annual report, "a number of communities have organized some of their established feeding facilities as the nucleus of their emergency feeding programs. Chicago, which has developed its program around the school cafeterias, has achieved operational readiness in this respect."[12]

Chicago, in fact, had outlined its civilian mass feeding program in 1951. Published by the Chicago Civil Defense Corps, the 268-page *Chicago Alerts: A City Plans Its Civil Defense Against Atomic Attack*, detailed every facet of the city's planned procedures following an atomic attack, encompassing administration, public safety, public works, emergency medical services, and emergency mass feeding.[13] The primary administrators of the program were men, even though most functions and responsibilities aligned with women's experience and skill set. For example, the plan called for personnel operating school lunchrooms to work under the Civilian Defense Mass Feeding Program, with the head cook of each school in charge of their personnel. The city estimated some 600,000 people being fed each day, with the city's 180 school cafeterias able to handle 400,000. This left 200,000 people to be fed in approximately 600 church cafeterias under an agreement with the Church Federation of Greater Chicago requiring personnel working in church-operated kitchens to report to their respective emergency feeding stations in case of attack. To ensure against the unexpected "elimination" of lunchroom personnel, the plan called for the "complete indoctrination" of women members of Parent-Teacher Associations, Mothers Clubs, and Ladies Aid Societies of the various church organizations. Restaurants, although an essential part of the city's plans, were viewed as backup locations. The report read:

> We have not lost sight of the fact that many schools and churches would be obliterated or placed inactive. This loss of potential will be taken up by the use of existing restaurants, which have a high potential for mass feeding. Restaurants, however, have been set up as an auxiliary to the first two stages, meaning schools and churches, because

school and churches will also be used for housing, whereas restaurants do not have housing facilities.[14]

That same year, the Battle Creek (Michigan) Home Economics Association published *Manual for the Operation of Emergency Feeding Stations*. The manual contained sanitary regulations for food care; safety rules; a work outline detailing the responsibilities for cooks and their helpers; and menus and recipes for preparing emergency meals in 50-portion and 100-portion quantities. Caroline Edwards, territorial supervisor of home economics education, supervised the writing of the manual. She wrote: "As in all phases of any emergency or disaster, it is extremely important to remain calm. Always be on the alert. An emergency meal does more than keep the body alive—it helps to revive discouraged souls and builds morale."[15] The manual was a collaborative effort, with the Kellogg Company providing the cover, the Post Products Division of General Foods Corporation mimeographing the pages, and association members assembling the final publication. Commenting on the manual, Mary Barber, chairman of the civil defense committee of the food and nutrition division of the American Home Economics Association, said, "The philosophy of the Battle Creek organization is to preach preparedness without fear." Even though it was unlikely that an atomic bomb would hit the Battle Creek area, she pointed out, civil defense workers needed to be ready to care for evacuees. As part of this preparation, moreover, women needed to practice mass feeding procedures, and to follow the recipes and menus provided in the manual. "This gives experience in handling the equipment in their church or club [and] familiarizes them with amounts and costs of ingredients," said Barber.[16]

The state of New York also placed an emphasis on women's role in the aftermath of an atomic attack, with women fully supporting the state's civil defense efforts. Meeting in January 1951, 200 members of the Federation of Women's Republican Clubs of New York State endorsed Governor Thomas Dewey's defense emergency bill, soon to be enacted as the New York State Defense Emergency Act of 1951. Colonel Lawrence Wilkinson, director of the New York State Civil Defense Commission, told the meeting's attendees that the home front was essential in an atomic attack, as hundreds of thousands of people could be casualties and potentially homeless. "We must recognize that there is no other way of caring for the homeless on the evil day," Wilkinson said.[17] As part of the plan, the commission issued a directive on emergency feeding to more than 100 local, county, and city civil defense directors throughout the state. The directive contained recommendations for utilizing various eating establishments for mass feeding operations because of the difficulty in obtaining food through normal channels. In addition, directors were encouraged to advise housewives to keep small supplies of nonperishable food on hand. "Food will be served or distributed at emergency feeding installations to those who drive from their homes, without charge or obligation," said Wilkinson, "until it becomes administratively possible to determine who can pay and who cannot pay." In addition, Wilkinson called for the creation of 324 mobile welfare teams capable of moving throughout the state and to neighboring states in case of atomic disaster. The teams, each one to consist of ten members, were to provide welfare services, emergency feeding, registration and information, and financial assistance. Wilkinson did not specify gender; he merely recommended that the emergency feeding team include a manager, two cooks, a fireman, two food servers, and four helpers.[18]

In June 1951, the city of Niagara Falls, New York, conducted a theoretical atomic attack, called "Operation Niagara," to test the city's civil defense operation. The test involved 9,000 volunteers to care for an estimated 40,000 casualties. Included were fifteen radiological teams, firefighters from seven counties, 550 nurses, and 150 doctors, as well as civil defense teams from surrounding areas. Among the demonstrations were emergency hospitals and mass feeding operations.[19] The New York State Civil Defense Commission, under the direction of Lieutenant General C. R. Huebner, expanded the state's emergency care and feeding plans in 1952, announcing that parks, open fields, and even roadside areas would need to be used to care for an estimated 50,000 to 100,000 homeless persons following an atomic attack. Men were needed to dig latrines and install first-aid stations, while women were essential in overseeing outdoor stoves and kitchen facilities, and setting up mass feeding areas. "For their own protection, feeding, and proper care," said Huebner, "many thousands must be assembled if necessary in open areas for at least a few hours and perhaps days. They will be put into buildings when buildings can be found, and as soon as possible they will be moved to other communities where buildings and home areas are available."[20]

In 1953, the state of Pennsylvania developed a cooperative plan with the food industry for the distribution of food during an emergency, and began a training program in mass feeding techniques. Women's groups in several states sponsored training classes in various civil defense capacities, including the mass care and feeding of evacuees.[21] Chicago, considered one of the nation's target cities for atomic attack, emphasized the FCDA's emergency welfare program in its civil defense efforts, while the state of Indiana expanded its food program and published a comprehensive list of food resources. What some consider to be the nation's first mass feeding demonstration took place on November 6, 1954, conducted by the Chicago Civil Defense Corps in cooperation with volunteers from women's organizations. The demonstration was under the direction of Frank Washam of the Chicago board of education and chairman of the Civil Defense Corps' emergency mass feeding committee. Using four locations, personnel prepared the food in metal barrels and pails over wood fires using bricks and rubble for fireplaces. Liquefied petroleum gas also was used as fuel in commercial cooking ranges. Anthony Mullaney, director of the Civil Defense Corps, estimated that some 100,000 people would be fed by 1 p.m. that day. John Thompson, reporting for the *Chicago Tribune*, wrote, "The exercise is designed both as a test for the corps personnel and a demonstration to women on what can be done in emergency feeding should atomic or hydrogen bombs devastate Chicago in an enemy air attack."[22]

The FCDA initiated several efforts related to mass feeding in 1953, including the creation of a National Advisory Committee on Emergency Feeding. It continued to work with the American Red Cross to develop training programs and conferences on disaster operations, both enemy-caused and natural. The agency also worked with several national social work associations to encourage their members' participation in national emergencies, and to develop a publication titled *The Social Worker in Civil Defense*. The FCDA held meetings throughout the year on mass disaster feeding with a wide range of associations, including the Family Service Association of America and Child Welfare League—both with many women members—as well as school lunch officials and home economists—also representing many women.[23]

The FCDA's 1953 annual report cites the fact that "a number of magazines in the feeding industry" published articles on mass feeding in civil defense. The report also pointed out that state civil defense offices were working with their respective state welfare departments to promote civil defense preparedness and mass feeding programs. Specifically, Arizona, California, Connecticut, Georgia, Mississippi, Tennessee, New York, Utah, and Wyoming published pamphlets on emergency feeding and mass care, among other topics. California took the extra step of conducting a survey of lodging and feeding facilities, and identified 5,630 buildings capable of sheltering two million people. Plus, the survey located an additional 5,000 public eating establishments that, along with the 5,630 shelter facilities, could serve close to four million meals per day. Among its major accomplishments was the introduction of the Emergency Mass Feeding Instructor Training Program, developed in cooperation with the U.S. Department of Defense. Eleven courses were conducted at various Army Food Schools, with the pilot training course having some 350 persons representing twenty organizations involved with mass feeding. In addition, an estimated 2,000 instructors were trained in follow-up courses in all of the FCDA's regions.[24] The FCDA also published a training manual, *Emergency Mass Feeding*, designed to be modified and reprinted by individual states for their specific needs. The manual covered all facets of mass feeding, including the construction of makeshift ovens, grills, cooking, and eating utensils. Finally, the federal Housing and Home Finance Agency and its advisory groups worked with FCDA on material to assist states and local civil defense organizations to explore the possible use of private homes for lodging in an emergency.[25]

The FCDA continued its instructor training course in 1954, graduating more feeding specialists and civil defense workers in mass feeding techniques.[26] Moreover, state and local civil defense organizations around the country began conducting mass feeding demonstrations, such as a 1955 outdoor workshop conducted by the Texas Division of Defense and Disaster Relief, where 125 people were fed in seven minutes; a drill conducted in Connecticut to demonstrate the mobilization ability to feed the masses on short notice; and the evacuation of workers from the State Office Building to the State Fairgrounds in Springfield, Illinois, followed by a mass feeding demonstration.[27]

In 1956, the FCDA actually conducted an emergency mass feeding

This photograph depicts participants at an Emergency Mass Feeding Course at Fort Dix, New Jersey (National Archives).

demonstration at a food writer's conference it hosted. As a result, newspapers around the country published articles on emergency feeding and emergency food supplies.[28] The FCDA reported that for the first time, state and local civil defense agencies had taken a serious approach to determining the potential scope of a post-atomic scenario, including the number of workers and lodging accommodations required.

Mass feeding drills continued to be held throughout the 1950s, as states emphasized the importance of post-attack programs to help survivors. The *Missouri Survival Plan*, published in 1958, provides a representative example of how many states approached the problem of how to respond following an atomic attack. Missouri Governor James Blair, Jr., set the tone in the introduction, writing: "Missouri is now susceptible to attack with little or no warning. This condition has come about because a strong military dictatorship, which supports a fanatic ideology of world domination, has developed thermonuclear weapons and the capability of delivering them upon this state." The detailed plan covered all aspects of the state's civil defense operations that would be needed in the aftermath of an atomic disaster, including attack warning, communications, intelligence, police, transportation, and welfare (e.g., housing, clothing, financial assistance, and feeding).[29]

The mission of the Feeding Service was "to feed survivors, injured and non-injured, workers and non-workers as well as emergency service personnel and emergency hospital staffs in a mass feeding situation, and by the issuance of rations for preparation in private homes." Missouri's official welfare planner, Thomas Singleton, oversaw the state, district, county, and municipality feeding programs. The plan called for him to utilize representatives from organizations such as the American Red Cross, Salvation Army, and Restaurant Association, as well as staff members in the home economics department at the University of Missouri. Women in these organizations became front-line workers, along with women volunteers from schools, churches, and other groups, in the state's mass feeding plan:

> The County Feeding Chief will be responsible for all feeding activities within his county.... The County Feeding Chief will form an organization and train the necessary staff to carry out the County Feeding mission. He will utilize the American Red Cross chapters in both the training and operational phase since their mass feeding training program and disaster committee will both fit into a mass feeding situation. He will utilize the clubs with which his Home Economist is working as well as the restaurant association, school lunch program, churches, lodges and any other groups set up for mass feeding and distribution of unprepared rations.[30]

Admittedly, mass disaster feeding programs took advantage of women's abilities as homemakers and cooks. At the same time, these programs also acknowledged and capitalized on women's experience and requisite skills in food management and preparation—skills needed to care for the countless thousands, even millions, of injured and homeless survivors of a nuclear attack. In 1960, for example, women volunteers in Galveston, Texas, completed a course in emergency mass feeding sponsored by the local chapter of the American Red Cross, and the Polk County Civil Defense Agency in Bartow, Florida, sponsored a mass feeding demonstration with 300 men and women, primarily lunchroom personnel, participating. The next year, the Southern Orange County Chapter of the American Red Cross in Santa Ana, California, offered a mass feeding course; in February 1962, women in Muncie, Indiana, graduated from a similar course and were certified as cooks for mass feeding emergencies; and women in Klamath Falls, Oregon, completed the first phase of a mass feeding course in May 1963 sponsored by the American Red Cross and Klamath County Civil Defense. Emergency mass feeding training and demonstrations, in fact, took place well into the 1960s.[31]

Even though in many cases men held senior positions in state and local

This photograph depicts two people baking biscuits at an emergency mass feeding course at Fort Dix, New Jersey (National Archives).

welfare agencies, women played an essential role in mass feeding. In a 1976 interview, for instance, Jean Wood Fuller, former director of women's activities for the FCDA, remembered an Iowa woman who, in the 1950s, enlisted an array of men and women volunteers to conduct a disaster feeding drill in Des Moines—a drill that received national attention and illustrated women's capabilities in civil defense. "They just set up a regular disaster scene and the National Guard pitched in and, of course, the policemen and firemen and the cooks and bakers in town," Fuller remembered. "They all gathered and it was an exercise in emergency cooking with the barest utensils possible."[32]

Historian Kenneth Rose has argued that the very real probability of a nuclear war with the Soviet Union served to undermine the government's appeal to female domesticity. "Women were being called on by the government to perform their traditional, nurturing roles in the extremities of an unprecedented cataclysm," he writes, "and despite the homey analogies used by government publications to enlist women in this effort, it was obvious to most that a nuclear attack would present problems far beyond the resources of poor grandma's pantry."[33] Rose is absolutely correct that focusing on the family food pantry glossed over the harsh realities of what would occur in a nuclear war. But women's involvement in mass feeding programs illustrates how women took the initiative and assumed a more important role in helping the nation prepare for a nuclear disaster. In other words, the so-called domestication of civil defense takes on a different connotation when one looks more closely at the government's nationwide mass feeding program—a program that involved comprehensive training and the contributions of volunteers representing women's organizations, groups, and professions, such as school lunch workers, dietitians, home economists, and, of course, homemakers.

21. "Emergency Mass Feeding Instructor Course"

In 1954, the Federal Civil Defense Administration, in cooperation with the Department of Defense, published Emergency Mass Feeding Instructor Course, *the first comprehensive manual for teaching personnel who would be responsible for feeding the survivors of an atomic attack, which could number in the millions. The government's mass feeding program had begun the prior year but greatly expanded in 1954. Members of various women's organizations, such as the Home Economics Association, conducted mass feeding demonstrations in Alabama, Georgia, Oklahoma, Texas, West Virginia, and other states. Colorado, Kansas, and Missouri even constructed permanent mass feeding facilities. The following excerpt provides a better understanding not only of the program's scope, but also of the knowledge and skills necessary for participants, including women, to successfully manage and conduct mass feeding.*

Feeding Problems

In any general natural or man-made disaster—whether it be fire, flood, hurricane, tornado, earthquake or atomic, thermo-nuclear, or saturation bombing—certain emergency conditions will generally prevail.

Wholesale destruction of dwellings, stores, or warehouses by enemy attack will leave thousands of people not only homeless, but without sources of food and feeding facilities. It is essential that provision be made for feeding facilities to be placed in operation immediately after attack. The program must be planned and operated to take care of hungry people wherever they may be. The fundamental importance of any such emergency feeding program automatically gives its organization and development a high priority in civil defense planning.

The content of this course was determined only after considerable discussion between the Federal Civil Defense Administration and the Quartermaster Corps of the Department of the Army. It has also had the benefit of the criticisms, suggestions, and recommendations of the representatives of the organizations and agencies who participated in the pilot program.

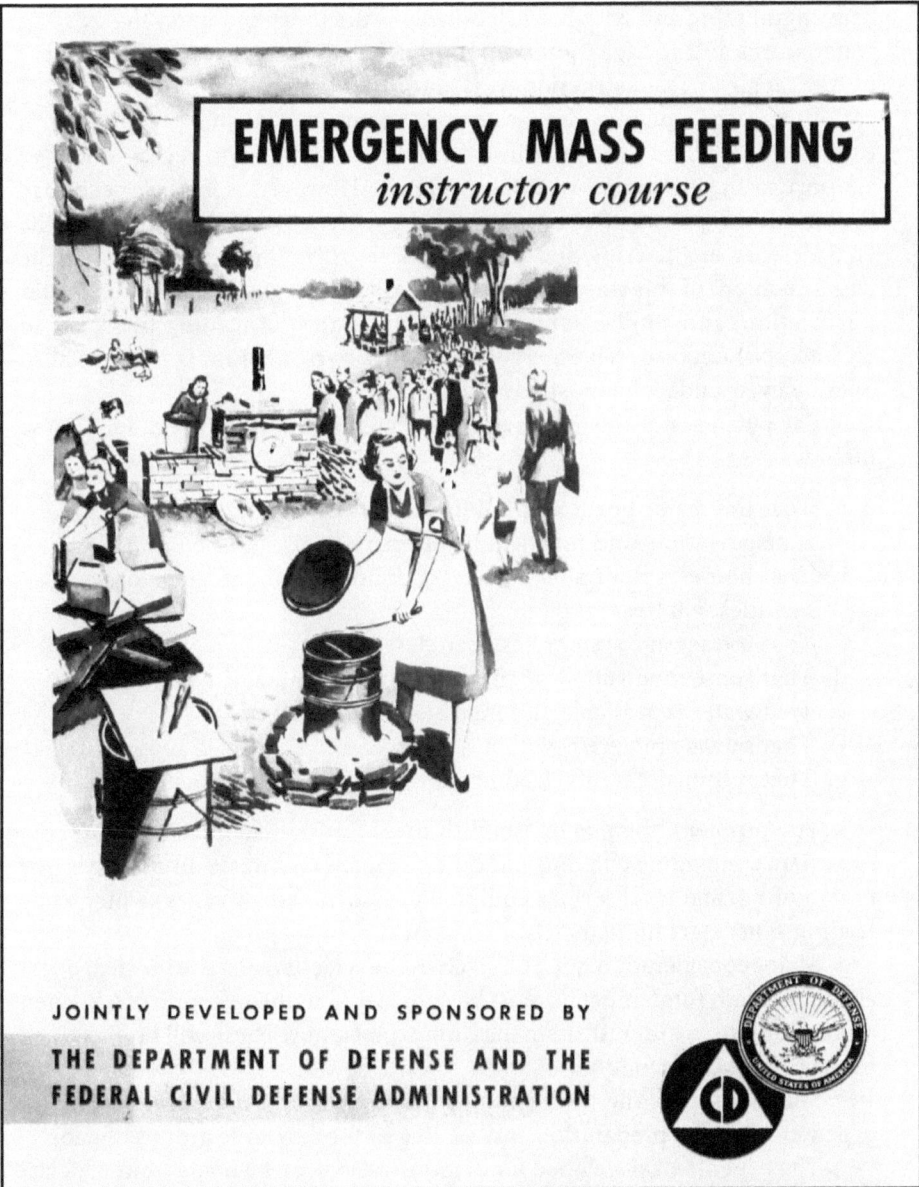

The course content includes lessons on sanitation and water purification. In a civil defense emergency, emergency feeding will look to the engineering and health services to provide safe water for cooking and drinking purposes, and to provide adequate facilities for disposal of wastes. It will also look to the health services for assistance on all other matters relating to sanitation.

The engineering and health services will, in turn, depend upon the existing water works and sewage utilities organizations to assume leadership in necessary repair or reconstruction work and the existing public health organizations to assure quality of the water and adequacy of sanitary facilities. It is expected that these services will be properly organized to render effective support to the emergency feeding program. However, it may be necessary for an interim period after attack to feed people without the support of the civil defense engineering and health services. It is for this reason that the course content of this training program includes lessons on sanitation, water purification, and similar subjects. The importance of feeding people is so vital to civil defense that emergency feeding personnel must be trained to operate even under the most adverse conditions.

For purposes of this instruction, certain assumptions are made. These include:

a. That the major portion of public utilities, including electricity, gas, transportation, and fuel, will be destroyed.
b. That homes, restaurants, cafeterias, food equipment, and storage facilities will be unusable.
c. That the sewage system has been destroyed.
d. That some food supplies, unaffected by the damage, are available.
e. That water is available and may be used if purified.
f. That salvage materials will be available.
g. That responsibility for feeding will rest upon civilian agencies.

The problem, then, is to establish mass feeding facilities utilizing field expedients, including cooking and eating utensils and waste disposal systems in lieu of normal food service equipment. For full effectiveness, emergency feeding must start immediately after attack.

Major consideration must be given to the selection of a site for such operations. Certain fundamentals must be considered in the selection of a kitchen and eating site in order to attain maximum efficiency. These will be explained in detail in the instruction.

Simplicity must be the key word in an operation dependent solely on expedients for the preparation and serving of food to large groups of people.

The expedients developed for demonstration can be made from material normally available. These facilities and utensils are of a type that can be made in the shortest possible time with a minimum of tools.

Groups of people with little or no mechanical ability can be instructed in the rudiments of this improvisation without difficulty.

The material covered is considered to be the minimum essential information necessary to meet the requirements of a disaster situation. Particular attention is called to the subjects of water purification, personal hygiene, sanitation, and food poisoning, as the rules pertaining to these are the ones most susceptible to violation.

Selecting the Site

When and if a disaster strikes, we will not have a modern cafeteria around the corner to go to for food. Therefore, it becomes necessary to think of the future and plan a method of preparing and serving food. An area or site must be chosen, with certain circumstances being considered, for the feeding of groups of people.

There are many problems that are encountered in choosing a site. Through actual experience we have developed seven rules or principles that should be followed in the setting up of a kitchen site.

1. Level, Self-Draining Ground

The kitchen should be level in order to facilitate ease of movement for cooks and food handlers. This will also be helpful in eliminating any accidents that are likely to occur when these workers carry heavy kettles and improvised stock pots over bumpy ground. Natural drainage should also be kept in mind for it is important to keep the kitchen area dry for sanitation reasons and, again, for the facilitation of movement. A sandy, loam type of site is best for water absorption. Hard clay is not desirable, because it becomes slippery and tends to hold water. Black muck or jumbo type ground becomes soft and bottomless and because of this, should be avoided.

2. Convenient to Diners

Many of the people that are to be fed may have difficulty in moving about because of injuries, age, etc. The distance should not be more than 15 minutes walking distance (approx. ¼ mile) for a normal person.

3. Accessible Roads

Thought should also be given to the heavy supplies that must be delivered to the kitchen from storage areas. It may be necessary to transport these items by large vehicles or hand carts. The roads should also be convenient for transporting certain patrons to and from the kitchen site.

4. Sanitary Area

The situation will require extreme care to preserve sanitation. Stagnant ponds or streams are infested with insects and should be avoided. Open or broken sewerage is ideal harborage for rodents and must be avoided. Insects and rodent infestation can cause serious outbreaks of sickness.

The presence of trees for shade is desirable, but thick shrub brush and growth restrict freedom of movement for all personnel and hampers efficient feeding.

5. Equipment Arrangement

The equipment should be constructed in a planned sequence. The first day construction should provide only the required equipment. Thereafter improvements should be made as conditions permit.

A recommended construction guide follows:

1st Day.
- a. Cross trench pre-dip sterilization.
- b. Open-fire cooking & heating facility.
- c. Cross trench washing facility.

2nd Day. First day's facilities plus:
- a. Cross trench barrel oven.
- b. Soakage pit & grease trap.
- c. Incinerator (horizontal & vertical barrel).
- d. Griddle.

3rd Day.
- a. Triple barrel utensil washing facility.
- b. Griddle & one barrel oven.
- c. Double barrel oven.

The equipment should be arranged similar to a cafeteria. First, a means of pre-dipping eating utensils, then the griddle tops (can be used for hot top) so that the service can be direct from the griddles. Next comes the ovens with the opening facing the cooking area away from the line. Another line of equipment can be arranged parallel and opposite the ovens and griddles at least 10 feet away. This equipment arrangement is used in the attached diagram. For safety and convenience of the cooks, a minimum of six feet between each open fire should be allowed. The end of the serving line should lead into the dining area. After the patrons have eaten, they leave the dining area without crossing the serving line and proceed to the utensil and washing facility.

A garbage disposal can should be placed in front of the utensil washing facility. This will be emptied after each meal and placed in the incinerator provided.

The facilities for washing the diners' utensils should be placed at the outer edge of the dining area, leading away from the kitchen site. The patrons clean and maintain their own eating utensils and bring them to meals.

The number of diners should be limited to 500 in any one kitchen with provisions made for the dining ·area to accommodate at least half that number.

The soakage pit and grease trap should be approximately 25 feet from the cooking area.

The location should be on the opposite side of the cooking area from the dining area.

The kitchen layout can be altered, provided one principle is constant. Keep a straight line flow through the serving line into the dining area and then to the washing area and the exit. Never rearrange to cause cross line traffic, because this can easily cause confusion and thus delay serving.

6. Personnel

The number of personnel required to maintain each feeding station will, of necessity, depend on the number of people being fed at that station. Assuming that the maximum (500) are being fed three meals per day they would require:

a Supervisor and Coordinator. One (1).
b. Cooks. Three (3). Actually preparing and serving food.
c. Cooks Assistants. Four (4) Assists cooks, deliver food, water, etc.
d. Assistant to Supervisor. One (1) per line. Required only at meal or serving time to direct traffic, etc.

7. Utilities

It is assumed that gas, electricity, and water will not be available through regular facilities.

Improvised lighting will be a necessity. This can be accomplished by means of homemade candles or through the use of sand or rag saturated with oil or gasoline. Pine knots can also be used for this purpose. As mentioned in a previous hour, potable water available for use at the kitchen site is a must.

Preparation and Service of Food

Simplicity of preparation and service of food is an absolute must in emergency mass feeding. Confusion will reign. Lack of organization can be expected. Shock may cause weakness and inertia. Personnel will, in the majority of cases, lack experience in improvising to meet feeding requirements.

Preparation of hot food should be limited to items which require no pre-preparation and lend themselves to cooking in a single pot. Canned foods meet these requirements. However, we do not mean to imply that emergency mass feeding is a "soup line" affair.

For obvious reasons we must continue to be nutrition conscious. Many persons lose sight of nutrition during times of emergency due to the fact that the desired food service equipment, personnel and subsistence are not as available as we have been accustomed to.

In this connection, no matter how humble our circumstances might be, it is possible to be nutrition wise. Under emergency conditions it becomes necessary to think in terms of nutrition as a "meal."

Under these conditions, it can be assumed that those being fed will not suffer from malnutrition. One kettle dishes can be nutritious and acceptable if care is exercised in the selection of the food items to be used. Of course the manner of serving will affect the acceptability of one-kettle dishes.

For the most part, the actual food items requiring cooking will be accomplished by the moist methods of cooking. For example, open kettles over direct and improvised steaming will be used.

The juices of all canned and cooked vegetables can be used to advantage on one-kettle cooked dishes. All canned foods that are opened must be transfer-rinsed to extract all food particles and juices, which can also be used. Toward the end of the cooking period, all juices should be thickened with any available thickening agent, prior to being served with solid foods. These juices are concentrations of valuable nutrients that are required by the body.

Normally we are very conscious of the eye appeal of food and its palatability. In striving to obtain eye appeal, we sacrifice food value many times. In this present emergency it will be necessary to reverse the procedure and sacrifice eye appeal slightly in order to retain maximum food value. An example of this is by retaining the original liquids from paste products and legumes, *i.e.*, noodles, rice, beans and using this liquid with the prepared dish. The scarcity of water and the fact that many vitamins are water soluble, makes this mandatory.

Another item that will be desirable and simple to make is a hot beverage. These hot drinks are excellent stimulants for initial shock and aid in reducing nervous tension. The stimulating effect derived from a hot beverage will improve morale and increase the comfort of the persons being fed. The method of preparation should be the same simple open kettle method for coffee, tea and cocoa or hot milk.

As the facilities improve with the introduction of improvised griddles and ovens, we can add grilled and baked dishes ... biscuits, corn bread, crisp spoon muffins or hot cakes are a few examples. Other baked items are potatoes, beans, macaroni or hash. Of course, with the implementation of baked food dishes, we could also have a soup, chowder or gumbo to accompany this meal. The omission of bread and yeast leavened products is intentional. The reason for this is the lack of special equipment that would be required. Time required for fermentation is a second consideration and the tremendous handling would increase possibilities of food infection.

By using the griddles, we can add rush dishes as fried meats, potatoes, noodles or thin breads. This also would enable the use of frying in fat to increase food value, use of leftover fats and a change in the type of food preparation.

Cooked hot cereals are excellent to serve for breakfast. It's a simple dish to prepare and is a very filling and sustaining food item. Simplicity in serving increases the desirability of this item. These dishes should be prepared quite moist and not cooked firm and dry.

Retention of Usable Material

Any material that is received by the kitchen site should be cleaned and retained for use. Food tins should be cleaned and used to make eating utensils, smoke stacks, food choppers, etc. Cardboard makes fine insulating material and wire or steel banding can be used for stack supports as well as supporting improvised ovens.

Children Feeding

Supervision of the field kitchen will require some thought to child or infant feeding. Fruit juices, puree of vegetable soups, mashed unseasoned vegetables and milk for each meal will probably be mandatory. If the number of infants and young children (1 to 18 months) is quite a considerable number, then it is advisable to establish separate infant kitchens.

22. "Basic Course in Emergency Mass Feeding Handbook"

The Basic Course in Emergency Mass Feeding Handbook *was originally published in 1957 and updated in 1966 by the Office of Civil Defense in cooperation with the American Red Cross and Welfare Administration, Department of Health, Education, and Welfare. The handbook covered the full gamut of the government's mass feeding program, from feeding procedures in community fallout shelters to guidelines for safe food and water to food service management. This section of food service management featured a comprehensive overview of the many facets of organizing food service work, which formed the front line of the program—and an area reliant on women's skills in food management, preparation, and service.*

Organizing Food Service Work

1. Feeding large groups is a complex task that requires good overall planning and coordination.
2. Any disruption or breakdown of automatic food service machinery can further complicate the feeding task. Sophisticated equipment may have to be replaced by human labor and improvised equipment.
3. Disaster mass feeding operations requires planning, coordination and organized effort as does feeding under normal conditions.
4. Because the number of people doing the work is small in relation to the number of people being fed, the feeding staff must work as a team to plan, prepare and serve to large groups.
5. To perform the tasks involved in carrying out the menu, food service workers need to master techniques and skills that simplify the work, reduce fatigue and promote greater efficiency.
6. Teamwork and coordination by the various food service workers units are required to get the work done efficiently on time. Coordination of all parts of the operation is also essential for smooth functioning.

AUGUST 1966

BASIC COURSE IN
EMERGENCY MASS FEEDING
HANDBOOK

H-15

ARC-2219A

Developed Jointly by
DEPARTMENT OF DEFENSE • OFFICE OF CIVIL DEFENSE
THE AMERICAN NATIONAL RED CROSS
and
WELFARE ADMINISTRATION
DEPARTMENT OF HEALTH, EDUCATION, AND WELFARE

a. *The four major divisions of work in any feeding operation are:*
      (1) Planning the meals, making the menus and procuring the food
      (2) Preparing the food
      (3) Serving the meal
      (4) Cleaning up
   b. *The duties of food workers in carrying out the four phases of a feeding task include:*
      (1) Planning
         (a) Plan and post menus, recipes, work schedules, indicating numbers to be fed, amount of food to be prepared and size of servings.
         (b) Requisition food, equipment and other supplies and receive, check, store and allocate supplies to work units.
         (c) Keep necessary records.
         (d) List jobs to be done and divide them into basic work units. Assign jobs of feeding team.
         (e) Supervise workers.
         (f) Enforce sanitary and safety practices in the feeding area.
         (g) Maintain liaison with other feeding units throughout the disaster area.
         (h) Recruit and assign licensed drivers for automotive units in mobile operations.
      (2) Preparing food
         (a) Follow menus, recipes and work schedules.
         (b) Schedule preparation of food to have it ready and in good condition at serving time.
         (c) Plan, collect and assign necessary equipment and food ingredients.
         (d) Arrange work space for efficiency.
         (e) Deliver food to serving counters.
         (f) Coordinate duties with those of the serving and cleaning groups.
         (g) Keep working areas clean.
         (h) Arrange for proper storage of disposal of leftovers.
         (i) Deliver soiled cooking utensils to dishwashing unit.
         (j) Keep close watch for spoiled or contaminated food.
         (k) Adhere to sanitation and safety regulations.

(3) Serving food
   (a) Before the meal is served:
       Decide upon the tasks involved; make a serving schedule and assign work duties; assemble the serving supplies and equipment; select the utensils and containers to be used if the food is being transported; organize and arrange the serving and dining areas.
       Systematize food arrangement on counter—cold foods first, hot foods last; assemble food accompaniments—such as salt, pepper, cream, sugar and drinking water and place them at point of use; wrap knives, forks and spoons in napkins and place them at start or end of the serving line; stack paper cups and bowls on clean trays, towels or paper, inverting them for easy grasping; establish lines for movement of diners from serving to eating area.
   (b) When ready to serve meal:
       Have proper serving utensils handy; determine portions to be served; assure enough servers for each station; serve food attractively; avoid overfilling and spilling; when serving thick soup or stew, see that everyone gets a fair share of both meat and vegetables; keep prepared food covered when not being served: keep serving area clean and neat "as you go."
   (c) After meal is served:
       Clear the serving counter; deliver leftover food to kitchen area for storage or disposal; dispose of trash and waste from serving area.
(4) Cleaning up
   (a) Sanitation and cleanup includes:
       General cleanliness and sanitation of the food service area; care and issuance of cleaning supplies to other team groups; provision of proper toilet and handwashing facilities and safe drinking water; proper handling of food and equipment; dishwashing and general cleaning.
   (b) Before the meal is served:
       Decide upon the tasks involved; assign work

duties to each member of group; issue cleaning supplies to all food units; clean and sanitize floors, tables and serving counters; set up trash and waste collection and disposal facilities; prepare the facilities for dishwashing.

(c) After the meal is served:
Wash and sanitize all soiled dishes and utensils; store properly; check all working surfaces, tables, shelves and ranges for cleanliness; wash and rinse dishcloths, serving towels, and cleaning cloths and hang them to dry in the air; sweep or mop floors and dust chairs; dispose of garbage and trash and sanitize the containers; put away cleaning supplies and equipment.

Conclusion:
The "Home" in Home Front

"Civil defense is the protection of the home front in the event of war or attack."[1]

So read an editorial in the *Postville Herald* in October 1951, near the end of the Federal Civil Defense Administration's first year of promoting the nation's civil defense program. Located in northeastern Iowa, the heart of the Midwest, Postville had first been settled in 1843 by Joel Post and his wife, Zeruiah, and became an "organized" town in 1873. Its most notable resident was 1946 Nobel laureate John R. Mott, son of Postville's first mayor, John S. Mott. With less than 2,000 residents and strong rural roots, Postville seemed well protected, even isolated, from foreign threats. Yet the Soviet Union's entrance into the atomic age had introduced a new, unprecedented threat that reached Postville's Main Street, just as it had permeated every American city, suburb, small town, and rural area. "Civil defense," the editorial continued, "is the farmer, signing up for the Ground Observer Corps; it's the store clerk, donating a pint of blood; it's the fireman, watching a movie on atomic warfare so that he can warn others; and it's the mother, showing her daughter how to make a splint. Civil defense is you, the reader, getting ready."[2]

Only the United States possessed an atomic bomb in 1945. And it remained that way until the Soviet Union detonated its first atomic bomb in August 1949, four years to the month after V-J Day. China fell to Mao Zedong and communism the same year. Then the North Koreans, backed by the Soviet Union and China, invaded South Korea in June 1952, launching another war with international repercussions. On November 1, the United States exploded a hydrogen bomb. Nine months later, the Soviet Union detonated its first H-bomb. The Cold War continued to escalate.

Within the eight years that President Harry S Truman served in office, from April 1945 following the death of President Franklin Roosevelt, through January 1953, when he gave way to Dwight Eisenhower, the nation had witnessed the birth of a new age, an atomic age, that forever changed the concept of warfare. Even more significant, the nation witnessed the emergence of an enemy, the Soviet Union, armed with atomic weapons. The nation's military objectives continued to change as the world situation changed, now focusing primarily on containing communist expansion in Eastern Europe and Asia, while, on the home front, President Truman created the FCDA to help prepare the American people for the possibility—and, as some believed, the probability—of an atomic attack by the Soviet Union. Surveys in the late 1940s and early 1950s, in fact, found many, if not most, Americans believing such an attack inevitable within their lifetime.

The United States had gone from the jubilation and relief of victory in a devastating, prolonged, deadly world war, to the embedded fear of mass destruction from atomic bombs. The home front, even a small town in Iowa, was no longer immune from war. The nation's borders, its protective shield, had been breached. "Civil defense is realistic," read the *Postville Herald*'s editorial, "based on the premise that the military cannot take the responsibility of guarding the home front, and that our vast oceans, geomilitarily, have been reduced to streams."[3]

When assessing the FCDA's civil defense strategy, the best approach is not with the hindsight of more than a half century of events, trends, and outcomes, but rather from the perspective of the early 1950s, as the events occurred. Within this context, the government's introduction of a domestic civil defense program—and its approach to women's involvement—makes perfect sense. The military believed the Soviet Union capable of destroying any city at any time with atomic bombs delivered by long-range bombers; and even in the most favorable scenario, it felt some bombers would get through. The only recourse, therefore, was the establishment of a civil defense program to ensure that Americans were prepared to survive the attack and, more important, help rebuild the nation.

Truman's mandate for the FCDA was straightforward: "to promote and facilitate the civil defense of the United States in cooperation with the several States [and to] conduct or arrange for training programs for the instruction of State and local civil-defense leaders and specialists in the organization, operation, and techniques of civil defense."[4] If this were accomplished, the American people could protect themselves and, concurrently, protect the home front. Achieving this objective, however, required public support and participation in civil defense programs, which, according to the FCDA, required 17 to 20 million volunteers, with some 80 percent being women. Women's importance could "scarcely be overstated," proclaimed the FCDA.[5]

Historians have seized on the FCDA's approach to enlisting women volunteers as evidence that the government "contained" women within the home, "reinforced" traditional gender roles, "militarized" the family, "domesticated" and "feminized" civil defense, and imposed "social control" on the American populace. Whether the FCDA's proclamation on women reflects gender bias or contemporary social attitudes is debatable, and not significant if the agency's policies and actions are viewed from a contemporary perspective.

"Women must take the lead in providing home fallout shelters, stocking provisions, and knowing proper emergency procedures," Dorothy Pearl, deputy assistant director of women's activities, Office of Civil and Defense Mobilization, told attendees at a 1959 workshop held in Chapel Hill, North Carolina. She went on to outline steps women needed to take to be ready in case of atomic attack, including knowing first aid and fire prevention techniques, as well as local civil defense plans and signals. In a 1961 talk titled "Home Preparedness—A Woman's Cause," Pearl again addressed women's critical role in civil defense. "[W]e who are building the non-military, deterrent force cannot afford to overlook any means of accomplishing our goal," she said. "Therefore, I urge you to take stock of your greatest resource—women. Take cognizance of their innate ability. Take note of their stamina, courage, fortitude, faith.... Provide her with the proper survival plans in which she can and will do her share. Then and only then, I believe, we will have a non-military defense, a deterrent to war which will stop any aggressor."[6]

The fact is that most Americans remained apathetic or indifferent to civil defense during the 1950s and 1960s. By 1965, moreover, civil defense had become overtaken with public concerns targeted to the Vietnam War and the civil rights movement. This is not debatable. Yet this does not negate the fact that countless men and women actively participated in civil defense during the early Cold War, and many more at least learned about civil defense by reading government pamphlets, newspapers, or magazine articles; watching television programs; and listening to the radio.

In addition, millions of members of women's organizations attended civil defense presentations at conferences and meetings. Women became involved with civil defense in schools through their membership in Parent-Teacher Associations. Professional women such as doctors, nurses, and educators, to name a few, participated in civil defense. Women in business lent their management skills, and broadcasters, telephone operators, restaurant staff, office administrators, and many others contributed to the nation's civil defense program. Women served in the Ground Observer Corps, participated in mass feeding programs, became block wardens, and joined the welfare, health, transportation, and communications services. They taught civil defense courses and home preparedness and home nursing workshops. Through all of these civil defense activities, women strengthened their skills and expanded their capabilities far beyond their homes' confining walls.

The year after the *Postville Herald* editorial appeared, Dorothy Mann, coordinator of women's activities for the Michigan Office of Civil Defense, wrote a guest column for the *Lansing State Journal*, once again emphasizing the connection between the home front and the home. "Defense of the home is a basic instinct of the American people," Mann wrote. "The fundamental feeling transcends mere self-preservation. It embraces the protection of family, friends, neighbors, community, and country. It is the essence of our national unity and the foundation of our national strength and security."[7]

This connection between home and home front formed the core of civil defense. During this period, the government, in cooperation with various organizations and associations, distributed some 450 million pamphlets, booklets, brochures, posters, and other civil defense materials—many of which dealt directly or indirectly with educating families about how to survive a nuclear attack. From the "Pledge for Home Defense" campaign to the Home Protection Program to the Home Preparedness Award Program, the FCDA and its successors, the Office of Civil and Defense Administration and the Office of Civil Defense, remained consistent in their message that protecting the home front began with each family protecting itself and their home.

Although the anecdotal evidence presented in this study is sure to come under scrutiny if not criticism, the evidence clearly illustrates the wide breadth of women's proactive support for civil defense at the national, regional, state, and local levels. From major "target" cities like Chicago and New York, to small towns like Postville, Iowa, women joined together for the common cause of civil defense. As mentioned elsewhere, women in Emporia, Kansas, joined with women across the nation in 1952 to enlist civil defense volunteers as part of the FCDA's "Pledge for Home Defense" campaign. The same year, women from several western states met in Oakland, California, to attend a civil defense training conference. Representatives of 17 women's organizations sponsored a civil defense conference in Tucson, Arizona, in May 1952. Farm women in rural Pennsylvania met in 1955 to learn more about the FCDA's welfare service and the Ground Observer Corps. Members of the Pleasant Grove [Utah] Women's Civil Defense Organization were among the groups attending a 1955 regional civil defense conference in Salt Lake City. In March 1957, women from six counties in West Virginia attended a Home Protection Exercise Course in Beckley. More than 200 women attended an April 1958 meeting in Eugene, Oregon, conducted by the American Red Cross; and 100 women in Wilmington, Delaware, took a home preparedness course that November.[8]

The theme of the 1960 National Women's Conference on Civil Defense, held September 26 and 27 in Washington, D.C., was "Building Our Home Defense." The conference, under the leadership of OCDM's Dorothy Pearl, featured demonstrations of radiological defense techniques, updates on the nation's fallout shelter status, and a review of processed food for post-attack survival. In 1961, the Mesa, Arizona, city council chamber "was filled to capacity," according to a newspaper report, by women interested in learning first aid and home preparedness, while women in cities and towns across the country, such as those in Butte, Montana, enrolled in home preparedness courses. Wayne Whitt wrote in the June 18, 1961, issue of *The Tennessean*, "If an emergency comes to Tennessee ... the women are more likely to be prepared than the men." Each year, he pointed out, hundreds of women participated in civil defense training courses.[9]

A renewed sense of urgency occurred in October 1962, when the United States and the Soviet Union came dangerously close to a nuclear gunfight over missiles in Cuba. The nation's governors and mayors called emergency meetings to discuss civil defense mobilization. New York Governor Nelson Rockefeller called a meeting of the National Governors Committee on Civil Defense to ensure "that the states take every step necessary to be in maximum readiness." Arkansas Governor Orval Faubus met with top civil defense and military leaders to review the state's readiness. New Mexico Governor Edwin Mechem invoked the state's Civil and Defense Mobilization Act. F. Ray Keyser, governor of Vermont, ordered a review of the state's civil defense operations. In Rhode Island, Governor John Notte ordered the marking of fallout shelters and urged citizens not to get panicky. Oregon Governor Mark Hatfield placed the state's Civil Defense Agency on 24-hour alert. In Florida, Governor Farris Bryant delivered a statewide radio and television address to reassure citizens of the state's readiness and to ease their nervousness. He was joined by Assistant U.S. Secretary for Civil Defense Steuart Pittman, Florida Civil Defense Director H.W. Tarking, and Adjutant General Henry McMillian, head of the Florida National Guard.[10]

People's anxiety was evident in cities across the nation. Robert Keyes, Montana's civil defense director, commented that people had not taken civil defense very seriously before, "but they're worried about it now." In Tampa, Florida, for example, residents bought up canned goods, guns and ammunition, and transistor radios, while school officials reviewed procedures for protecting students. The city also was deluged with requests for civil defense booklets. The Kansas City, Missouri, civil defense office reported more than 400 telephone calls in a single day inquiring about area fallout shelters and information on how to survive a nuclear attack. In response, the city announced the locations of 130 public shelters, and hoped to have 500 shelters available within a week.[11]

Civil defense groups held impromptu meetings and conferences to address the readiness of their programs. Representatives from 16 women's organizations in St. Louis attended the first meeting of the St. Louis Women's

Civil Defense Council, and were introduced to "survival biscuits," a mainstay of fallout shelters. In California, more than 400 women attended the Women's Civil Defense Conference held in Anaheim. The conference theme was "Disaster Preparedness Is Everyone's Job." Howard Janney, civil defense director for Fayette County, West Virginia, asked each family in the county to send at least one member to an emergency civil defense meeting to address the current situation. The Waterbury (Vermont) Women's Council for Civil Defense met to discuss a course in medical self-help. And Washington Governor Albert Rosellini and General Ensley Llewellyn, state director of civil defense, addressed a gathering of 500 concerned women in Olympia, the state capital.[12]

Were these women contained, militarized, controlled, or indoctrinated? The answer is, "No." Women were genuinely interested in learning more about civil defense and seizing the opportunities open to them. Women served as assistant regional directors of civil defense; state directors of women's civil defense programs; presidents and chairs of national, regional, state, and local committees; and managers and coordinators of a wide range of civil defense programs and activities.

The FCDA clearly focused on women's involvement with civil defense. It established a National Women's Advisory Council; named women directors at the regional level; distributed millions of printed materials directed toward home and family protection; worked diligently to enlist women into civil defense, both individually and as members of women's organizations; and supported women's regional, state, and local civil defense activities. The FCDA and its successors, however, due in part to a lack of funding but more specifically to adhere to the original mission of relying primarily on community support, did not represent a monolithic, manipulative government entity. In fact, when reading the annual reports of the FCDA, OCDM, and Office of Civil Defense, it becomes apparent that these agencies continuously introduced new projects, new publications, and new strategies in an attempt to overcome public apathy and attract more men and women.

Grace Martin served as coordinator of women's activities for the Texas Department of Civil Defense during the early Cold War. In this capacity, she traveled the state attending women's meetings, conferences, and other gatherings, and speaking about the necessity for joining civil defense. In her presentations, Martin reflected the same message often heard at civil defense meetings across the country, namely that protecting the home and the home front were inexplicably connected. From the highest levels of government on down to the state, county, and local levels, she made it clear that women had a responsibility to protect both, and that their home skills were equivalent to nation-saving skills.

"The purpose of volunteer registration in every Texas community as in other communities of the United States is to encourage people to stand up and be counted as willing workers for civil defense," she told members of 22 women's organizations in Denton, Texas, in 1952. Eight years later, with the country still entrenched in a Cold War, Martin told members of home demonstration clubs in Corsicana, Texas, "We are in danger. If the home front crumbles, men have nothing to fight with and nothing to fight for."[13]

If there is a conclusion to be reached from this study, it is that the federal government consciously and with purpose solicited women for the national civil defense program. It did so because women, or so the government believed, were more readily available during daytime hours, had special home and family protection skills, and knew their communities better than men. Although it is inarguable that women in civil defense often performed duties based on their traditional gender roles, it is important to note that these women were not a monolithic cohort. Rather, they represented different age groups, ethnicities, educational levels, marital status, professional experience, skill sets, and economic background. They lived in major cities, suburbs, small towns, and rural areas in all parts of the country. Many were professionals; many were housewives. Upon examination of their participation in the warden service, health service, police and nursing services, transportation service, emergency mass feeding program, Ground Observer Corps, communications service, training programs, and other civil defense activities, it is evident that these women performed a multitude of duties and exhibited a wide range of experience and skills. These women, very simply, chose to make a positive contribution to the nation's defense during an era when it seemed, to them at least, that protecting their families, their homes, and the home front was a very serious and important endeavor—and they performed their duties well.

APPENDIX:
SELECTED CHAPTERS
FROM "CIVIL DEFENSE IN OUTLINE"

Shortly after its formation in 1951, the Federal Civil Defense Administration published a comprehensive study guide on its structure, policies, and services for state, regional, and local organizations. Civil Defense in Outline: A Study Guide for the National Civil Defense Program *provided a detailed explanation of every phase of FCDA operations, including an extensive description of each service area, including warden, transportation, health services, emergency welfare,, communications, police, and supply—all areas of particular interest to women. This appendix includes an excerpt from Chapter 1, and Chapters 7, 10, 11, 12, 15, 16 and 18 in their entirety.*

CHAPTER 1: CIVIL DEFENSES ORGANIZATION
(AN EXCERPT)

The responsibility of the Federal organization:

1. Formulates a Nation-wide civil defense training program.
2. Develops training policies and plans as guides for State and local authorities.
3. Provides staff guidance and assistance to State and local authorities.
4. Operates a staff college for key civil defense authorities at State and regional levels.
5. Operates technical training schools for selected personnel who, in turn, will train State and municipal civil defense workers.
6. Issues administrative guides, manuals, and other training aids.

205

CIVIL DEFENSE IN OUTLINE

*A Study Guide for the
National Civil Defense Program*

FEDERAL CIVIL DEFENSE ADMINISTRATION
WASHINGTON, D. C.

State Civil Defense Organization

The responsibility of the State organization:

1. Organizes and operates State training programs.
2. Assists local authorities in establishing and operating their training programs.

Local Civil Defense Organization

The local organization is responsible for training local civil defense personnel and educating the general public to protect itself in case of enemy attack. This program will include training in all the various services.

Financing Civil Defense

Government at all levels should bear the burden.

1. Federal Government will supply 50 percent of organizational equipment costs on a matching basis.
2. State and local governments will supply 50 percent of organizational equipment costs.

Civil Defense Legislation

Federal

The Federal Civil Defense Act of 1950 sets forth Federal responsibilities.

State

The Model Civil Defense Act drafted by FCDA:

1. Creates a State civil defense agency.
2. Gives the Governor emergency powers in case of enemy-caused disasters and sabotage.
3. Provides for appointment of a full-time director.
4. Gives authority to create State area offices.
5. Gives authority to enter into mutual aid plans with other States.
6. Gives authority to use States' resources for civil defense.
7. Provides for surveys of available food, clothing, and other material for distribution to points of disaster in time of emergency.

8. Provides for precautionary measures against air raids.
9. Directs all State, district, and local officials and volunteer agencies with regard to evacuation.
10. Designates health and sanitation measures to safeguard health.
11. Provides for enforcement of all civil defense laws and regulations.
12. Provides additional authority during war.
13. Provides for appropriations.

Local

Because of variations in definition of the powers of local government, a comprehensive model for local legislation has not been prepared.

Local legislation should follow the enabling legislation enacted by the States.

Initial Steps in Civil Defense Planning

The first step in putting civil defense policies into operation is to plan practical methods for using existing public and private resources to the best advantage, thus providing for a realistic, full-fledged civil defense organization.

The plan should indicate, in broad terms, what is to be done and by whom. The civil defense director should:

1. Determine responsibilities and assign these to officials, departments, and agencies.
2. List existing resources-personnel, supplies, and equipment.
3. Provide for additional resources which are not currently available but will be needed in time of attack.

A state of civil defense readiness will not exist until:

1. Deficiencies in resources have been filled and funds made available for planning and operation. A force of volunteer civil defense workers has been trained and equipped. The public understands what to do in time of emergency.

Planning Project

To initiate his planning project, the civil defense director of each Planning State should arrange for one of its designated critical target areas or one of its larger cities and surrounding urban communities to undertake the development of a civil defense plan as a model for the State and its other municipalities.

After the plan is drafted, it should be presented to conference meetings of State and local officials. Representatives of the Federal Civil Defense Administration would attend.

Representatives of other States and municipalities may be asked to participate in the meetings as observers. These observers will return home with an improved understanding of the problems involved. Such a program can aid the progressive development of municipal, State, and Federal civil defense planning in general, as well as that of the city whose plans are under discussion.

Following the meeting, the city should coordinate its civil defense plan with the plans of neighboring communities. Mutual aid and mobile support plans then can be considered in more detail and a metropolitan area plan drawn up and coordinated with the State plan.

Value of Such a Plan

Such a plan is valuable to the city because it:

1. Puts the city in a state of readiness in keeping with predetermined courses of action—namely, operating procedures and effective utilization of existing resources.
2. Indicates the need and stimulates development of outside resources to make up deficiencies.
3. Stimulates other cities through their observers to make similar efforts.
4. Informs Federal, State, and local officials of problems raised, solutions suggested, and deficiencies indicated, thus advancing long-range State and local programs on a Nation-wide basis.

Execution of a Plan

In order to carry out the project, the participants must have a working knowledge of the problems of civil defense.

They should keep informed through current reading materials (available from the Superintendent of Documents, Washington 25, D.C.).

Required local legislation should be enacted creating an official civil defense agency. In the absence of such authority, a temporary organization should be established.

It is necessary to enlist the aid of appropriate existing State, county, and local officials and selected private agencies in order to utilize all local resources for civil defense.

Chapter 7: The Warden Service

The civil defense warden service furnishes the administration and leadership for the organized self-protection program, which embraces both individual and extended self-protection. In this program, the warden is the point of contact between the Civil Defense Corps and the public.

The warden renders on-the-spot guidance and assistance to mobile civil defense units. His post forms a communications network and base of operations for the civil defense services.

The warden is a volunteer who should be well known and respected in the neighborhood and community, and whose leadership is acceptable.

Women, particularly housewives, should play an important role in the warden service. Experience has proved that women are particularly qualified for this type of responsibility and generally are present in residential neighborhoods at all hours.

The family unit constitutes the basis for individual self-protection.

An individual and his family should be trained in measures they may take for self-protection, so that they may form the first line of civil defense.

Specifically, individuals should be encouraged to:

1. Take training and refresher courses such as basic first aid; fire prevention; bacteriological, chemical, and atomic warfare defense; and rescue methods.
2. Equip themselves with necessary tools, supplies, and other essentials for the preservation of the home and family.

All communities in critical target areas should provide for their common protection and orderly joint action in event of attack. Extended self-protection should be organized:

1. Where people live.
2. Where people work.
3. Where people assemble.

The people in each of these areas should be organized under direction of the warden service into units of volunteers for firefighting, rescue, first aid, and other essential elements of self-protection.

Outside of critical target areas, a similar but modified extended self-protection organization should be established by the warden service to:

1. Afford protection in event of attack.
2. Organize reception of evacuees and other supporting programs.

Organized on a block-by-block basis, the warden service is the civil defense pipeline to the people of the neighborhoods and to the civil defense agencies. The men and women of the warden service will:

1. Assist in organizing individual self-protection training courses in cooperation with local Red Cross and other agencies in the community civil defense program.
2. Organize the extended self-protection program.
3. Instruct the public on civil defense methods and regulations and inform neighborhoods, families, and employee groups of current civil defense developments.
4. Assemble pertinent data and essential information concerning occupants of buildings, businesses, physical features, and available protective equipment.

Following an attack, wardens will:

1. Mobilize organized self-protection units.
2. Report casualties, damages, and general conditions.
3. Render first aid, fight small fires, assist in rescue work, and prevent panic, utilizing the resources of the neighborhood.
4. Call for needed assistance from mobile civil defense services when the situation is beyond the control of the organized self-protection forces of the immediate area. Assist in unexploded ordnance reconnaissance.
5. Assist mobile support teams at the scene of damage.
6. Collaborate with civil defense officials responsible for evacuation, police, fire, communications, and other services.
7. Assist families during rehabilitation and reconstruction programs.

Men and women wardens should receive comprehensive training in:

- Organization, duties, and responsibilities of the warden service.
- First aid.
- Fire fighting.
- Chemical warfare defense.
- Biological warfare defense.
- Basic rescue procedure.

Chapter 10: Transportation

In a war-caused disaster, transportation will be needed for the movement of:

1. Special civil defense teams and equipment.
2. Casualties and the homeless.
3. Food and emergency supplies, including water.
4. Medical and health teams.
5. Emergency labor parties.
6. Engineering and utility crews.
7. Persons or property under mutual aid arrangements.

Civil defense authorities must plan, coordinate, organize, and at times train personnel for the transportation services. Deficiencies of some types of transportation may require the acquisition of vehicles for special use. All forms of transportation will be needed in civil defense.

Transportation services should be part of civil defense at all levels of organization.

The State chief of transportation should assist local transportation chiefs in developing their plans and determining that they are adequate. He should coordinate all local plans into a State-wide plan and also organize the transportation elements of mobile support.

A central transportation division should be established within the framework of the local civil defense organization.

Duties of the local transportation division:

1. Receives the transportation requirements of all local civil defense services, noting their estimated needs for various types of equipment and facilities, including warehousing.
2. Makes an inventory of available facilities, including railroads, intercity bus companies, intercity truck lines, air transport, taxicabs, local garages, public rental cars and trucks, local transit systems, sightseeing buses, ferries and other types of watercraft, truck fleets of private companies, school buses, public and private ambulances, private automobiles, and private aircraft.
3. Develops plans to meet emergency needs—such as converting trucks, buses, or station wagons into ambulances by adapters to support litters.
4. Makes mutual aid or other arrangements through the State or area civil defense director for the use of stand-by facilities outside the

local area to cover estimated deficits in facilities, and to provide additional mobile support.

The transportation division should sponsor the establishment of emergency storage and hauling facilities for fuels and other operating supplies, including designated service stations equipped with auxiliary pumping units. It should establish and equip emergency repair stations and arrange temporary local priorities for use of supplies and facilities in case of disaster.

The transportation division should direct the preparation of plans and procedures for the emergency utilization of the facilities of all transport agencies, permitting each to supervise its own operation to the fullest extent possible.

It should mobilize unorganized transportation equipment.

Plans should be made, in cooperation with the police service, for "freezing" private automobiles and other highway vehicles not engaged in essential work.

Points of assembly should be designated on the outskirts of a local area, and each vehicle operator should be assigned an assembly place in event of an alert.

A central dispatching office should be set up at the local control center and secondary dispatching control centers established as necessary.

The transportation division should consult with the engineering services on plans for the restriction of roadways, waterways, and bridges to essential traffic, and with the police and engineering services on control and coordination of vehicular movement.

The local civil defense transportation service should sponsor programs for training personnel, if required, in the concept of organized movements.

To the extent possible, persons capable of repairing automotive vehicles should be relied upon to furnish a reservoir of men for emergency repairs in case of disaster.

The public must be kept informed of civil defense transportation plans, the success of which depends on understanding and cooperation.

CHAPTER 11: HEALTH SERVICES AND SPECIAL WEAPONS DEFENSE

Because of technical and professional requirements, civil defense health services and special weapons defense must remain a responsibility of existing health agencies and individuals. These agencies and individuals will perform their wartime functions under civil defense rules and regulations.

Close liaison between civil defense organizations and peacetime health services is imperative.

In each State, the State health officer generally should be placed in charge of all state civil defense health and medical services.

Cities should appoint local health officers in the same manner.

Maintenance of usual health services during wartime is the responsibility of existing health agencies and professional and technical health experts. The relief of suffering immediately after a civilian wartime disaster, provision of emergency lifesaving measures, and preservation or restoration of health services normally existing in peacetime are the responsibilities of civil defense.

A single organizational blueprint could not be applied to every State or local community. For this reason, health and medical services are described in functional rather than organizational units.

The functions of each service are discussed below in general terms only.

Each service listed is sufficiently important in the over-all program to require direction by a separate chief reporting to the chief of health services and special weapons defense.

A complete system of first-aid stations should be devised in certain areas designated by State civil defense authorities.

Emergency equipment should be stored at fringe areas and be ready for prompt transportation to implement the stations' functions. Vans might serve as first-aid stations if no suitable buildings are available.

Physicians, dentists, nurses, pharmacists, first-aid workers, litter bearers, and clerks for recording vital statistics should be assigned to these stations early to take part in the planning as well as in the operation of the stations.

Screening of casualties for further treatment will be done at first-aid stations. Competent dispatching service will be required to route casualties to other treatment centers.

A complete inventory of facilities around critical target areas should be made to determine the available space that can be converted to hospital use. Use of hotels and apartments is not generally recommended.

Emergency equipment such as beds, instruments, and medical supplies should be placed in condition for ready shipment from storage points to equip the hospitals. Staffs for the improvised hospitals, including volunteer workers, should be drawn from nearby areas to treat cases of shock and burns, for surgical operations, and for other services that may be needed.

Existing hospitals in nearby and distant communities should be used for patients who can be transported to them, and for those exposed to dangerous amounts of radiation but with no other significant injuries.

Close cooperation with the transportation service will be necessary.

In general, trucks will be used as emergency ambulances.

All hospitals should have emergency water, electric, and gas supplies available in event of failure of normal supplies.

Casualty services are made up primarily of surgical teams, including shock-treatment and burn-treatment units. These teams should be organized locally and—supplemented by teams from other cities—organized as affiliated hospital units.

A system of distribution of drugs, chemicals, instruments, equipment, antibiotics, biologicals, and surgical textiles should be established.

Adequate local storage of all such supplies would be excessively expensive, duplicate precious supplies, and require a great number of skilled supply workers. The reserves of surgical supplies are not adequate to meet major wartime disasters. To augment existing supplies, the Federal Government plans to stockpile these items. They will be located outside critical areas but will be readily accessible by rail, truck, and air shipping facilities to more than one critical area.

The American National Red Cross is assigned the major responsibility for Nation-wide coordination of donor recruitment, blood procurement, and the storage, processing, and preparation of blood for shipment.

In localities where there are no blood banks, steps should be taken promptly to establish them; these banks should participate in the national blood program.

Transportation of blood within the State is largely the responsibility of the State civil defense transportation agencies. Shipment of blood from Federal civil defense supply depots will be a Federal responsibility, subject to Public Health Service interstate shipping standards for biological products.

These services are necessary for such functions as blood matching; clinical, public health, and sanitation laboratory measures; and functions relating to biological and chemical warfare.

Federal mobile laboratories may be available for prompt reinforcement of laboratory services at disaster areas.

Preservation of the health of the surviving population after a disaster is vital. The following basic responsibilities, utilizing aid from adjacent communities, should be planned for:

1. Maintenance or restoration of water sanitation, plus safe treatment of temporary emergency water supplies.
2. Adequate food inspection, especially in emergency kitchens and canteens.
3. Extension or revision of existing milk sanitation regulations to meet the possibility that local pasteurization plants will be disabled.

4. Maintenance or restoration of sanitation standards in disposal of sewage or solid waste.
5. Regulation of sanitation in shelters and emergency billeting.
6. Decontamination measures relating to atomic, biological, or chemical warfare.

In order to carry out these responsibilities both during and after a disaster, the local sanitation services would require volunteer workers.

Such volunteers should be trained in specialized fields and given necessary authority to perform their duties.

It is suggested that the State health officer, with the assistance of existing agencies, establish the standards for nutritional services. Model standards and instructions are available from the Department of Agriculture and the Federal Security Agency. Responsibilities would include planning emergency diets and food priority systems to guide the emergency welfare service, which is responsible for emergency provision of food.

Milk rationing would be the most urgent consideration.

Medical services must be planned to assure non-casualty care for survivors who were ill before the disaster or who become ill following disaster.

Responsibilities of the veterinary service:

1. Protection of food animals, especially in event of biological warfare. Care must be taken against contamination of animals or crops.
2. Safeguarding of pets, other small animals, and animals in zoos and similar institutions. Local civil defense health organizations must keep uniform records of all medical evacuees, injured or ill persons, and the dead.

The current epidemic reporting program should be augmented to insure prompt reporting of increased incidence of diseases produced by biological warfare. Service records should be maintained of all personnel working on this aspect of civil defense, both regular and volunteer.

Provision for adequate morgue and identification facilities is imperative.

Plans should include provision for prompt removal of the dead from damaged areas by the rescue service, and from badly needed hospital facilities by the health service. Temporary morgues where the dead may be identified and prepared for burial will be necessary. Preparation of graves should be the responsibility of the engineering services.

The welfare services should be assigned the responsibility for notifying next of kin and giving sympathetic assistance.

The local civil defense transportation service should be responsible for providing all transportation for the health services. The health service is responsible for notifying the transportation service of its needs.

Types of essential transportation include first-aid station vans, emergency ambulances, morgue trucks, casualty evacuation and hospital-patient evacuation vehicles, and vehicles for essential health personnel.

It is essential that there be liaison with the civil defense communications service to insure adequate communication for the health service.

Training should be given in steps so as to train the maximum number of people with minimum dislocation of their normal activities.

As an example, courses in the medical aspects of atomic warfare have been conducted for medical school faculty members in key States and for nurses by the Federal Government, thereby qualifying them to become instructors. In the larger cities, instructors should conduct courses for persons in order that the latter can become instructors. This new group then should be responsible for training local professional health personnel in their own cities and nearby towns.

It is suggested that States and localities do not begin training courses for professional and technical personnel until the Federal Civil Defense Administration has completed and issued training manuals for teachers.

After an atomic attack, a radiological survey should be started immediately by radiological monitoring teams of the local health service.

Radiation hazards to civil defense workers and the general population of the area will be checked by medical specialists.

All civil defense personnel assigned to radiologically contaminated areas should be issued radiological dosage devices by the appropriate branch of the health service.

Suggested specifications for individual dosage devices and other radiological monitoring instruments will be provided by the Federal Civil Defense Administration.

Special Federal or State radiological monitoring teams would be provided for continued surveys, requiring special skills and equipment, in the post-disaster period.

Biological sampling and laboratory analysis should be the responsibility of local health department laboratories. Exact identification may be referred to existing State and Federal public health laboratories organized and equipped for that purpose.

Monitoring and other protective services for biological warfare against food animals are the responsibility of the Federal, State, and local veterinary agencies. Similar services to protect crops against special weapons are the responsibility of the Federal, State, and local agricultural agencies.

Chemical warfare monitoring should be the responsibility of local health departments, through monitoring devices or teams, and of individual physicians, through recognition of clinical symptoms of victims.

CHAPTER 12: EMERGENCY WELFARE SERVICE

The emergency welfare service in civil defense is considered to embrace all the service and assistance required to meet the human need for food, clothing and shelter, and information and counseling on personal and family problems that arise from enemy action or threat of such action.

In planning the emergency welfare service, provision must be made for four principal types of activities:

1. Registration and information.
2. Mass care.
3. Temporary rehabilitation.
4. Evacuation (reception).

In civil defense operations, the registration and information units of the emergency welfare service will:

1. Obtain and maintain information concerning affected civilians, separated families, homeless persons, and persons receiving mass care and other assistance.
2. Furnish information to individuals, other civil defense divisions, and cooperating agencies caring for affected civilians.
3. Refer families and individuals to other appropriate welfare agencies.

Personnel to operate this service should be enlisted from social-work agencies with the assistance of trained volunteers.

Mass feeding, emergency clothing, and temporary shelter may be needed by a large number of persons after an attack. A survey should be made of all local eating establishments, commercial and private, to determine their normal feeding capacity and possible degree of expansion; also of mobile canteens, food trains, available cooking and serving equipment, and food supplies (retail, wholesale, and government).

A survey should also be made to identify persons experienced in preparing and serving large quantities of food. Agreements should be negotiated with food facility owners for use of their establishments and release of supplies and equipment when needed for emergency feeding.

Mass-feeding menus should be secured in advance from the health and medical services.

Inventories of facilities, equipment, supplies, and personnel, together with copies of negotiated agreements, should be used by local and State civil defense agencies in planning mutual aid operations.

Civil defense planning should provide for temporary mass shelter.

Homeless persons and families should be housed in homes of friends and relatives, in homes of others who volunteer space, and in unoccupied or partially occupied houses and buildings. A survey should be made of local available facilities for rehousing.

Volunteers experienced in hotel work, settlement work, and building management should be enlisted to record the potential capacity for housing the homeless. The housing survey should note structural soundness, degree of safety from attack, and adequacy of water, heating, sanitation, lighting, cooking, serving, and storage facilities.

An appraisal of potential mass-care facilities should include such equipment as cots, blankets, emergency lighting, toilet facilities, and general maintenance items.

An inventory should be made of all available clothing supplies from both retail and wholesale outlets and arrangements made for immediate procurement if necessary.

Essential garments should be listed according to population groups.

Inventories should be made available to State civil defense authorities for mutual aid purposes.

The welfare service should:

1. Arrange for meeting the material needs of families and individuals.
2. So far as possible, preserve normal group associations—family, neighborhood, and school.
3. Help evacuees to adjust to the new environment.
4. Facilitate communications between evacuees and persons remaining in the evacuated area.

The welfare service in reception areas is responsible for:

1. Selecting homes for evacuees.
2. Placing evacuees.
3. Providing information to evacuation headquarters regarding arrival and address of evacuees.
4. Supervising evacuees under care.
5. Initiating case-work services as necessary.
6. Cooperating with educational authorities to assure school attendance.

7. Cooperating with health and medical services to provide necessary medical and health supervision.
8. Helping to provide employment opportunities.
9. Organizing special community facilities, such as social centers, commercial feeding centers, laundries, nursery centers, and recreation facilities.

The services of existing welfare agencies in reception areas must be expanded to care for the evacuated population.

At the scene of attack it is the responsibility of the emergency welfare service to organize feeding facilities, including mobile facilities, for civil defense workers. Mobile support units from other localities should be self-sufficient at least for the first 2 days.

Chapter 15: Communications

The nerve system of civil defense is communications. Effective and rapid communication must be maintained between Federal and State and between State and local civil defense organizations and within these organizations if they are to function when needed.

Every contingency must be provided for, and sound flexible plans developed so that in an emergency communications in some form will be available.

Security problems will arise in the use of communication channels, which may be subject to enemy interception. Radio is particularly vulnerable. All plans for communication systems and procedures must take into account this security factor to avoid unnecessary disclosure of information valuable to an enemy.

The Federal Civil Defense Administration is responsible for the overall planning of communications for civil defense and for coordination with the Department of Defense, the Federal Communications Commission, other governmental agencies, and commercial communication and broadcasting networks. It will determine the technical specifications and advise civil defense organizations on their communication systems.

In formulating communication plans, each State and local civil defense organization should take the following steps:

1. Identify the communication needs that exist in an emergency, and anticipate the volume and kind of traffic and any special problems.

2. Take an inventory of existing communication facilities and make arrangements for their emergency use in accordance with anticipated requirements.
3. Provide in every instance secondary systems of communications.

Normally, communication requirements in critical target areas would include facilities for:

1. Communication between civil defense control centers.
2. Attack warning networks.
3. Communication systems for:
    (a) fire
    (b) police
    (c) transportation
    (d) rescue
    (e) warden
    (f) health
    (g) engineering
    (h) reconnaissance teams
4. Air-ground communication systems at State control centers for use with aircraft employed in civil defense activities.

Local communications plans should embrace all forms of communication, including telephone, telegraph, facsimile, AM (broadcasting), shortwave radio, teletype, messenger service, or other practical emergency communications.

Wherever possible, wire line circuits should be back-stopped by radio. Self-powered mobile radio equipment is especially desirable.

State civil defense agencies should develop an itemized list of requirements, and these should be reviewed, coordinated, and consolidated by the State organization for submission to the Federal Civil Defense Administration when requested.

State civil defense control centers should be located with special regard to security, the availability of communications, and transportation.

Local civil defense control centers should also be located with regard to security and ready availability to all kinds of communication facilities and to local civil defense services. Alternate control centers should be planned.

Equipment of local control centers should be as simple as possible; however, they should be capable of maintaining communications for the following purposes:

1. Receipt and dissemination of air-raid warning information.
2. Operation of sirens and public-address systems to alert and convey

warnings to the public, to industrial installations, and to civil defense volunteer workers.
3. Summoning of key civil defense personnel to duty.
4. Reports and requests for assistance from the established local services and civil defense operating units.
5. Contact with State and other control centers to facilitate exchange of assistance.
6. Constant two-way communication with local police, fire, rescue, medical, engineering, and other operating services and with key radio broadcasting services.

Provision should be made for a force of messengers and automobiles, motorcycles, bicycles, or other transportation.

Broadcasting stations (including television) should be used to inform the public of its responsibility in civil defense and to teach civil defense procedures. AM broadcasting stations will be available for dissemination of civil defense instructions during and after air raids, but only under classified operating regulations prepared by the Federal Communications Commission.

Under an organized plan, amateur radio operators will make an important contribution to civil defense communications. Their knowledge and radiotelephone and continuous-wave equipment can be utilized in augmenting the established safety services (police and fire) and in providing radio facilities for the civil defense services that have no radio facilities at present (such as warden and medical).

Chapter 16: Police Service

Police services are represented by coordinators at State, sectional, county and metropolitan levels in addition to the local chief of police services.

The State coordinator develops police resources, plans, and procedures to assure maximum civil defense effectiveness of the police services in the State. He—

1. Coordinates functions of sectional coordinators and all police agencies within the State.
2. Coordinates activities of the police services with other civil defense services.
3. Develops and activates police and auxiliary police training programs with particular emphasis on general civil defense tactical problems and coordinated activities.

4. In conjunction with military agencies, develops training methods for explosive ordnance agents.
5. Facilitates the flow of instructions and information from Federal and State civil defense offices to police agencies.
6. Directs the inventory and maintenance of master records of police facilities, personnel, and equipment in the State.
7. Develops plans for organization and implementation of police mobile support involving, under special orders from the Governor, the command of intrastate and interstate police resources.
8. Stimulates and organizes auxiliary police training and maintains liaison with State civil defense offices in the development of police training material, training aids, and texts.

The sectional coordinator implements police civil defense planning, coordinates civil defense functions and activities of all police agencies, and integrates such functions and activities with those of other civil defense services within the section. He—

1. Directs the State civil defense program for sectional police services.
2. Coordinates civil defense functions of all police agencies in the section and integrates them with those of other civil defense services.
3. Assists and advises in the development of mutual aid compact between sectional police agencies, including units of the State police.
4. Inventories sectional police resources at specific intervals for the State coordinator.
5. Assists in developing and improving police communications.

The metropolitan coordinator implements metropolitan police civil defense planning and coordinates all police activities with those of other civil defense services. He—

1. Coordinates police functions with those of other civil defense services; implements police planning for civil defense, including mutual aid agreements; keeps current inventory of police personnel, equipment, and facilities in his area; and transmits data to the State coordinator.
2. Assists in developing police communication networks and stimulates the recruitment, organization, and training of auxiliary police, as well as special training of regular police in civil defense.

The local chief of police develops police resources, plans, and procedures to assure maximum civil defense effectiveness, and establishes a basis for coordination of police services with other county or local civil defense services. He—

1. Allocates additional responsibilities and implements police organizational pattern in compliance with plans of the local civil defense organization.
2. Develops and augments police resources to assure maximum civil defense effectiveness.
3. Serves on the staff of the local director of civil defense as advisor and operating head of the police services.
4. Evaluates and expands operational controls and procedures.
5. Mobilizes personnel and equipment.
6. Actuates police and auxiliary police training programs, with emphasis on tactical problems and coordinated activities.
7. Recruits and trains auxiliary police as a part of the regular police services.
8. Maintains a current inventory of police resources, personnel, and equipment within his jurisdiction and supplies the State coordinator with this data at regular intervals.
9. Coordinates the activities of police services with other civil defense services.
10. Develops mutual aid plans.

Auxiliary police are volunteers enrolled through the local civil defense office or in the regular police recruiting program. They serve as an integral part of the regular police organization in emergencies.

Duties of auxiliary police:

1. Under direction of regular police personnel, perform police duties as assigned.
2. Patrol assigned area on foot or in vehicles.
3. Direct traffic and provide right-of-way for emergency vehicles.
4. Enforce laws and emergency regulations; apprehend violators and detain suspicious persons.
5. Protect life and property and prevent looting and other illegal actions.
6. Guard docks, warehouses, bridges, and other vulnerable points.
7. Prevent and control panic, hysteria, and mob action.
8. Assist wardens and explosive ordnance reconnaissance agents.
9. Assist in evacuation of persons from dangerous areas and prevent unauthorized persons from entering such areas.
10. Render first aid.

Volunteer forces should not be hastily organized, clothed with police authority, and armed with police weapons. All auxiliaries should be carefully selected and trained before participating in police activities.

Police must be trained in the methods and techniques of civil defense, with special attention to the following:

1. Prevention of panic.
2. Maintenance of communications. It is vitally important that all possible alternate and auxiliary communication systems be developed. Disruption of police communications will not only impair effectiveness of the police force but may mean loss of additional lives and property.
3. Traffic and highway control. Police services should work with the transportation service in establishing control points and regulating traffic. Routes should be designated through local urban centers. Plans and procedures should be developed for dispatching convoys and for operating traffic under controlled dispatch and priorities. Police training for civil defense should include measures to be taken when an alert is given.
4. Police should be prepared to receive reports of explosive ordnance, to send explosive ordnance reconnaissance officers to check on reports, and, where necessary, to take adequate precautions. Actual disposal of unexploded ordnance is the responsibility of the armed forces.

Chapter 18: Supply Service

Adequate supply and equipment for civil defense should be a joint responsibility of the Federal, State, and local governments.

Supply planning must keep step with general organizational and operational planning for civil defense.

Normal peacetime supply organizations in States, counties, and cities should absorb most of the burden of procurement, storage, and distribution of civil defense supplies. Civil defense authorities should study existing supply organizations to determine what changes may be necessary or desirable.

Continuing estimates should be made of stocks of supplies and equipment for civil defense.

Mutual aid and State mobile support patterns must be considered before determining requirements for new supplies.

The Federal Government can make appropriate allocations of national resources for civil defense needs when total State requirements are determined.

A standardized specification manual will be issued by the Federal Civil Defense Administration.

Procurement of civil defense supplies should be divided among Federal, State, and local civil defense organizations.

Civil defense supplies procured at Federal expense will be of two kinds:

1. Those not normally stored in peacetime, and peculiar to civil defense, which must be furnished to and through States to localities for use in developing and organizing their civil defense systems.
2. Those which would be used by the Federal Government for replacing supplies and equipment destroyed or worn out in emergency civil defense operations, and for emergency relief at the time of disaster.

When necessary materials are unavailable, the Federal Civil Defense Administration should be called upon to determine essential priority requirements and assist in procuring necessary authorizations.

State and city storage warehouses should be located at dispersal points.

Federal warehouses, situated at strategic points within 4-hour delivery time of a critical target area, will be used for items supplied by the Federal Government for disaster operations.

Expenditures of Federal funds must accord with accounting procedures prescribed by the Federal Civil Defense Administration. The local civil defense director should designate a responsible property officer, who will handle details in connection with municipal civil defense supplies and maintain proper records.

Qualified persons in the various State and local organizations should be held responsible for continuing studies of inventory requirements and supply.

Chapter Notes

Preface

1. James Baughman, "Television Comes to America," *Illinois History* (March 1993): 42.
2. For a discussion of the hydrogen bomb's impact on American society, see Allan M. Winkler, *Life Under a Cloud: American Anxiety About the Atom* (New York: Oxford University Press, 1993).
3. "'Atomic Attack' on TV," *The Evening Sun* (Hanover, PA), May 15, 1954: 6; "TV Key," *The Brooklyn Daily Eagle* (Brooklyn, NY), May 18, 1954: 13; C. E. Butterfield, "Highlights: Radio, TV," *The Evening Independent* (Massillon, OH) May 21, 1954: 10; "Look and Listen With Donald Kirkley," *The Baltimore Sun*, May 18, 1954: 12.
4. Betty Friedan, *The Feminine Mystique* (New York: W.W. Norton & Company, 1963).
5. Elaine Tyler May, *Homeward Bound: American Families in the Cold War Era* (New York: Basic Books, 1988), 105.
6. Susan Hartmann, "Women's Employment and the Domestic Ideal in the Early Cold War Years," in Joanne Meyerowitz, editor, *Not June Cleaver: Women and Gender in Postwar America, 1945-1960* (Philadelphia: Temple University Press, 1994), 86.
7. See Elaine Tyler May's review of Laura McEnaney, *Civil Defense Begins at Home: Militarization Meets Everyday Life in the Fifties*, *Wisconsin Magazine of History* (Summer 2002): 61–62.
8. Laura McEnaney, *Civil Defense Begins at Home: Militarization Meets Everyday Life in the Fifties* (Princeton, NJ, Princeton University Press, 2000), 89.
9. *Ibid.*, 109.
10. *The Warden's Handbook* (Washington, D.C.: Government Printing Office, 1951), 1.
11. *Federal Civil Defense 1954 Annual Report* (Washington, D.C., Government Printing Office, 1954), 33–45.
12. *Ibid.*, 90.
13. *Ibid.*, 4.

Chapter 1

1. Speech at Fuller Lodge to honor work at Los Alamos, October 16, 1945. Quoted in Kai Bird, Martin J. Sherwin, *American Prometheus: the Triumph and Tragedy of J. Robert Oppenheimer* (New York: Alfred A. Knopf, 2005), 323.
2. *Challenge for Security and Survival: Manual for Women in Civil Defense* (Ohio Civil Defense, 1965), 5
3. For an overview of the civil rights movement in the 1950s and 1960s, see Bruce Dierenfield, *The Civil Rights Movement: Revised Edition* (New York: Routledge, 2008).
4. For an overview of the Berlin Crisis and Cuban Missile Crisis, see Jeremy Isaacs and Taylor Downing, *Cold War* (London: Little Brown Book Group, 2014).
5. David Lilienthal, "Science and Man's Fate," *Nation*, July 13, 1946: 40–41.
6. Paul Boyer, *By the Bomb's Early Light: American Thought and Culture at the Dawn of the Atomic Age* (New York: Pantheon Books, 1985), 15.
7. For an overview of the Berlin Airlift, the iron curtain, NATO, and the fall of China, see Jeremy Isaacs and Taylor Downing, *Cold War*.
8. "Truman Urges Civil Defense Preparations," *The Journal News* (White Plains, NY), September 18, 1950: 1.
9. "Women's Defense Responsibilities Are Outlined," *The Daily Clintonian* (Clinton, IN), October 4, 1950: 1; "Plans Are Being Made to Mobilize Nation's Woman Power," *Carsicana Semi-Weekly Light* (Corsicana, TX), December 22, 1950: 2.
10. *Ibid.*
11. "Robbie Johnson's Chat With Women," *Times Herald* (Olean, NY), September 27, 1950: 7; John M. McCullough, "Women Here to Train in Civil Defense Roles," *The Philadelphia Inquirer*, December 1, 1950: 8; Katherine Dunlap, "Civil Defense Leaders Appeal for 100,000 Women Volunteers," *The Philadelphia Inquirer*, December 15, 1950: 39+; "Civil Defense Session

Today," *The Des Moines Register* (Des Moines, IA), September 21, 1950: 3; "Women to Be Active in S.C. Civil Defense," *Florence Morning News* (Florence, SC) October 20, 1950: 14; "Conference On Civil Defense Opens in Capital," *The Mount Pleasant News* (Mount Pleasant, IA), October 2, 1950: 1.

12. Harry S Truman: "Executive Order 10186—Establishing the Federal Civil Defense Administration in the Office for Emergency Management of the Executive Office of the President," December 1, 1950. Gerhard Peters, and John T. Woolley, *The American Presidency Project*. Retrieved from http://www.presidency.ucsb.edu/ws/?pid=78352.

13. The provisions of Executive Order 10222 of Mar. 8, 1951, appear at 16 FR 2247, 3 CFR, 1949–1953 Comp., p. 736, unless otherwise noted. Retrieved from https://www.archives.gov/federal-register/codification/executive-order/10222.html.

14. *Federal Civil Defense Administration 1951 Annual Report* (Washington, D.C.: U.S. Government Printing Office, 1951), 19.

15. *Georgia Women in Civil Defense* (Georgia Civil Defense, c. 1954), 32.

16. *Ibid.*, 16–17.

17. *FCDA 1951 Annual Report*, XI, 9; *Homemaker's Manual of Atomic Defense* (Columbia Broadcasting System, 1951): 2.

18. Susan Stoudinger Northcutt, "Women and the Bomb: Domestication of the Atomic Bomb in the United States," *International Social Science Review* 74, No. 3/4 (1999): 130; Kenton Clymer, "The Ground Observer Corps: Public Relations and the Cold War in the 1950s," *Journal of Cold War Studies* 15,1 (Winter 2013): 34–52; also see Mitro Toossi, "A Century of Change: The U.S. Labor Force, 1950–2050" (Bureau of Labor Statistics, 2002).

19. *Federal Civil Defense Administration 1953 Annual Report* (Washington, D.C.: U.S. Government Printing Office, 1953), 167.

20. Quote cited in McEnaney, *Civil Defense Begins at Home*, 109.

21. Kristina Zarlengo, "Civilian Threat, the Suburban Citadel, and Atomic Age Women," *Institutions, Regulation, and Social Control* 24, 4 (Summer 1999), 943–944.

22. *Ibid.*

23. Elaine Tyler May, *Homeward Bound: American Families in the Cold War Era* (New York: Basic Books, 1988), 103–104; Zarlengo, "Civilian Threat, the Suburban Citadel, and Atomic Age Women," 951.

24. Zarlengo, "Civilian Threat, the Suburban Citadel, and Atomic Age Women," 951.

25. Susan Stoudinger Northcutt, "Women and the Bomb: Domestication of the Atomic Bomb in the United States," 130.

26. Mary Brennan, *Wives, Mothers, and the Red Menace* (Boulder: University of Colorado Press, 2008), 93.

27. *Challenge for Security and Survival*, 10.

28. *Women in Civil Defense* (Washington, D.C.: U.S. Government Printing Office, 1952).

29. *Ibid.*, 1–3.

30. Clara McMahon, "Civil Defense and Education Goals," *The Elementary School Journal* 53 (April 1953): 440–442. Also see Michael Scheibach, *Atomic Narratives and American Youth: Coming of Age with the Atom, 1945–1955* (Jefferson, NC: McFarland, 2003); and *Atomics in the Classroom: Teaching the Bomb in the Early Postwar Years* (Jefferson, NC: McFarland, 2015).

31. See Scheibach, *Atomic Narratives and American Youth*, and Scheibach, *Atomics in the Classroom*.

32. *120 Years of American Education: A Statistical Portrait* (Washington, D.C.: National Center for Education Statistics, U.S. Department of Education, 1993), 28.

33. Andrew Grossman, *Neither Dead Nor Red: Civilian Defense and American Political Development During the Early Cold War* (New York: Routledge, 2001), 102–103.

34. *Ibid.*, 103.

Chapter 4

1. President Harry S Truman's address at a dinner of the 1951 Civil Defense Conference, The American Presidency Project. Retrieved from http://www.presidency.ucsb.edu/ws/?pid=14079.

2. Quoted in Andrew Grossman, *Neither Dead Nor Red: Civilian Defense and American Political Development During the Early Cold War* (New York: Routledge, 2001): 103.

3. *Ibid.*, 19–20.

4. Laura McEnaney on "Women's Role in Civil Defense," PBS American Experience Interview. Retrieved from http://www.pbs.org/wgbh/amex/bomb/filmmore/reference/interview/mcenaney09.html.

5. Grossman, 103.

6. To learn more about the Korean War, see David Halberstam, *The Coldest Winter: America and the Korean War* (New York: Hyperion, 2007).

7. Executive Orders, Harry S Truman (1945–1953), Harry S. Truman Library & Museum. Retrieved from https://www.trumanlibrary.org/executiveorders/index.php?pid=95&st=&st1=.

8. *Ibid.*

9. Harry S Truman: "Proclamation 2914—Proclaiming the Existence of a National Emergency," December 16, 1950. Gerhard Peters and

John T. Woolley, *The American Presidency Project*. Retrieved from http://www.presidency.ucsb.edu/ws/?pid=13684.

10. "Statement by the President Upon Signing the Civil Defense Act of 1950." The American Presidency Project. Retrieved from http://www.presidency.ucsb.edu/ws/?pid=13777.

11. See Halberstam, *The Coldest Winter*, 624–630.

12. Laura McEnaney, *Civil Defense Begins at Home: Militarization Meets Everyday Life in the Fifties* (Princeton, NJ: Princeton University Press, 2000): 7–8.

13. *Federal Civil Defense Administration 1951 Annual Report* (Washington, D.C.: U.S. Government Printing Office, 1951), VIII–IX.

14. *Federal Civil Defense Administration 1957 Annual Report* (Washington, D.C.: U.S. Government Printing Office, 1957): 54.

15. *FCDA 1951 Annual Report*, 1.

16. "Women's Role in Civil Defense," *New York Times* July 11, 1951: 34.

17. *FCDA 1951 Annual Report*, 65–66.

18. Ibid.

19. *This Is Civil Defense* (Washington, D.C.: U.S. Government Printing Office, 1951): 21–22.

20. "Message to the Congress Transmitting the First Annual Report of the Federal Civil Defense Administration," Public Papers of the President (1945–1953), Harry S. Truman Library & Museum.

21. McEnaney, *Civil Defense Begins at Home*, 25–26.

22. *Federal Civil Defense Administration 1952 Annual Report* (Washington, D.C.: U.S. Government Printing Office, 1952): 62.

23. *Federal Civil Defense Administration 1953 Annual Report* (Washington, D.C.: U.S. Government Printing Office, 1953): 71.

24. Ibid.

25. Ibid.

26. *Federal Civil Defense Administration 1954 Annual Report* (Washington, D.C.: U.S. Government Printing Office, 1954): 96.

27. Ibid., 164–165.

28. Ibid.

29. *Federal Civil Defense Administration 1956 Annual Report* (Washington, D.C.: U.S. Government Printing Office, 1956): 45.

30. *FCDA 1957 Annual Report*, 47–50.

31. *Office of Civil Defense and Mobilization 1959 Annual Report* (Washington, D.C.: U.S. Government Printing Office, 1959): 48.

32. Dee Garrison, *Bracing for Armageddon: Why Civil Defense Never Worked* (New York: Oxford University Press, 2006): 111–113.

33. "Civil Defense Fireside Chat," Theodore Sorensen Papers, Box 30, Civil Defense, John F. Kennedy Presidential Library and Museum.

34. Ibid.

35. *Civil Defense 1965* (Washington, D.C.: U.S. Government Printing Office, 1965): 4–5.

36. See *Civil Defense 1965* for a discussion of civil defense activities.

37. Kathleen Johnson, "Women Defend the Nation," The Cold War Museum. Retrieved from http://www.coldwar.org/articles/50s/women_civildefense.asp.

Chapter 7

1. *Texans on the Alert for Civil Defense and Disaster Relief* (Texas Division of Defense and Disaster Relief, 1956), 8–13.

2. *Federal Civil Defense Administration 1951 Annual Report* (Washington, D.C.: U.S. Government Printing Office, 1951): 19–20.

3. *Challenge for Security and Survival: Manual for Women in Civil* Defense (Ohio Civil Defense, 1965).

4. Ibid.

5. *Federal Civil Defense Administration 1952 Annual Report* (Washington, D.C.: U.S. Government Printing Office, 1952): 62.

6. *Federal Civil Defense Administration 1953 Annual Report* (Washington, D.C.: U.S. Government Printing Office, 1953): 34.

7. *Women in Civil Defense* (Washington, D.C.: U.S. Government Printing Office, 1952): 18–19.

8. Remarks at the Conference of the National Women's Advisory Committee on Civil Defense. The American Presidency Project. Retrieved from http://www.presidency.ucsb.edu/ws/?pid=10109.

9. Terry Dickson, "Your Part in Civil Defense," *St. Louis Post-Dispatch* (St. Louis, MO), January 10, 1954: 64.

10. "Women Asked to Help Out in Civil Defense," *The Odgen Standard-Examiner* (Ogden, UT), November 11, 1952: 11.

11. *FCDA 1952 Annual Report*: 54.

12. Ibid.; "Texans to Be Registered for Home Defense," *The Courier-Gazette* (McKinney, TX), November 11, 1952: 4.

13. *FCDA 1953 Annual Report*: 68.

14. Ibid., 77.

15. Florence Ward, "Home Demonstration Work Under the Smith-Lever Act, 1914–1924," *U.S. Department of Agriculture Circular No. 43* (June 1929): 29.

16. Josephine Brighenti, "State Fair," *The Clare Sentinel* (Clare, MI), August 3, 1951: 16.

17. "Deaf Smith Home Demonstration Clubs Take Lead in Civil Defense Activities," *Pampa Daily News* (Pampa, TX), May 7, 1952: 16.

18. Claudia G. Williams, "Home Demonstration's Note Book," *The Paris News* (Paris, TX), August 6, 1953: 11.

19. "Civil Defense and Citizenship," *North*

Carolina Federation of Home Demonstration Clubs News Letter 8, 4 (October 1953): 5, 10.

20. Arthur Adams, "Decade of Decision," *Journal of Home Economics* 43, 7 (September 1951): 508.

21. "Women in Civil Defense," *New York Times* October 17, 1950: 18.

22. "Hospital Aid Group Joins Civil Defense," *The Philadelphia Inquirer*, January 12, 1951: 42.

23. "Women Called to Hear Civil Defense Orders," *Washington C.H. Record-Herald* (Washington Court House, OH), January 10, 1951: 2.

24. "Speakers' Training Courses," *Pittsburgh Post-Gazette* (Pittsburgh, PA), February 17, 1951: 5.

25. "Women's Civil Defense Division Organized," *The Palm Beach Post* (West Palm Beach, FL), February 8, 1951: 1.

26. "County Nurses Mobilize for Civil Defense," *The Tustin News* (Tustin, CA), April 6, 1951: 1.

27. "Defend Home First, Expert Tells Women," *Arizona Republic* (Phoenix, AZ), December 14, 1951: 7.

28. "Tells Women Civil Defense Role," *The News-Palladium* (Benton Harbor, MI), May 23, 1952: 4.

29. "Urgency of Civil Defense Stressed to Clubwomen," *The Salt Lake Tribune* (Salt Lake City, UT), May 6, 1952: 31; "Women to Form Civil Defense Unit at Conclave," *The Salt Lake Tribune* (Salt Lake City, UT), September 6, 1952: 32.

30. "32 Women Will Spearhead Civil Defense in Community," *Tucson Daily Citizen* (Tucson, AZ), May 24, 1952: 4.

31. "Women Get Civil Defense Call, Begin Plans for Own Group," *Lincoln Evening Journal* (Lincoln, Nebraska) July 2, 1952: 14.

32. "Women's Civil Defense Role Stressed at Session Here," *Daily World* (Opelousas, LA), August 24, 1952: 23.

33. "Women Are Being Offered Course in Civil Defense," *The News-Herald* (Franklin, PA), October 4, 1952: 9.

34. "Truman Lashes Defense Budget Cuts By Ike," *The Salem News* (Salem, OH), June 27, 1953: 1.

35. "Advise Russians of U.S. Atom Power, Dean Urges," *Chicago Daily Tribune* June 26, 1953: 15.

36. "Death Fear, Breeder of Panic, Greatest Perils in Disaster, Defense Parley Told," *The Los Angeles Times*, June 26, 1953: 53; "Civil Defense Course Slated," *Long Beach Independent* (Long Beach, CA), June 17, 1953: 14.

37. *George Women in Civil Defense* (Georgia Civil Defense Department, 1954).

38. "Parley on Civil Defense," *New York Times*, October 24, 1954: 113.

39. "Farm Women Urged to Help Civil Defense," *The Gettysburg Times* (Gettysburg, PA), March 12, 1955: 1.

40. "Pleasant Grove Women Slated for Major Role in Region CD Meeting," *The Daily Herald* (Provo, UT), January 11, 1955: 3.

41. "Home Protection in Civil Defense Outlined by Women's Director," *The Daily Herald* (Provo, UT), February 27, 1955: 21.

42. "Women Asked to Increase Awareness to Civil Defense," *Denton Record-Chronicle* (Denton, TX), February 3, 1955: 12.

43. "The Women's Civil Defense Council," *Anderson Herald* (Anderson, IN), January 31, 1958: 4.

44. "Civil Defense Advisory Group Holds Meeting," *Reno Gazette-Journal* (Reno, NV), November 18, 1958: 7.

45. "Home Preparedness Courses Finished by Women's Groups," *The Evening Review* (East Liverpool, OH), November 21, 1959: 3.

46. "National Civil Defense Experts to Appear at Provo Leadership Meet," *The Daily Herald* (Provo, UT), June 3, 1956: 5; "Preparedness at Home Cuts War Possibility," *The Daily Herald* (Provo, UT), June 20, 1956: 3.

47. "CD Women in Meeting," *The Salina Journal* (Salina, KS), March 30, 1958: 9.

48. "Home Preparedness Is Key to Survival if Attacked," *Herald and News* (Klamath Falls, OR), January 29, 1960: 4.

49. "Women Are the Key to Civil Defense," *Argus-Leader* (Sioux Falls, SD), January 27, 1960: 5.

50. "Civil Defense Interests Many Women in Mesa," *Arizona Republic* (Phoenix, AZ), July 27, 1961: 14.

51. Tracy Davis, *Stages of Emergency: Cold War Nuclear Civil Defense* (Durham, NC: Duke University Press, 2007), 42.

52. "Women's CD Council for Orick Area," *Eureka Humboldt Standard* (Eureka, CA), April 4, 1962: 12.

53. "Humboldt Represented at State Civil Defense Meet," *Eureka Humboldt Standard* (Eureka, CA), October 26, 1962: 8.

54. "CD Is a Project for Family," *The News Journal* (Wilmington, DE), April 21, 1965: 18.

55. "She Co-ordinates Home, Civil Defense," *The Los Angeles Times*, January 3, 1965: 179; "DeRidder Banquet to Be Tuesday," *The Times* (Shreveport, LA), January 27, 1965: 27; "Secretaries Will Hear Mrs. Moore," *The Town Talk* (Alexandria, LA), November 15, 1965: 24.

Chapter 10

1. *Federal Civil Defense Administration 1951 Annual Report* (Washington, D.C.: U.S. Government Printing Office, 1951), 19.

2. *United States Civil Defense* (Washington, D.C.: U.S. Government Printing Office, 1950), 44.

3. *FCDA 1951 Annual Report*, 19.

4. *Challenge for Security and Survival* (Ohio Civil Defense, 1965), 23; *FCDA 1951 Annual Report*, 44.

5. Kenton Clymer, "The Ground Observer Corps, *Journal of Cold War Studies* 15, 1 (Winter 2013): 34–52; "Women to Aid Recruit of CD Ground Corps," *The Times* (San Mateo, CA), April 17, 1953: 4; "Women's Ground Observer Corps Open Meeting," *Carrol Daily Times Herald* (Carroll, IA), May 10, 1955: 9; "Chief Air Spotter Is Mother of 3, Businesswoman, Amateur Painter," *The Daily Tribune* (Wisconsin Rapids, WI), April 25, 1953: 1; "Busy Woman Aids GOC," *Herald and News* (Klamath Falls, OR), June 22, 1954: 10.

6. Andrew Gross, *Neither Dead Nor Red: Civilian Defense and American Political Development During the Early Cold War* (New York: Routledge, 2001), 89.

7. Ibid., 87–88.

8. "Wardens Have Important Role in Civil Defense," *The San Bernardino County Sun* (San Bernardino, CA), November 11, 1952: 10.

9. Ibid.

10. *FCDA 1951 Annual Report*, 64; *Federal Civil Defense Administration 1955 Annual Report* (Washington, D.C.: U.S. Government Printing Office, 1955), 9.

11. *Federal Civil Defense Administration 1952 Annual Report* (Washington, D.C.: U.S. Government Printing Office, 1952), 69, 71.

12. "Recruiting and Training of Workers Under Way," *The Evening Independent* (Massillon, OH), January 3, 1951: 2.

13. "City Seeks Senior Raid Wardens," *Detroit Free Press*, February 4, 1951: 3.

14. "Block Warden Organization Explained at City Meeting," *The Morning News* (Wilmington, DE), February 9, 1951: 37.

15. *FCDA 1952 Annual Report*, 87–88; Grossman, *Neither Dead Nor Red*, 88.

16. *Federal Civil Defense Administration 1953 Annual Report* (Washington, D.C.: U.S. Government Printing Office, 1953), 91–92.

17. "Defense Training Set for Women," *The Philadelphia Inquirer*, October 24, 1952: 19; "Women to the Rescue," *The Decatur Daily-Review* (Decatur, IL), February 16, 1953: 10; "Women's Warden Courses Offered," *The Daily Notes* (Canonsburg, PA), October 29, 1952: 1.

18. Grossman, *Neither Dead Nor Red*, 88; *FCDA 1953 Annual Report*: 31, 35.

19. "3 Women Form Defense Groups," *The Post-Standard* (Syracuse, NY), March 19, 1952: 39.

20. "Into Operational Stage," *The Daily Messenger* (Canandaigua, NY), November 23, 1953: 1.

21. "C.D. Training for Women," *The Journal News* (White Plains, NY), August 8, 1953: 10.

22. Ibid.

23. "Block Warden Plans Outlined at Meeting," *Williamsport Sun-Gazette* (Williamsport, PA), January 8, 1953: 1; "Community Civil Defense Fire School Scheduled," *The Daily Herald* (Provo, UT), May 13, 1953: 3.

24. "Train Leaders in Civil Defense," *Pittsburgh Post-Gazette* (Pittsburgh, PA), November 13, 1953: 14.

25. "Should Prepare for Germ Warfare, Peterson Says," *The Winona Republican-Herald* (Winona, MN), November 3, 1953: 1; "Civil Defense Vital, State Leaders Told," *The Daily Telegram* (Eau Claire, WI), November 2, 1953: 3.

26. "Civil Defense Conference to Take Place Here Over Week End," *The Cincinnati Enquirer* (Cincinnati, OH), November 12, 1953: 14.

27. *FCDA 1953 Annual Report*, 36, 90, 119.

28. *Federal Civil Defense Administration 1954 Annual Report* (Washington, D.C.: Government Printing Office, 1954), 141–142.

29. "Speigletown Women See Defense Test," *The Times Record* (Troy, NY), May 18, 1954: 18.

30. "Pima Civil Defense Wardens Begin Intensified Training," *Tucson Daily Citizen* (Tucson, AZ), April 8, 1954: 8.

31. Ibid., 33–35; "Mock Raids' Toll Vast; Civil Defense Unready," *The Cincinnati Enquirer* (Cincinnati, OH), June 15, 1954: 3; "Public Response to Civil Defense Raid Alert Spotty," *Pittston Gazette* (Pittston, PA), October 26, 1954: 1.

32. "Women's Corps to Aid Raid Test," *The Philadelphia Inquirer*, June 1, 1954: 7; "Orem to Participate in Nation-Wide Defense Alert," *The Daily Herald* (Provo, UT), June 13, 1954: 6; "Preparations Readied for A-Test Here," *The Oneonta Star* (Oneonta, NY), February 18, 1954: 5.

33. "Seek to Organize Women's Warden Service in Village," *The Chicago Heights Star* (Chicago Heights, IL), November 9, 1954: 2.

34. *FCDA 1955 Annual Report*, 120–121.

35. "Farm Leaders to Map Rural Civil Defense," *Battle Creek Enquirer* (Battle Creek, MI), February 1, 1956: 10.

36. "Rural C.D. Can Save America," *The Fairmount News* (Fairmount, IN), September 6, 1956: 2.

37. "New 'Grass Roots' CD Setup Charted," *Battle Creek Enquirer* (Battle Creek, MI), June 5, 1956: 2.

38. "CD Women Plan 'Warden' System," *The Salina Journal* (Salina, KS), August 26, 1956: 28; "Need 300 Wardens, Women Volunteers," *Janesville Daily Gazette* (Janesville, WI),

March 26, 1957: 9; "3 Speakers Chart CD Efforts for 100 AAUW Members," *Battle Creek Enquirer* (Battle Creek, MI), January 18, 1957: 4; "Women's Meeting On Civil Defense September 24–25," *The Edinburg Daily Courier* (Edinburg, IN), August 28, 1957: 1.

39. "The Women's Civil Defense Council," *Anderson Herald* (Anderson, IN), January 31, 1958: 4; "BRF Women Prepare for Civil Defense," *The La Crosse Tribune* (La Crosse, WI), January 12, 1958: 24; "Civil Defense Training Course for Women to Begin April 10," *The Burlington Free Press* (Burlington, VT), March 29, 1958: 4.

40. "Women Civil Defense Leaders Will Meet," *Alton Evening Telegraph* (Alton, IL), November 12, 1958: 10.

41. *Office of Civil Defense and Mobilization 1959 Annual Report* (Washington, D.C.: U.S. Government Printing Office, 1959), 4–5.

42. Philip Benjamin, "H-Bomb Test Raid Stills Bustling City," *New York Times*, April 18, 1959: 1.

43. "PL Grove Civil Defense School Slated," *The Daily Herald* (Provo, UT), March 30, 1960: 9; "Civil Defense Wardens Information Up To Date," *Steuben Republican* (Angola, IN), March 16, 1960: 1.

44. Speech by President John Kennedy on the Berlin Crisis (Washington, July 25, 1961), John F. Kennedy Presidential Library and Museum. Retrieved from https://www.jfklibrary.org/Research/Research-Aids/JFK-Speeches/Berlin-Crisis_19610725.aspx.

45. "Drive Opens for Recruiting Raid Wardens," *El Paso Herold-Post* (El Paso, TX), July 27, 1961: 1; "Women's Civil Defense Group Expands Program," *The Advocate-Messenger* (Danville, KY), August 29, 1961: 1; "107 District CD Wardens Needed for Preparedness," *The Galveston Daily News* (Galveston, TX), August 18, 1961: 3; "State School Personnel Must Act As Wardens," *The Bee* (Danville, VA), September 20, 1961: 36.

46. "Women Leaders Invited to Civil Defense Meet," *The Lincoln Star* (Lincoln, Nebraska) February 21, 1965: 11; "Woman, Once House Member, in Civil Defense," *The Courier-Journal* (Louisville, KY), December 19, 1965: 115.

47. Percy Maxim Lee, "The Family in Our Democratic Society," *Journal of Home Economics* 44, 7 (September 1952): 501.

48. *Women in Civil Defense* (Washington, D.C.: U.S. Government Printing Office, 1952): 1.

Chapter 13

1. Radio Address to the American People on Armistice Day, November 11, 1951. Harry S. Truman Library & Museum. Retrieved from https://trumanlibrary.org/publicpapers/viewpapersphp?pid=556.

2. *Women in Civil Defense* (Washington, D.C.: U.S. Government Printing Office, 1952), 15.

3. *United States Civil Defense Police Services* (Washington, D.C.: U.S. Government Printing Office, 1951).

4. "Women's Defense Responsibilities Are Outlined," *The Daily Clintonian* (Clinton, IN), October 4, 1950: 1; *United States Civil Defense Police Services*.

5. Dorothy Moses Schulz, "Policewomen in the 1950s: Paving the Way for Patrol," *Women & Criminal Justice*, 4, 2 (1993): 6.

6. "Police Auxiliary of 40,000 Planning for City's Defense," *New York Times*, August 8, 1950: 1.

7. "Civil Defense Drive Gets 130 Recruits," *New York Times*, July 19, 1951: 5; Women Get Chance to Swap Rolling Pin for a Blackjack," *The News Journal* (Wilmington, DE), November 24, 1950: 44.

8. Schulz, 9–10.

9. Ibid., 6.

10. *Federal Civil Defense Administration 1952 Annual Report* (Washington, D.C.: U.S. Government Printing Office, 1951), 58; *United States Civil Defense Polices Services*: 43.

11. "City Charts Tasks for Civil Defense," *New York Times*, January 3, 1951: 17; "Police Auxiliary of 40,000 Planned for City's Defense: 1; "City Defenses Head Asks Women's Aid," *New York Times*, December 27, 1950: 8; "Civil Defense Call Gets Good Results," *New York Times*, January 5, 1951: 9.

12. *Federal Civil Defense Administration 1951 Annual Report* (Washington, D.C.: U.S. Government Printing Office, 1951), 58.

13. "Leach Heads Biological War Defense Group," *The News Journal* (Wilmington, DE), February 7, 1951: 18.

14. "20 Women Join Auxiliary Police," *Oakland Tribune* (Oakland, CA), August 9, 1951: 29; "1,000 Women Volunteers for Oakland Auxiliary Police Force Asked by Chief," *Oakland Tribune* (Oakland, CA), July 18, 1951: 21.

15. "Civil Defense Bureau Will Open in City Hall," *Hartford Courant* (Hartford, CT), January 17, 1951: 17; "130 Men and Women Police Auxiliaries Congratulated at Defense Graduation," *Hartford Courant* (Hartford, CT), October 5, 1951: 21; "Police Seek Auxiliary of 300 Persons," *Hartford Courant* (Hartford, CT), December 2, 1950: 8; "Greenwich Organizes Civil Defense Groups," *New York Times*, November 19, 1950: 92.

16. *FCDA 1952 Annual Report*, 56, 83–84; *Federal Civil Defense Administration 1953 Annual Report* (Washington, D.C., U.S. Government Printing Office, 1953), 35, 125.

17. "Legion Plans Drive for Civil Defense Auxiliary Police," *St. Louis Post-Dispatch* (St. Louis, MO), March 8, 1952: 7.
18. "Eatontown to Organize Women for Civil Defense Police Duty," *Asbury Park Press* (Asbury Park, NJ), December 12, 1952: 19.
19. "700 Civil Defense Police to Graduate," *The Star Tribune* (Minneapolis, MN), June 7, 1953: 36; "Women's Auxiliary Police for School Crossings," *Kingsport Times* (Kingsport, TN), August 4, 1953: 12; "Two Named Delegates to Auxiliary Meeting," *Council Bluffs Nonpareil* (Council Bluffs, IA), August 16, 1953: 20; "Defense Council Plans Raid Test on Saturday," *The Morning News* (Wilmington, DE), February 25, 1953: 28; "Civil Defense Police to End Instruction," *The Indianapolis Star* (Indianapolis, IN), December 20, 1953: 10; "Training Class Held for Women in Police Unit," *The Evening Times* (Sayre, PA), March 31, 1954: 7.
20. *Federal Civil Defense Administration 1954 Annual Report* (Washington, D.C., U.S. Government Printing Office, 1954), 131–132.
21. *Ibid*.
22. "Women's Civil Defense Police Trained," *The Indianapolis Star* (Indianapolis, IN), January 15, 1955: 5; "Seip Named Deputy C.D. Police Head," *The Pocono Record* (Stroudsburg, PA), June 10, 1955: 20; "Auxiliary to Get First Aid Work," *Press and Sun-Bulletin* (Binghamton, NY), February 2, 1955: 3; "CD Meeting Slated Sunday at Republic," *The Evening Standard* (Uniontown, PA), February 15, 1957: 21.
23. "To Aid in Civil Defense," *The Kansas City Times* (Kansas City, MO), October 30, 1959: 105; "CD Lecture Courses Open Tonight," *Naugatuck Daily* (Naugatuck, CT), April 20, 1960: 1; "More Women Join CD Ranks," *The Morning News* (Wilmington, DE), June 13, 1964: 29; *Office of Civil and Defense Mobilization 1960 Annual Report* (Washington, D.C.: U.S. Government Printing Office, 1960), 22.
24. "Training Home Nurses," *The Burlington Free Press* (Burlington, VT), December 16, 1950: 6.
25. *FCDA 1952 Annual Report*, 52; *Red Cross Home Nursing Civil Defense Supplement* (Washington, D.C., American National Red Cross, 1951), 1; "Nurses to Enroll for Civil Defense," *Monroe Evening Times* (Monroe, WI), February 26, 1951: 6; "Tenth District Nurses to Attend Civil Defense Class," *The Daily Telegram* (Eau Claire, WI), May 29, 1951: 5; "Complete Roll of All County Nurses for Civil Defense," *Warren Times* (Warren, PA), September 17, 1951: 8; "Civil Defense Is Discussed Before Nurses," *Palladium-Item* (Richmond, IN), May 21, 1951: 4; "Nurses Prepare for Civil Defense," *The Town Talk* (Alexandria, LA), March 22, 1951: 16; "Nurses Plan Civil Defense Organization," *Cumberland Evening Times* (Cumberland, MD), April 30, 1952: 11; "Role of Nurses in Civil Defense Noted at Course," *The Winona Republican-Herald* (Winona, MN), November 30, 1951: 3.
26. "Baytown Nurses Attend Civil Defense Meeting," *The Baytown Sun* (Baytown, TX), September 24, 1954: 2; "Muncie Nurses Attend Civil Defense Event," *Muncie Evening Press* (Muncie, IN), November 20, 1954: 6; "Local Nurses to Be Organized for Civil Defense," *Hartford Courant* (Hartford, CT), February 1, 1954: 25; "Many Nurses Volunteer for Civil Defense," *Pittston Gazette* (Pittston, PA), September 10, 1954: 2.
27. Margaret Schafer, "Civil Defense Service," *American Journal of Nursing* 56, 10 (October 1956): 1291–1292; Ann Magnussen, "Red Cross Service," *American Journal of Nursing* 56, 10 (October 1956): 1290–1291.
28. *Federal Civil Defense Administration 1956 Annual Report* (Washington, D.C.: U.S. Government Printing Office, 1956), 114,
29. "Nurses Set Civil Defense Program," *The Lawton Constitution* (Lawton, Oklahoma) June 5, 1957: 12; "Nurses Plan Civil Defense Series," *Great Falls Tribune* (Great Falls, MT), May 5, 1957: 16; "Nurses Take Civil Defense Rescue Course," *Asbury Park Press* (Ashbury Park, NJ), January 31, 1958: 4; "Civil Defense Nurses Course Well Attended," *Wellsville Daily Reporter* (Wellsville, NY), March 7, 1958: 2; "Area Nurses Plan Civil Defense Meet," *Idaho State Journal* (Pocatello, ID), November 13, 1960: 18.
30. "Nurses Attend Civil Defense Training Meet," *The Escanaba Daily* (Escanaba, MI), September 26, 1961: 12; "CD Meet Underway," *Lansing State Journal* (Lansing, MI), June 1, 1961: 46.
31. "San Medic Speaks to Nurses on Civil Defense," *The Magee Courier* (Magee, MS), November 1, 1962: 5; "Plan Nurses Civil Defense Study Series," *The Troy Record* (Troy, NY), January 20, 1964: 11; "Hospital-Civil Defense Disaster Test June 2," *Fitchburg Sentinel* (Fitchburg, Massachusetts) May 6, 1965: 13.
32. Catherine Sullivan, "The Civil Defense Role of Nurses," *Journal of the American Medical Association* (169) January 24, 1959: 388.
33. *Ibid.*, 388.

Chapter 16

1. "Home Demonstration Clubs" (October 21, 2010). Delmar Historical and Art Society. Retrieved from http://www.delmarhistoricalandartsociety.blogspot.com/2010/10/home-demonstration-clubs.html.
2. "Dorothy Mann Battles Both Apathy and Fear," *Lansing State Journal* (Lansing, MI), January 6, 1957: 47.

3. *Federal Civil Defense Administration 1952 Annual Report* (Washington, D.C.: U.S. Government Printing Office, 1952), 55.

4. *Federal Civil Defense Administration 1953 Annual Report* (Washington, D.C.: U.S. Government Printing Office, 1953), 77.

5. *Federal Civil Defense Administration 1954 Annual Report* (Washington, D.C.: U.S. Government Printing Office, 1954), 164.

6. *Challenge for Security and Survival: Manual for Women in Civil Defense* (Ohio Civil Defense, 1965), 24.

7. Laura McEnaney, *Civil Defense Begins at Home: Militarization Meets Everyday Life in the Fifties* (Princeton, New Jersey: Princeton University Press, 2000), 76–77.

8. "Home Defense Pledges Listed Goal of Intense Campaign," *The Salt Lake Tribune* (Salt Lake City, UT), October 27, 1952: 9.

9. Andrew Grossman, *Neither Dead Nor Read: Civilian Defense and American Political Development During the Early Cold War* (New York: Routledge, 2001), 102.

10. *Home Protection Exercises* (Government Printing Office, Office of Civil Defense and Mobilization, 1960), 4.

11. "Dorothy Mann Battles Both Apathy and Fear," 47.

12. "H-Bomb Is Everybody's Business," *The San Bernardino County Sun* (San Bernardino, CA), April 29, 1954: 35.

13. "Defense Teams to Demonstrate at Alexandria," *The Monroe News-Star* (Monroe, LA), April 9, 1954: 2.

14. "Protection Parley Set," *Lansing State Journal* (Lansing, MI), September 28, 1954: 4.

15. "Home Protection Discussion Topics for Culture Club," *Moberly Monitor-Index* (Moberly, MO), October 11, 1954: 6.

16. *Federal Civil Defense Administration 1955 Annual Report* (Washington, D.C.: U.S. Government Printing Office, 1955), 174.

17. "Home Protection in Civil Defense Outlined By Women's Director," *The Daily Herald* (Provo, UT), February 27, 1955: 21.

18. "Women from 6 Counties Invited to Take Home Protection Class," *The Raleigh Register* (Beckley, West VA), March 25, 1957: 2.

19. "5 States' Homemakers to Meet for Civil Defense Conference," *The Indianapolis Star* (Indianapolis) August 29, 1957: 11; "Altrusta Club to Sponsor Home Preparedness Plan," *The Town Talk* (Alexandria, LA), September 24, 1957: 14; "Women's C.D. Council Meets," *The Daily Herald* (Provo, UT), September 8, 1957: 4.

20. "CD Workshop for Women Announced," *The Eugene Guard* (Eugene, OR), April 13, 1958: 8.

21. "Civil Defense Preparedness Course Offered," *The Montana Standard* (Butte, MT), May 3, 1058: 12.

22. "26 Women Complete Preparedness Course," *The Morning News* (Wilmington, DE), December 15, 1958: 4; "100 Area Women to Take CD Home Preparedness Course," *The Morning News* (Wilmington, DE), November 1, 1958: 5.

23. "34 Complete Home Protection Defense Course," *The Palm Beach Post* (West Palm Beach, FL), January 21, 1959: 13.

24. "Civil Defense Leader in Reno for Home Preparedness Drill," *Reno Gazette-Journal* (Reno, NV), January 22, 1959: 16.

25. "County Homemakers Hear About Home Protection in CD Program," *The Morning Herald* (Hagerstown, MD), September 22, 1959: 7.

26. "Workshop in Civil Defense Held Here," *McKinney Weekly Democrat-Gazette* (McKinney, TX), July 2, 1959: 1.

27. "'Women Are the Key to Civil Defense,'" *Argus-Leader* (Sioux Falls, SD), January 27, 1960: 5.

28. Ibid.; "Yuma Women Urged to Form CD Council," *The Yuma Daily Sun* (Yuma, AZ), September 22, 1960: 5.

29. "Civil Defense Group Launches 'Home Preparedness' Program," *Jefferson City Post-Tribune* (Jefferson City, MO), January 31, 1960: 7; "Committee Chairmen Appointed Women's Civil Defense Council," *Jefferson City Post-Tribune* (Jefferson City, MO), January 21, 1960: 5; "Women's Civil Defense Council in TV Series," *Jefferson City Post-Tribune* (Jefferson City, MO), January 15, 1960: 12; "Mrs. Walter Rottman, Jr., Wins First Home Preparedness Award," *Jefferson City Post-Tribune* (Jefferson City, MO), May 18, 1960: 5.

30. "5 Points to Preparedness; New Class Starts Monday," *St. Cloud Times* (St. Cloud, MN), March 18, 1960: 3.

31. "Second Home Preparedness Workshop Scheduled Tonight," *The Montana Standard* (Butte, MT), August 16, 1961: 3.

32. Wayne Whitt, "Women Better Versed," *The Tennessean* (Nashville, TN), June 18, 1961: 94.

33. "Home Preparedness Class Planned for Scottdale in Civil Defense Training," *The Daily Courier* (Connellsville, PA), October 23, 1961: 10.

34. "CD Seminar to Alert Home Defenses," *The Post-Standard* (Syracuse, NY), November 6, 1961: 11.

35. Jim Waesche, "Somerset CD Agency Has Wide Number of Duties," *The Daily Times* (Salisbury, MD), October 26, 1962: 15.

36. 1968—Statement by the president on the need for federal, state, and local cooperation

in civil defense and emergency preparedness, April 13, 1968. American Presidency Project. Retrieved from http://www.presidency.ucsb.edu/ws/index.php?pid=28800.
37. Ibid.

Chapter 20

1. Remarks marking the opening day of Civil Defense Week in 1957. Quoted in *Public Papers of the Presidents of the United States* (U.S. National Archives), 675–676.
2. "The Cold War Homefront: Civil and Home Defense." Retrieved from http://www.authentichistory.com/1946-1960/4-cwhomefront/3-civildefense/1-educating/index.html.
3. "Grandma's Pantry Belongs in Your Kitchen," *By, For, And About Women in Civil Defense* (Washington, D.C.: Government Printing Office, 1955), 2.
4. Ibid.
5. "Grandma's Pantry Goes on Wheels," *By, For, And About Women in Civil Defense* (Washington, D.C.: Government Printing Office, 1956), 1.
6. *Grandma's Pantry Was Always Ready—Is Your Pantry Prepared?* (New York: New York State Civil Defense Commission, circa 1955).
7. *Federal Civil Defense Administration 1956 Annual Report* (Washington, D.C.: Government Printing Office, 1956), 45.
8. Dee Garrison, *Bracing for Armageddon: Why Civil Defense Never Worked* (New York: Oxford University Press, 2006), 205.
9. Elaine Tyler May, *Homeward Bound: American Families in the Cold War Era* (New York: Basic Books, 1988), 104.
10. *Federal Civil Defense Administration 1952 Annual Report* (Washington, D.C.: U.S. Government Printing Office, 1952), 96.
11. Paul Murphy and James Hundley, "Food Supply and Emergency Feeding in Civil Defense," *Public Health Reports, 1896–1970* (September 1952): 862.
12. *FCDA 1952 Annual Report*, 95–96.
13. *Chicago Alerts: A City Plans Its Civil Defense Against Atomic Attack* (Chicago: The Chicago Civil Defense Corps, 1951).
14. Ibid., 224.
15. Mary Barber, "The Home Economist and Civil Defense," *Journal of Home Economics* 48, 10 (December 1951): 781; "From the Editor's Mail," *Journal of Home Economics* 48, 8 (October 1951): 657.
16. Barber, *Journal of Home Economics*, 781.
17. "Back Defense Bill, Women Are Urged," *New York Times*, January 27, 1951, 8.
18. "Feeding of Million in Attack Planned," *New York Times*, April 3, 1951, 15.
19. "'Atom-Bombing' Test Set for Niagara Falls, *New York Times*, June 10, 1951, 39.
20. "Outdoor Care Set in Event of Attack," *New York Times*, September 21, 1952, 32.
21. *Federal Civil Defense Administration 1953 Annual Report* (Washington, D.C.: Government Printing Office, 1953), 140.
22. "Civil Defense Mass Feeding Set for Today," *Chicago Tribute* November 6, 1954, 16.
23. *FCDA 1953 Annual Report*, 139.
24. Ibid.
25. *FCDA 1954 Annual Report*, 140.
26. Ibid., 204.
27. *FCDA 1956 Annual Report*, 45.
28. *Texans on the Alert for Civil Defense and Disaster Relief* (Austin: State of Texas, 1956): 42; *FCDA 1954 Annual Report*, 89, 226.
29. *Missouri Survival Plan* (Jefferson City: State of Missouri, 1958).
30. Ibid.
31. Bob Wagner, "CD Agency Illustrates Methods," *The Orlando Sentinel* (Orlando, FL), February 24, 1960: 37; "Red Cross Slates Mass Feeding Class," *The Los Angeles Times*, February 19, 1961: 392; Mrs. Ed Harris, "Runge Park Cookout Is Examination in Red Cross, CD-Sponsored Course," *The Galveston Daily News* (Galveston, TX), July 10, 1960: 7; "Mass Food Class Ends First Half," *Herald and News* (Klamath Falls, OR), May 8, 1963: 22; "23 Women to Complete Mass Feeding Course," *The Star Press* (Muncie, IN), February 11, 1962; 8.
32. "Jean Wood Fuller: Women in Politics Project," 191.
33. Kenneth Rose, *One Nation Underground: The Fallout Shelter in American Culture* (New York: New York University Press, 2001), 148–149.

Conclusion

1. "Civil Defense Is Home Front Protection," *Postville Herald* (Postville, IA), October 24, 1951: 2.
2. Ibid.
3. Ibid.
4. Harry S Truman, Executive Order 10186—Establishing the Federal Civil Defense Administration in the Office for Emergency Management of the Executive Office of the President. American Presidency Project. Retrieved from http://www.presidency.ucsb.edu/ws/?pid=78352.
5. *Federal Civil Defense Administration 1951 Annual Report* (Washington, D.C.: U.S. Government Printing Office, 1951), 19.
6. "Ready Family Doubles Its Survival Chances," *The Daily Tar Heel* (Chapel Hill, NC), July 29, 1959: 4; Pearl, Mrs. Norton (Dorothy).

"Women and Civil Defense," in *The Cold War: A History in Documents and Eyewitness Accounts*, edited by Jussi M. Hanhimaki and Odd Arne Westad. (New York: Oxford University Press, 2011), 298–299.

7. Mrs. Joseph W. Mann, "A Pledge for Home Defense," *Lansing State Journal* (Lansing, MI), November 16, 1952: 12.

8. "New Civil Defense Campaign Launched," *The Emporia Weekly Gazette* (Emporia, KS), November 6, 1952: 4; "Women's Defense Parley Set at St. Mary's College," *Oakland Tribune* (Oakland, CA), January 30, 1952: 20; "32 Women Will Spearhead Civil Defense in Community," *Tucson Daily Citizen* (Tucson, AZ), May 24, 1952: 4; "Farm Women Urged to Help Civil Defense," *The Gettysburg Times* (Gettysburg, PA), May 12, 1955: 1; "Pleasant Grove Women Slated for Major Role in Region CD Meeting," *The Daily Herald* (Provo, UT), January 11, 1955: 3; "Women from 6 Counties Invited to Take Home Protection Class," *The Raleigh Register* (Beckley, West VA), March 25, 1957: 2; "CD Workshop for Women Announced," *The Eugene Guard* (Eugene, OR), April 13, 1958: 8; "100 Area Women to Take CD Home Preparedness Course," *The Morning News* (Wilmington, DE), November 1, 1958: 5; "Home Preparedness Course Set," *The Montana Standard* (Butte, MT), August 7, 1961: 5.

9. Women's Leaders Confer in Capital on Home Defense," *Battle Creek Enquirer* (Battle Creek MI), September 27, 1960: 8; Mitzi Zipf, "Civil Defense Interests Many Women in Mesa," *Arizona Republic* (Phoenix, AZ), July 27, 1961: 14; Wayne Whitt, "Women Better Versed," *The Tennessean* (Nashville, TN), June 18, 1961: 94.

10. "Civil Defense Actions Pushed In Cities Across the Nation," *The Town Talk* (Alexandria, LA), October 25, 1962 5; "Oregon's Civil Defense Alert," *Statesman Journal* (Salem, OR), October 23, 1962: 8; "State Steps Up Civil Defense," *The Palm Beach Post* (West Palm Beach, FL), October 30, 1962: 1; "Crisis Brings Urgent Civil Defense Move," *Palladium-Item* (Richmond, IN), October 26, 1962: 10.

11. "Crisis Brings Urgent Civil Defense Move," *Palladium-Item* (Richmond, IN), October 26, 1962: 10; "CD Office in Kansas City Swamped With Calls," *The Hays Daily News* (Hays, KS), October 24, 1962: 5.

12. "Humboldt Represented at State Civil Defense Meet," *Eureka Humboldt Standard* (Eureka, CA), October 26, 1962: 8; "Websterite Elected by State Women," *Democrat and Chronicle* (Rochester, NY), May 27, 1964: 8; "CD Meeting Set," *The Daily Chronicle* (Centralia, WA), October 19, 1962: 8; "Waterbury Women to State Self-Care Course," *The Burlington Free Press* (Burlington, VT), October 16, 1962: 3; "Women Give Taste Test to Survival Biscuits," St. Louis Post-Dispatch (St. Louis, MO), October 5, 1962: 16.

13. "Volunteers Needed," *Denton Record-Chronicle* (Denton, TX), November 2, 1952: 18; "Woman's Responsibility in Fight for Survival Stressed at HD Camp," *Corsicana Daily Sun* (Corsicana, TX), August 5, 1960: 4.

BIBLIOGRAPHY

Adams, Arthur. "Decade of Decision." *Journal of Home Economics* 43, 7 (September 1951): 508–511.

"Advise Russians of U.S. Atom Power, Dean Urges." *Chicago Daily Tribune* June 26, 1953: 15.

"Altrusta Club to Sponsor Home Preparedness Plan." *The Town Talk* (Alexandria, LA). September 24, 1957: 14.

"Area Nurses Plan Civil Defense Meet." *Idaho State Journal* (Pocatello, ID). November 13, 1960: 18.

"'Atomic Attack' on TV." *The Evening Sun* (Hanover, PA). May 15, 1954: 6.

"'Atom-Bombing' Test Set for Niagara Falls, *New York Times*. June 10, 1951: 39.

"Auxiliary to Get First Aid Work." *Press and Sun-Bulletin* (Binghamton, NY). February 2, 1955: 3.

"Back Defense Bill, Women Are Urged." *New York Times*. January 27, 1951: 8.

Badore, Angela. "Gender of a Nation: Propaganda in World War II and the Atomic Age." *The Cupula* (Spring 2014): 1–36.

Barber, Mary, "The Home Economist and Civil Defense." *Journal of Home Economics* 48, 10 (December 1951): 780–781.

Basic Course for Civil Defense (Washington, D.C.: U.S. Government Printing Office, 1955).

"Block Warden Organization Explained at City Meeting." *The Morning News* (Wilmington, DE). February 9, 1951: 37.

"Block Warden Plans Outlined at Meeting." *Williamsport Sun-Gazette* (Williamsport, PA). January 8, 1953: 1

Baughman, James. "Television Comes to America." *Illinois History* (March 1993): 42.

"Baytown Nurses Attend Civil Defense Meeting." *The Baytown Sun* (Baytown, TX). September 24, 1954: 2.

Boyer, Paul. *By the Bomb's Early Light: American Thought and Culture at the Dawn of the Atomic Age* (New York: Pantheon Books, 1985).

Brennan, Mary. *Wives, Mothers, and the Red Menace* (Boulder, Colorado: University of Colorado Press, 2008).

"BRF Women Prepare for Civil Defense." *The La Crosse Tribune* (La Crosse, WI). January 12, 1958: 24.

Brighenti, Josephine. "State Fair." *The Clare Sentinel* (Clare, MI). August 3, 1951: 16.

"Busy Woman Aids GOC." *Herald and News* (Klamath Falls, OR). June 22, 1954: 10.

Butterfield, C. E. "Highlights: Radio, TV." *The Evening Independent* (Massillon, OH). 2 May 1954: 10.

"C.D. Training for Women." *The Journal News* (White Plains, NY). August 8, 1953: 10.

"CD Is a Project for Family." *The News Journal* (Wilmington, DE). April 2, 1965: 18.

"CD Lecture Courses Open Tonight." *Naugatuck Daily* (Naugatuck, CT). April 20, 1960: 1.

"CD Meet Underway." *Lansing State Journal* (Lansing, MI). June 1, 1961: 46.

"CD Meeting Set." *The Daily Chronicle* (Centralia, WA). October 19, 1962: 8.

"CD Meeting Slated Sunday at Republic." *The Evening Standard* (Uniontown, PA). February 15, 1957: 21.

"CD Office in Kansas City Swamped With Calls." *The Hays Daily News* (Hays, KS). October 24, 1962: 5.

"CD Seminar to Alert Home Defenses." *The Post-Standard* (Syracuse, NY). November 6, 1961: 11.

"CD Women in Meeting." *The Salina Journal* (Salina, KS). March 30, 1958: 9.

"CD Women Plan 'Warden' System." *The Salina Journal* (Salina, KS). August 26, 1956: 28.

"CD Workshop for Women Announced." *The Eugene Guard* (Eugene, OR). April 13, 1958: 8.

Challenge for Security and Survival: Manual for Women in Civil Defense (Ohio Civil Defense, 1965).

Chicago Alerts: A City Plans Its Civil Defense Against Atomic Attack (Chicago: The Chicago Civil Defense Corps, 1951).

"Chief Air Spotter Is Mother of 3, Businesswoman, Amateur Painter." *The Daily Tribune* (Wisconsin Rapids, WI). April 25, 1953: 1.

"City Charts Tasks for Civil Defense." *New York Times*. January 3, 1951: 17.

"City Seeks Senior Raid Wardens." *Detroit Free Press*. February 4, 1951: 3.

"Civil Defense Actions Pushed In Cities Across the Nation." *The Town Talk* (Alexandria, LA). October 25, 1962: 5.

"Civil Defense Advisory Group Holds Meeting." *Reno Gazette-Journal* (Reno, NV). November 18, 1958: 7.

"Civil Defense and Citizenship." *North Carolina Federation of Home Demonstration Clubs News Letter* 8, 4 (October 1953): 5, 10.

"Civil Defense Bureau Will Open in City Hall." *Hartford Courant* (Hartford, CT). January 17, 1951: 17.

"Civil Defense Call Gets Good Results." *New York Times*, January 5, 1951: 9.

"Civil Defense Conference to Take Place Here Over Week End." *The Cincinnati Enquirer* (Cincinnati, OH). November 12, 1953: 14.

"Civil Defense Course Slated." *Long Beach Independent* (Long Beach, CA). June 17, 1953: 14.

"Civil Defense Drive Gets 130 Recruits." *New York Times*, July 19, 1951: 5

"Civil Defense Group Launches 'Home Preparedness' Program." *Jefferson City Post-Tribune* (Jefferson City, MO). January 3, 1960: 7.

"City Defenses Head Asks Women's Aid." *New York Times*. December 27, 1950: 8.

"Civil Defense Interests Many Women in Mesa." *Arizona Republic* (Phoenix, AZ). July 27, 1961: 14.

"Civil Defense Is Discussed Before Nurses." *Palladium-Item* (Richmond, IN). May 21, 1951: 4.

"Civil Defense Is Home Front Protection." *Postville Herald* (Postville, IA). October 24, 1951: 2.

"Civil Defense Leader in Reno for Home Preparedness Drill." *Reno Gazette-Journal* (Reno, NV). January 22, 1959: 16.

"Civil Defense Mass Feeding Set for Today." *Chicago Tribune*. November 6, 1954: 16.

Civil Defense 1965 (Washington, D.C.: U.S. Government Printing Office, 1965).

"Civil Defense Nurses Course Well Attended." *Wellsville Daily Reporter* (Wellsville, NY). March 7, 1958: 2.

"Civil Defense Police to End Instruction." *The Indianapolis Star* (Indianapolis, IN). December 20, 1953: 10.

"Civil Defense Preparedness Course Offered." *The Montana Standard* (Butte, MT). May 3, 1958: 12.

"Civil Defense Session Today." *The Des Moines Register* (Des Moines, IA). September 2, 1950: 3.

"Civil Defense Training Course for Women to Begin April 10." *The Burlington Free Press* (Burlington, VT). March 29, 1958: 4.

"Civil Defense Vital, State Leaders Told." *The Daily Telegram* (Eau Claire, WI). November 2, 1953: 3.

"Civil Defense Wardens Information Up To Date." *Steuben Republican* (Angola, IN). March 16, 1960: 1.

Clymer, Kenton. "The Ground Observer Corps: Public Relations and the Cold War in the 1950s." *Journal of Cold War Studies* 15 (Winter 2013): 34–52.

"Committee Chairmen Appointed Women's Civil Defense Council." *Jefferson City Post-Tribune* (Jefferson City, MO). January 2, 1960: 5.

"Community Civil Defense Fire School Scheduled." *The Daily Herald* (Provo, UT). May 13, 1953: 3.

"Complete Roll of All County Nurses for Civil Defense." *Warren Times* (Warren, PA). September 17, 1951: 8.

"Conference On Civil Defense Opens in Capital." *The Mount Pleasant News* (Mount Pleasant, IA). October 2, 1950: 1.

"County Homemakers Hear About Home Protection in CD Program." *The Morning Herald* (Hagerstown, MD). September 22, 1959: 7.

"County Nurses Mobilize for Civil Defense." *The Tustin News* (Tustin, CA). April 6, 1951: 1.

"Crisis Brings Urgent Civil Defense Move." *Palladium-Item* (Richmond, IN). October 26, 1962: 10.

"Deaf Smith Home Demonstration Clubs Take Lead in Civil Defense Activities." *Pampa Daily News* (Pampa, TX). May 7, 1952: 16.

"Death Fear, Breeder of Panic, Greatest Perils in Disaster, Defense Parley Told." *The Los Angeles Times* June 26, 1953: 53.

"Defend Home First, Expert Tells Women." *Arizona Republic* (Phoenix, AZ). December 14, 1951: 7.

"Defense Council Plans Raid Test on Saturday." *The Morning News* (Wilmington, DE). February 25, 1953: 28.

"Defense Teams to Demonstrate at Alexandria." *The Monroe News-Star* (Monroe, LA). April 9, 1954: 2.

"Defense Training Set for Women." *The Philadelphia Inquirer*. October 24, 1952: 19.

"DeRidder Banquet to Be Tuesday." *The Times* (Shreveport, LA). January 27, 1965: 27.

Dickson, Terry. "Your Part in Civil Defense." *St. Louis Post-Dispatch* (St. Louis, MO). January 10, 1954: 64.

Davis, Tracy. *Stages of Emergency: Cold War*

Nuclear Civil Defense (Durham, NC: Duke University Press, 2007).
"Dorothy Mann Battles Both Apathy and Fear." Lansing State Journal (Lansing, MI). January 6, 1957: 47.
"Drive Opens for Recruiting Raid Wardens." El Paso Herold-Post (El Paso, TX). July 27, 1961: 1.
Dierenfield, Bruce, The Civil Rights Movement: Revised Edition (New York: Routledge, 2008).
Dunlap, Katherine. "Civil Defense Leaders Appeal for 100,000 Women Volunteers." The Philadelphia Inquirer. December 15, 1950: 39+.
Eisenhower, Dwight. Remarks at the Conference of the National Women's Advisory Committee on Civil Defense, October 31, 1954. The American Presidency Project. Retrieved from http://www.presidency.ucsb.edu/ws/?pid=10109.
_____. Remarks marking the opening day of Civil Defense Week in 1957. Quoted in Public Papers of the Presidents of the United States (U.S. National Archives): 675–676.
Friedan, Betty. The Feminine Mystique (New York: W.W. Norton & Company, 1963).
Fuller, Jean Wood. "Jean Wood Fuller: Women in Politics Oral History Project." The Bancroft Library, University of California Berkeley, 1977: 191. Retrieved from: https://archive.org/stream/orgwomenvolpolgo00fullrich#page/n13/mode/2up.
"Farm Leaders to Map Rural Civil Defense." Battle Creek Enquirer (Battle Creek, MI). February 1956: 10.
"Farm Women Urged to Help Civil Defense." The Gettysburg Times (Gettysburg, PA). May 12, 1955: 1.
Family Food Stockpile for Survival (Washington, D.C.: U.S. Government Printing Office, 1966).
Federal Civil Defense Administration 1950 Annual Report (Washington, D.C.: U.S. Government Printing Office, 1950).
Federal Civil Defense Administration 1951 Annual Report (Washington, D.C.: U.S. Government Printing Office, 1951).
Federal Civil Defense Administration 1952 Annual Report (Washington, D.C.: U.S. Government Printing Office, 1952).
Federal Civil Defense Administration 1953 Annual Report (Washington, D.C.: U.S. Government Printing Office, 1953).
Federal Civil Defense Administration 1954 Annual Report (Washington, D.C.: U.S. Government Printing Office, 1954).
Federal Civil Defense Administration 1955 Annual Report (Washington, D.C.: U.S. Government Printing Office, 1955).
Federal Civil Defense Administration 1956 Annual Report (Washington, D.C., U.S. Government Printing Office, 1956).
Federal Civil Defense Administration 1957 Annual Report (Washington, D.C.: U.S. Government Printing Office, 1957).
"Feeding of Million in Attack Planned." New York Times. April 3, 1951: 15.
"5 Points to Preparedness; New Class Starts Monday." St. Cloud Times (St. Cloud, MN), March 18, 1960: 3.
"5 States' Homemakers to Meet for Civil Defense Conference." The Indianapolis Star. August 29, 1957: 11.
Fox, Corinne. "American Women in the 1950s: The Years Between the War and Liberation." Saber and Scroll 2, 3 (Summer 2013): 30–36.
"From the Editor's Mail." Journal of Home Economics 48, 8 (October 1951): 657.
Garrison, Dee, Bracing for Armageddon: Why Civil Defense Never Worked (New York: Oxford University Press, 2006).
Georgia Women in Civil Defense (Georgia Civil Defense Department, 1954).
Grandma's Pantry Was Always Ready—Is Your Pantry Prepared? (New York: New York State Civil Defense Commission, circa 1955).
"Greenwich Organizes Civil Defense Groups." New York Times. November 19, 1950: 92.
Grossman, Andrew. Neither Dead Nor Read: Civilian Defense and American Political Development During the Early Cold War (New York: Routledge, 2001).
"Grandma's Pantry Belongs in Your Kitchen." By, For, And About Women in Civil Defense (Washington, D.C.: Government Printing Office, 1955).
"Grandma's Pantry Goes on Wheels." By, For, And About Women in Civil Defense (Washington, D.C.: Government Printing Office, 1956).
"H-Bomb Is Everybody's Business." The San Bernardino County Sun (San Bernardino, CA). April 29, 1954: 35.
Halbarstam, David. The Coldest Winter: America and the Korean War (New York: Hyperion, 2007).
Harris, Mrs. Ed. "Runge Park Cookout Is Examination in Red Cross, CD-Sponsored Course." The Galveston Daily News (Galveston, TX). July 10, 1960: 7.
Hartmann, Susan. "Women's Employment and the Domestic Ideal in the Early Cold War Years." in Joanne Meyerowitz, editor, Not June Cleaver: Women and Gender in Postwar America, 1945–1960 (Philadelphia: Temple University Press, 1994), 84–100.
Home Protection Exercises (Government Printing Office, Office of Civil Defense and Mobilization, 1960).

Homemaker's Manual of Atomic Defense (Columbia Broadcasting System, 1951).

"Home Defense Pledges Listed Goal of Intense Campaign." *The Salt Lake Tribune* (Salt Lake City, UT). October 27, 1952: 9.

"Home Demonstration Clubs" (October 21, 2010). Delmar Historical and Art Society. Retrieved from http://www.delmarhistoricalandartsociety.blogspot.com/2010/10/home-demonstration-clubs.html.

"Home Preparedness Class Planned for Scottdale in Civil Defense Training." *The Daily Courier* (Connellsville, PA). October 23, 1961: 10.

"Home Preparedness Course Set." *The Montana Standard* (Butte, MT). August 7, 1961: 5.

"Home Preparedness Courses Finished by Women's Groups." *The Evening Review* (East Liverpool, OH). November 2, 1959: 3.

"Home Preparedness Is Key to Survival if Attacked." *Herald and News* (Klamath Falls, OR). January 29, 1960: 4.

"Home Protection Discussion Topics for Culture Club." *Moberly Monitor-Index* (Moberly, MO). October 1, 1954: 6.

"Home Protection in Civil Defense Outlined by Women's Director." *The Daily Herald* (Provo, UT). February 27, 1955: 21.

"Hospital Aid Group Joins Civil Defense." *The Philadelphia Inquirer*. January 12, 1951: 42.

"Hospital-Civil Defense Disaster Test June 2." *Fitchburg Sentinel* (Fitchburg, MA), May 6, 1965: 13.

"Humboldt Represented at State Civil Defense Meet." *Eureka Humboldt Standard* (Eureka, CA). October 26, 1962: 8.

"Into Operational Stage." *The Daily Messenger* (Canandaigua, NY). November 23, 1953: 1.

Isaacs, Jeremy Isaacs and Taylor Downing. *Cold War* (London: Little Brown Book Group, 2014).

Johnson, Kathleen. "Women Defend the Nation." The Cold War Museum. Retrieved from http://www.coldwar.org/articles/50s/women_civildefense.asp.

Johnson, Lyndon. Statement by the President on the Need for Federal, State, and Local Cooperation in Civil Defense and Emergency Preparedness, April 13, 1968. American Presidency Project. Retrieved from http://www.presidency.ucsb.edu/ws/index.php?pid=28800.

Kennedy, John. "Civil Defense Fireside Chat." Theodore Sorensen Papers, Box 30, Civil Defense, John F. Kennedy Presidential Library and Museum.

———. Speech by President John Kennedy on the Berlin Crisis (Washington, July 25, 1961), John F. Kennedy Presidential Library and Museum. Retrieved from https://www.jfklibrary.org/Research/Research-Aids/JFK-Speeches/Berlin-Crisis_19610725.aspx.

"Leach Heads Biological War Defense Group." *The News Journal* (Wilmington, DE). February 7, 1951: 18.

Lee, Percy Maxim. "The Family in Our Democratic Society." *Journal of Home Economics* 44, 7 (September 1952): 496–501.

"Legion Plans Drive for Civil Defense Auxiliary Police." *St. Louis Post-Dispatch* (St. Louis, MO). March 8, 1952: 7.

Lichtman, Sarah. "Do-It-Yourself Security: Safety, Gender, and the Home Fallout Shelter in Cold War America." *Journal of Design History* 19, 1 (Spring 2006): 39–55.

Lilienthal, David. "Science and Man's Fate." *Nation*, July 13, 1946: 40–41.

"Local Nurses to Be Organized for Civil Defense." *Hartford Courant* (Hartford, CT). February 1, 1954: 25.

"Look and Listen With Donald Kirkley." *The Baltimore Sun*. May 18, 1954: 12.

Mann, Mrs. Joseph W. "A Pledge for Home Defense." *Lansing State Journal* (Lansing, MI). November 16, 1952: 12.

"Many Nurses Volunteer for Civil Defense." *Pittston Gazette* (Pittston, PA). September 10, 1954: 2.

"Mass Food Class Ends First Half." *Herald and News* (Klamath Falls, OR). May 8, 1963: 22.

May, Elaine Tyler. *Homeward Bound: American Families in the Cold War Era* (New York: Basic Books, 1988).

May, Elaine Tyler. Review of Laura McEnaney, *Civil Defense Begins at Home: Militarization Meets Everyday Life in the Fifties*, *Wisconsin Magazine of History* (Summer 2002), 61–62.

McCullough, John M. "Women Here to Train in Civil Defense Roles." *The Philadelphia Inquirer*. December 1950: 8.

McEnaney, Laura. *Civil Defense Begins at Home: Militarization Meets Everyday Life in the Fifties* (Princeton, NJ: Princeton University Press, 2000).

———. McEnaney on "Women's Role in Civil Defense." PBS American Experience Interview. Retrieved from http://www.pbs.org/wgbh/amex/bomb/filmmore/reference/interview/mcenaney09.html.

McMahon, Clara. "Civil Defense and Education Goals." *The Elementary School Journal* 53 (April 1953): 440–442.

Magnussen, Ann. "Red Cross Service." *American Journal of Nursing* 56, 10 (October 1956): 1290–1291.

Missouri Survival Plan (Jefferson City: State of Missouri, 1958).

"More Women Join CD Ranks." *The Morning News* (Wilmington, DE). June 13, 1964: 29.

Murphy, Paul and James Hundley. "Food Supply and Emergency Feeding in Civil Defense." *Public Health Reports, 1896–1970* (September 1952): 862.

"Mock Raids' Toll Vast; Civil Defense Unready." *The Cincinnati Enquirer* (Cincinnati, OH). June 15, 1954: 3.

"Mrs. Walter Rottman, Jr., Wins First Home Preparedness Award." *Jefferson City Post-Tribune* (Jefferson City, MO). May 18, 1960: 5.

"Muncie Nurses Attend Civil Defense Event." *Muncie Evening Press* (Muncie, IN). November 20, 1954: 6.

"National Civil Defense Experts to Appear at Provo Leadership Meet." *The Daily Herald* (Provo, UT). June 3, 1956: 5.

"Need 300 Wardens, Women Volunteers." *Janesville Daily Gazette* (Janesville, WI). March 26, 1957: 9.

Nelson, Craig. *The Age of Radiance: The Epic Rise and Fall of the Atomic Era* (NY: Scribner, 2014).

"New 'Grass Roots' CD Setup Charted." *Battle Creek Enquirer* (Battle Creek, MI). June 5, 1956: 2.

"New Civil Defense Campaign Launched." *The Emporia Weekly Gazette* (Emporia, KS). November 6, 1952: 4.

Northcutt, Susan Stoudinger. "Women and the Bomb: Domestication of the Atomic Bomb in the United States," *International Social Science Review* 74, No. 3/4 (1999): 129–139.

"Nurses Attend Civil Defense Training Meet." *The Escanaba Daily* (Escanaba, MI). September 26, 1961: 12.

"Nurses Plan Civil Defense Organization." *Cumberland Evening Times* (Cumberland, MD). April 30, 1952: 11.

"Nurses Plan Civil Defense Series." *Great Falls Tribune* (Great Falls, MT). May 5, 1957: 16.

"Nurses Prepare for Civil Defense." *The Town Talk* (Alexandria, LA). March 22, 1951: 16.

"Nurses to Enroll for Civil Defense." *Monroe Evening Times* (Monroe, WI). February 26, 1951: 6.

"Nurses Set Civil Defense Program." *The Lawton Constitution* (Lawton, Oklahoma) June 5, 1957: 12.

"Nurses Take Civil Defense Rescue Course." *Asbury Park Press* (Ashbury Park, NJ). January 31, 1958: 4.

Office of Civil Defense and Mobilization 1959 Annual Report (Washington, D.C.: U.S. Government Printing Office, 1959).

Office of Civil and Defense Mobilization 1960 Annual Report (Washington, D.C.: U.S. Government Printing Office, 1960).

"100 Area Women to Take CD Home Preparedness Course." *The Morning News* (Wilmington, DE). November 1958: 5.

"107 District CD Wardens Needed for Preparedness." *The Galveston Daily News* (Galveston, TX). August 18, 1961: 3.

"130 Men and Women Police Auxiliaries Congratulated at Defense Graduation." *Hartford Courant* (Hartford, CT). October 5, 1951: 21.

120 Years of American Education: A Statistical Portrait (Washington, D.C.: National Center for Education Statistics, U.S. Department of Education, 1993).

"1,000 Women Volunteers for Oakland Auxiliary Police Force Asked by Chief." *Oakland Tribune*. July 18, 1951: 21.

Oppenheimer, J. Robert. Speech at Fuller Lodge to honor work at Los Alamos, October 16, 1945. Quoted in Kai Bird, Martin J. Sherwin, *American Prometheus: The Triumph and Tragedy of J. Robert Oppenheimer* (New York: Alfred A. Knopf, 2005), 323.

"Oregon's Civil Defense Alert." *Statesman Journal* (Salem, OR). October 23, 1962: 8.

"Orem to Participate in Nation-Wide Defense Alert." *The Daily Herald* (Provo, UT). June 13, 1954: 6.

"Outdoor Care Set in Event of Attack." *New York Times*. September 2, 1952, 32.

"Parley on Civil Defense." *New York Times*. October 24, 1954: 113.

Pearl, Mrs. Norton (Dorothy). "Women and Civil Defense." In *The Cold War: A History in Documents and Eyewitness Accounts*, edited by Jussi M. Hanhimaki and Odd Arne Westad. New York: Oxford University Press, 2011: 298–299.

Peterson, Val. "Co-Ordinating and Extending Federal Assistance." *The Annals of the American Academy of Political and Social Science* 309 (January 1957): 52–64.

"Pima Civil Defense Wardens Begin Intensified Training." *Tucson Daily Citizen* (Tucson, AZ). April 8, 1954: 8.

"PL Grove Civil Defense School Slated." *The Daily Herald* (Provo, UT). March 30, 1960: 9.

"Plan Nurses Civil Defense Study Series." *The Troy Record* (Troy, NY). January 20, 1964: 11.

"Plans Are Being Made to Mobilize Nation's Woman Power." *Corsicana Semi-Weekly Light* (Corsicana, TX). December 22, 1950: 2.

"Pleasant Grove Women Slated for Major Role in Region CD Meeting." *The Daily Herald* (Provo, UT). January 1, 1955: 3.

"Police Auxiliary of 40,000 Planning for City's Defense." *New York Times*, August 8, 1950: 1.

"Police Seek Auxiliary of 300 Persons." *Hartford Courant* (Hartford, CT). December 2, 1950: 8.

Political Development During the Early Cold War (New York: Routledge, 2001).

"Preparations Readied for A-Test Here." *The*

Oneonta Star (Oneonta, NY). February 18, 1954: 5.

"Preparedness at Home Cuts War Possibility." *The Daily Herald* (Provo, UT). June 20, 1956: 3.

"Protection Parley Set." *Lansing State Journal* (Lansing, MI). September 28, 1954: 4.

"Public Response to Civil Defense Raid Alert Spotty." *Pittston Gazette* (Pittston, PA). October 26, 1954: 1.

"Ready Family Doubles Its Survival Chances." *The Daily Tar Heel* (Chapel Hill, NC). July 29, 1959: 4.

"Recruiting and Training of Workers Under Way." *The Evening Independent* (Massillon, OH). January 3, 1951: 2.

"Red Cross Slates Mass Feeding Class." *The Los Angeles Times* (Los Angeles, CA). February 19, 1961: 392.

"Robbie Johnson's Chat With Women." *Times Herald* (Olean, NY). September 27, 1950: 7.

"Role of Nurses in Civil Defense Noted at Course." *The Winona Republican-Herald* (Winona, MN), November 30, 1951: 3.

Rose, Kenneth. *One Nation Underground: The Fallout Shelter in American Culture* (New York University Press, 2001).

"Rural C.D. Can Save America." *The Fairmount News* (Fairmount, IN). September 6, 1956: 2.

"San Medic Speaks to Nurses on Civil Defense." *The Magee Courier* (Magee, MS). November 1, 1962: 5.

Schafer, Margaret. "Civil Defense Service." *American Journal of Nursing* 56, 10 (October 1956): 1291–1292.

Scheibach, Michael. *Atomic Narratives and American Youth: Coming of Age with the Atom, 1945–1955* (Jefferson, NC: McFarland, 2003).

_____. *Atomics in the Classroom: Teaching the Bomb in the Early Postwar Years* (Jefferson, NC: McFarland, 2015).

Scheuer, Steven. "'Atomic Attack' Shows Terror of New Arms." *The Brooklyn Daily Eagle* (Brooklyn, NY). May 18, 1954: 13.

Schulz, Dorothy Moses. "Policewomen in the 1950s: Paving the Way for Patrol." *Women & Criminal Justice*, 4, 2 (1993): 5–30.

"Second Home Preparedness Workshop Scheduled Tonight." *The Montana Standard* (Butte, MT). August 16, 1961: 3.

"Secretaries Will Hear Mrs. Moore." *The Town Talk* (Alexandria, LA). November 15, 1965: 24.

"Seek to Organize Women's Warden Service in Village." *The Chicago Heights Star* (Chicago Heights, IL). November 9, 1954: 2.

"Seip Named Deputy C.D. Police Head." *The Pocono Record* (Stroudsburg, PA). June 10, 1955: 20.

"700 Civil Defense Police to Graduate." *The Star Tribune* (Minneapolis, MN), June 7, 1953: 36.

"She Co-ordinates Home, Civil Defense." *The Los Angeles Times* (January 3, 1965): 179.

"Should Prepare for Germ Warfare, Peterson Says." *The Winona Republican-Herald* (Winona, MN), November 3, 1953: 1.

"Speaker's Training Classes." *Pittsburgh Post-Gazette* (Pittsburgh, PA). February 17, 1951: 5.

"Speigletown Women See Defense Test." *The Times Record* (Troy, NY). May 18, 1954: 18.

"State School Personnel Must Act As Wardens." *The Bee* (Danville, VA). September 20, 1961: 36.

"State Steps Up Civil Defense." *The Palm Beach Post* (West Palm Beach, FL).October 30, 1962: 1.

Sullivan, Catherine. "The Civil Defense Role of Nurses." *Journal of the American Medical Association* 169 (January 24, 1959): 388–389.

"Tells Women's Civil Defense Role." *The News-Palladium* (Benton Harbor, MI). May 23, 1952: 4.

"Tenth District Nurses to Attend Civil Defense Class." *The Daily Telegram* (Eau Claire, WI). May 29, 1951: 5.

"Texans to Be Registered for Home Defense." *The Courier-Gazette* (McKinney, TX). November 1, 1952: 4.

Texans on the Alert for Civil Defense and Disaster Relief (Austin: State of Texas, 1956).

"The Cold War Homefront: Civil and Home Defense." Retrieved from http://www.authentichistory.com/1946-1960/4-cwhomefront/3-civildefense/1-educating/index.html.

The Home Demonstration Agent (Washington, D.C.: U.S. Government Printing Office, 1951).

This Is Civil Defense (Washington, D.C.: U.S. Government Printing Office, 1951).

"3 Speakers Chart CD Efforts for 100 AAUW Members." *Battle Creek Enquirer* (Battle Creek, MI). January 18, 1957: 4.

"3 Women Form Defense Groups." *The Post-Standard* (Syracuse, NY). March 19, 1952: 39.

"To Aid in Civil Defense." *The Kansas City Times* (Kansas City, MO). October 30, 1959: 105.

Toossi, Mitro. "A Century of Change: The U.S. Labor Force, 1950–2050" (Bureau of Labor Statistics, 2002).

"The Women's Civil Defense Council." *Anderson Herald* (Anderson, IN). January 3, 1958: 4.

"34 Complete Home Protection Defense Course." *The Palm Beach Post* (West Palm Beach, FL). January 2, 1959: 13.

"32 Women Will Spearhead Civil Defense in

Community." *Tucson Daily Citizen* (Tucson, AZ). May 24, 1952): 4.

"Train Leaders in Civil Defense." *Pittsburgh Post-Gazette* (Pittsburgh, PA). November 13, 1953: 14.

"Training Class Held for Women in Police Unit." *The Evening Times* (Sayre, PA). March 31, 1954: 7.

"Training Home Nurses." *The Burlington Free Press* (Burlington, VT). December 16, 1950: 6.

Truman, Harry S. Address at a Dinner of the 1951 Civil Defense Conference, The American Presidency Project. Retrieved from http://www.presidency.ucsb.edu/ws/?pid=14079.

_____. Executive Orders, Harry S Truman (1945–1953), Harry S. Truman Library & Museum. Retrieved from https://www.trumanlibrary.org/executiveorders/index.php?pid=95&st=&st1=.

_____. "Executive Order 10186—Establishing the Federal Civil Defense Administration in the Office for Emergency Management of the Executive Office of the President." December 1, 1950. Online by Gerhard Peters and John T. Woolley, The American Presidency Project. http://www.presidency.ucsb.edu/ws/?pid=78352.

_____. "Message to the Congress Transmitting the First Annual Report of the Federal Civil Defense Administration." Public Papers of the President (1945–1953), Harry S. Truman Library & Museum.

_____. "Proclamation 2914—Proclaiming the Existence of a National Emergency." December 16, 1950. Online by Gerhard Peters and John T. Woolley, The American Presidency Project. http://www.presidency.ucsb.edu/ws/?pid=13684.

_____. Radio Address to the American People on Armistice Day, November 11, 1951. Harry S. Truman Library & Museum. Retrieved from https://trumanlibrary.org/publicpapers/viewpapersphp?pid=556.

_____. "Statement by the President Upon Signing the Civil Defense Act of 1950." The American Presidency Project. Retrieved from http://www.presidency.ucsb.edu/ws/?pid=13777.

_____. The provisions of Executive Order 10222 of Mar. 8, 1951, appear at 16 FR 2247, 3 CFR, 1949–1953 Comp., p. 736, unless otherwise noted. Retrieved from https://www.archives.gov/federal-register/codification/executive-order/10222.html.

"Truman Lashes Defense Budget Cuts By Ike." *The Salem News* (Salem, OH). June 27, 1953: 1.

"Truman Urges Civil Defense Preparations." *The Journal News* (White Plains, NY). September 18, 1950: 1.

"TV Key." *The Brooklyn Daily Eagle* (Brooklyn, NY). May 18, 1954: 13.

"Two Named Delegates to Auxiliary Meeting." *Council Bluffs Nonpareil* (Council Bluffs, IA). August 16, 1953: 20

"20 Women Join Auxiliary Police." *Oakland Tribune* (Oakland, CA). August 9, 1951: 29.

"26 Women Complete Preparedness Course." *The Morning News* (Wilmington, DE). December 15, 1958: 4.

"23 Women to Complete Mass Feeding Course." *The Star Press* (Muncie, IN). February 11, 1962: 8.

United States Civil Defense (Washington, D.C.: U.S. Government Printing Office, 1950).

United States Civil Defense Police Services (Washington, D.C.: U.S. Government Printing Office, 1951).

"Urgency of Civil Defense Stressed to Clubwomen." *The Salt Lake Tribune* (Salt Lake City, UT). May 6, 1952: 31.

"Volunteers Needed." *Denton Record-Chronicle* (Denton, TX). November 2, 1952: 18.

Waesche, Jim. "Somerset CD Agency Has Wide Number of Duties." *The Daily Times* (Salisbury, MD). October 26, 1962: 15.

Wagner, Bob. "CD Agency Illustrates Methods." *The Orlando Sentinel*. February 24, 1960: 37

Ward, Florence. "Home Demonstration Work Under the Smith-Lever Act, 1914–1924." *U.S. Department of Agriculture Circular No. 43* (June 1929): 29.

"Wardens Have Important Role in Civil Defense." *The San Bernardino County Sun* (San Bernardino, CA). November 1, 1952: 10.

"Waterbury Women to State Self-Care Course." *The Burlington Free Press* (Burlington, VT). October 16, 1962: 3.

"Websterite Elected By State Women." *Democrat and Chronicle* (Rochester, NY). May 27, 1964: 8.

Whitt, Wayne. "Women Better Versed." *The Tennessean* (Nashville, TN). June 18, 1961: 94.

Williams, Claudia G. "Home Demonstration's Note Book." *The Paris News* (Paris, TX). August 6, 1953: 11.

Winkler, Allan M. *Life Under a Cloud: American Anxiety About the Atom* (New York: Oxford University Press, 1993).

"Woman, Once House Member, in Civil Defense." *The Courier-Journal* (Louisville, KY). December 19, 1965: 115.

"Woman's Responsibility in Fight for Survival Stressed at HD Camp." *Corsicana Daily Sun* (Corsicana, TX). August 5, 1960: 4.

"Women Are Being Offered Course in Civil Defense." *The News-Herald* (Franklin, PA). October 4, 1952: 9.

"'Women Are the Key to Civil Defense,'" *Argus-Leader* (Sioux Falls, SD). January 27, 1960: 5.

"Women Asked to Help Out in Civil Defense."

The Ogden Standard-Examiner (Ogden, UT). November 1, 1952: 11.

"Women Asked to Increase Awareness to Civil Defense." *Denton Record-Chronicle* (Denton, TX). February 3, 1955: 12.

"Women Called to Hear Civil Defense Orders." *Washington C.H. Record-Herald* (Washington Court House, OH). January 10, 1951: 2.

"Women Civil Defense Leaders Will Meet." *Alton Evening Telegraph* (Alton, IL). November 12, 1958: 10.

"Women from 6 Counties Invited to Take Home Protection Class." *The Raleigh Register* (Beckley, WV). March 25, 1957: 2.

Women Get Chance to Swap Rolling Pin for a Blackjack." *The News Journal* (Wilmington, DE). November 24, 1950: 44.

"Women Get Civil Defense Call, Begin Plans for Own Group." *Lincoln Evening Journal* (Lincoln NE). July 2, 1952: 14.

"Women Give Taste Test to Survival Biscuits." *St. Louis Post-Dispatch*. October 5, 1962: 16.

"Women in Civil Defense." *New York Times*. October 17, 1950: 18.

Women in Civil Defense (Washington, D.C.: U.S. Government Printing Office, 1952).

"Women Leaders Invited to Civil Defense Meet." *The Lincoln Star* (Lincoln, NE). February 2, 1965: 11.

"Women to Aid Recruit of CD Ground Corps." *The Times* (San Mateo, CA). April 17, 1953: 4.

"Women to Be Active in S.C. Civil Defense." *Florence Morning News* (Florence, SC). October 20, 1950: 14.

"Women to Form Civil Defense Unit at Conclave." *The Salt Lake Tribune* (Salt Lake City, UT). September 6, 1952: 32.

"Women to the Rescue." *The Decatur Daily-Review* (Decatur, IL). February 16, 1953: 10.

"Women's Auxiliary Police for School Crossings." *Kingsport Times* (Kingsport, TN). August 4, 1953: 12.

"Women's C.D. Council Meets." *The Daily Herald* (Provo, UT). September 8, 1957: 4.

"Women's CD Council for Orick Area." *Eureka Humboldt Standard* (Eureka, CA). April 4, 1962: 12.

"Women's Civil Defense Council in TV Series." *Jefferson City Post-Tribune* (Jefferson City, MO). January 15, 1960: 12.

"Women's Civil Defense Division Organized." *The Palm Beach Post* (West Palm Beach, FL). February 8, 1951: 1.

"Women's Civil Defense Group Expands Program." *The Advocate-Messenger* (Danville, KY). August 29, 1961): 1.

"Women's Civil Defense Police Trained." *The Indianapolis Star* (Indianapolis, IN). January 15, 1955: 5.

"Women's Civil Defense Role Stressed at Session Here." *Daily World* (Opelousas, LA). August 24, 1952: 23.

"Women's Corps to Aid Raid Test." *The Philadelphia Inquirer*. June 1954: 7.

"Women's Defense Parley Set at St. Mary's College." *Oakland Tribune* (Oakland, CA). January 30, 1952: 20.

"Women's Defense Responsibilities Are Outlined." *The Daily Clintonian* (Clinton, IN). October 4, 1950: 1.

"Women's Ground Observer Corps Open Meeting." *Carrol Daily Times Herald* (Carroll, IA). May 10, 1955; 9.

Women's Leaders Confer in Capital on Home Defense." *Battle Creek Enquirer* (Battle Creek MI). September 27, 1960: 8.

"Women's Meeting on Civil Defense September 24–25." *The Edinburg Daily Courier* (Edinburg, IN). August 28, 1957: 1.

"Women's Role in Civil Defense." *New York Times*, July 1, 1951: 34.

"Women's Warden Course Offered." *The Daily Notes* (Canonsburg, PA). October 29, 1952: 1.

"Workshop in Civil Defense Held Here." *McKinney Weekly Democrat-Gazette* (McKinney, TX). July 2, 1959: 1.

"Yuma Women Urged to Form CD Council." *The Yuma Daily Sun* (Yuma, AZ). September 22, 1960: 5.

Zarlengo, Kristina. "Civilian Threat, the Suburban Citadel, and Atomic Age Women." *Institutions, Regulation, and Social Control* 24, 4 (Summer 1999), 925–958.

Zipf, Mitzi. "Civil Defense Interests Many Women in Mesa." *Arizona Republic* (Phoenix, AZ). July 27, 1961: 14.

INDEX

Adams, Arthur 64
Aids for Police Training Officers 117
Alert America 6
Allegheny County (Utah) Federation of Women's Clubs 91
Allen, Floyd 121
American Association of University Women 14, 61, 95
American Broadcasting Corporation (ABC) 1
American Council on Education 64
American Home Economics Association 6, 61, 98
American Hotel Association 15
American Legion 15, 120
American Legion Auxiliary 6, 42, 69, 95, 124
American Medical Association 42, 124
American National Dietetic Association 172
American Publishers Institute 42
American Red Cross 6, 15, 42, 69, 122–123, 147, 149–150, 175, 179, 181–182, 192, 200
American Women in Radio and Television (AWRT) 6, 39
AMVETS 71
Arlen, Margaret 15
Armstrong Circle Theatre 1
Association of Junior League of America 94–95
"Atomic Attack" 1, 96
Atomic Energy Commission 12, 67

Barber, Mary 177
The Basic Course in Emergency Mass Feeding Handbook 192-196
Berg, Olive 150
Berlin Airlift 13
Berlin Crisis 12. 43, 97, 124, 153–154
Bird, Mrs. Victor 68
Blair, James, Jr. 181
Boyer, Paul 12
Brennan, Mary 17–18
British Women's Voluntary Service 40
Brown vs. Board of Education 11
Bryant, Farris 201
By, For, and About Women in Civil Defense 172

By the Bombs Early Light: American Thought & Culture at the Dawn of the Atomic Age 12–13

Caldwell, Millard 14
California Women's Civil Defense Conference 70
Camp Fire Girls 71
Catholic War Veterans 95
Challenge for Security and Survival 10–12, 44
Chicago Alerts: A City Plans Its Civil Defense Against Atomic Attack 176
Chicago Civil Defense Corps 176
Child Welfare League 179
Churchill, Winston 13
Cincinnati-Hamilton County Civil Defense 92
Civil Defense Act of 1950 35, 38
Civil Defense and Vocational Education 42
Civil Defense Education Through Elementary and Secondary Schools 42
Civil Defense in Outline: A Study Guide for the National Civil Defense Program 205–226
Civil Defense Volunteer Registration Guide 39, 59
Civil Defense Women's Advisory Council 69; see also National Women's Advisory Committee/Council; Women's Civil Defense Auxiliary Committee
Civil Rights Act of 1964 11
Coe, Myrtle 123
Columbia Broadcasting System (CBS) 1, 15
Community Chest 175
CONELRAD 3–5, 35, 78, 80, 150–151, 153, 168
Congress of Women's Auxiliaries of the CO 61
Croddy, Mildred 65
Croxdale, Ressie 65
Cuban Missle Crisis 12, 98, 124, 154

Daughters of the American Revolution 16, 40
Dean, Gordon 67

Department of Agriculture 63, 175, 63
Department of Defense 13, 43, 192, 200, 202
Devine, Lester 119
Dewey, Thomas 177
Dougherty, Brig. Gen. Clyde 87
Dozler, Maj. Gen. James 14

Edwards, Caroline 177
Eisenhower, Dwight 16, 35, 38, 43, 48, 60, 66, 95, 96, 146, 155, 170, 172, 197
Emergency Feeding for Great Britain 176
Emergency Feeding Instructor Course 184–191
Emergency Mass Feeding Instructor Training Program 179
Emergency Traffic Control Training Course 119
Ewing, Sherley 1
Ewing, Mrs. Walter 61, 65
Executive Order 10186 34
Executive Order 10222 15

Family Action Program 145
Family Food Sheet 173
Family Service Association of America 179
Faubus, Orval 201
Federal Civil Defense Administration (FCDA) 4, 14–16, 32–45, 46–47, 58–70, 72–74, 84–87, 91–99, 114, 116–125, 145–148, 172–183, 198–202
Federation of Women's Clubs 40
Federation of Women's Republican Clubs of New York State 177
The Feminine Mystique 3
Fireside Theater 1
Ford Theater 1
Friedan, Betty 3
Fuller, Jean Wood 16, 68–69, 171, 172–173, 183
Future Homemakers of America 42, 124

Garrison, Dee 173
Georgia Civil Defense Department 67
Georgia Women in Civil Defense 20–27, 67
Gill, William 32
Girl Scouts of America 71, 148
Goddard, Gay 151
Godfrey, Michael 119
Grandma's Pantry 41, 171–174, 183
Grandma's Pantry Goes on Wheels 173
Grandma's Pantry Was Always Ready. Is Your Pantry? 173
Grossman, Andrew 34
Ground Observer Corps 15, 67, 69, 85

Handbook for Auxiliary Police 117
Hartmann, Susan 4
Hatfield, Mark 201
Haucke, Mrs. Frank 94
Hazell, Lois 71
Healy, Adelaide 91

Home Defense Action Program 62
Home Defense Corps 161–163
home demonstration clubs 42, 62–63, 69, 150, 203
Home Nursing Course 42
Home Protection Exercises 42, 62, 145–146
Home Services Corp 16
Homemaker's Manual of Atomic Defense 15
Homeward Bound: American Families in the Cold War Era 3, 16
Hostetler, Maj. Gen. Erwin 10
Housing and Home Finance Agency 180
Howard, Katherine 16, 48–55, 69, 147
Hueber, Lt. Gen. C.R. 89
Hundley, James 175

International Association of Chiefs of Police 117, 121
iron curtain 13

Janney, Howard 202
Jefferson City (Missouri) Women's Council for Civil Defense 151
Johnson, Lyndon 10–11, 44, 98

Kennedy, John F. 12, 43–44, 96–98, 153, 155
Kentucky Division of Civil Defense 98
Keyes, Robert 201
Keyser, F. Ray 201
Khrushchev, Nikita 12, 97; *see also* Soviet Union
Kirkley, Donald 1
Kohler, Walter 91
Korean War 13, 34–35, 38, 197
Kreber, Maj. Gen. Leo 64
Kurtz, Mrs. William 71

League of Women Voters 98
Lee, D. Preston 119
Lee, Percy Maxim 98
Lilienthal, David 12
Limited Test Ban Treaty 12
Llewellyn, Gen. Ensley 202
Long Island Federation of Women's Clubs 68
Louisiana Office of Civil Defense 66
Lowe, Bert 93

Madison County (Indiana) Women's Civil Defense Council 69
Magnussen, Ann 123
Maine Civil Defense Agency 171–172
Mann, Dorothy 65, 144–145, 199–200
Manual for the Operation of Emergency Feeding Stations 177
Martin, Grace M. 202–203
Maryland Civil Defense Agency 1
Maryland Federation of Women's Clubs 148
May, Elaine Tyler 3, 16, 173
McEnaney, Laura 4, 5, 145

Index 247

McMahon, Clara 18
McMillian, Adj. Gen. Henry 202
Mechem, Edwin 201
Michigan Office of Civil Defense 65, 124–125
Mills, Frances 98
Missouri Survival Plan 181
Moore, Ellen Bryan 71
Morrison, Frank 98
The Motorola Television Hour 1
Murphy, Paul 175

Nathan, Henry 150
National Advisory Committee on Emergency Feeding 179
National Advisory Committee on Women's Participation 39, 59–60
National Advisory Council for Rural Civil Defense 94
National Broadcasting Corporation (NBC) 1
National Civil Defense Training Center (Olney, MD) 39, 86
National Council of Catholic Women 14, 94
National Council of Jewish Women 14, 74
National Council of Negro Women 14, 61, 94
National Federation of Business and Professional Women's Clubs 6, 14, 37, 40, 61, 69
National Home Demonstration Council 61, 63
National Policy on Shelters 96
National School Boards Association 42
National Securities Resources Board 13–14, 32, 84
National Security Act of 1947 13
National Sheriffs' Association 117
National Women's Advisory Committee/Council 16, 40, 59; *see also* Civil Defense Women's Advisory Council; Women's Civil Defense Auxiliary Committee
Netteler, Joseph 120
New York State Civil Defense Commission 89, 91
New York State Civil Defense Rescue Training School 89
New York State Defense Emergency Act of 1951 177
North American Air Defense Command (NORAD) 71
North Atlantic Treaty Organization (NATO) 13
North Carolina Federal of Home Demonstration Clubs 63
North Korea *see* Korean War
Northcutt, Susan Stoudinger 16–17
Notte, John 201
Nutter, Donald 154

Office for Emergency Management of the Executive Office of the President 34
Office of Civil and Defense Mobilization (OCDM) 43–44, 70, 96, 149–150, 164, 175, 200, 202
Office of Civil Defense (OCD) 32, 43–44, 192, 200, 202
Office of Civil Defense Planning 32
Office of Cooperative Extension Work 62
Office of War Information 19
Ohio Civil Defense Department 44, 58
Operation Alert 4–6, 40, 93, 96
Operation Main Street 62
"Operation Mercy 1965" 125
Operation Niagara 178
Oppenheimer, J. Robert 10
Orange County (California) Nurses Association 65
Ossanna, Sue 153

Pangle, Mary Ellen 148
Parent-Teachers Association 6, 69
Patterson, Spencer 120
Pearl, Dorothy 199–200
Peterson, Evan 149
Peterson, Val 66, 91
Pittman, Stewart 201
Playhouse 90 1
Pleasant Grove (Utah) Women's Civil Defense 68, 200
"Pledge for Home Defense" 61, 72–74, 144
Plummer, William 121
Porch, Mrs. Marion 66
Proclamation 2914-Proclaiming the Existence of a National Emergency 35
Provo (Utah) City Civil Defense Program 148

Retail Grocers Association 41
Rockefeller, Nelson 201
Roosevelt, Franklin 197
Rose, Kenneth 183
Rosellini, Albert 202

St. Louis Women's Civil Defense Council 201–202
Salvation Army 181
Samuel, Bernard 14
Scales, Milton 98
Schafer, Margaret 123
Schatzmann, William 119
Silver Bow (Montana) Civil Defense Administration 149
Singleton, Thomas 181
Smith, Audrey 70
Snyder, A.E. 97
The Social Worker in Civil Defense 178
Southern California Women's Conference on Civil Defense 67
Soviet Union 1, 12–13, 17, 28, 35, 50, 69, 71, 98, 114, 116, 124, 147, 153, 164, 183, 197–198, 201; *see also* Khrushchev, Nikita
Studio One 1
Sullivan, Catherine 125

Sullivan, Lt. Col. J. Arnold 71
Survival Through Emergency Preparedness (STEP) 94
Survival Under Atomic Attack 61, 72
Symington, W. Stuart 13

Target Areas Media Civil Defense Conference 92
Tarking, H.W. 201
television households (U.S.) 1
Texans on the Alert for Civil Defense 76–81
Texas Division of Defense and Disaster Relief 76
Thaxter, Phyllis 3
This Is Civil Defense 37, 100–107
Thompson, John 179
Trainer, Leonard 175–176
Truman, Harry S 5, 13–16, 32, 34–35, 38, 43, 46–47, 66–67, 114, 146, 155, 197–198; *see also* Executive Order 10186; Executive Order 10222; Proclamation 2914-Proclaiming the Existence of a National Emergency

U.S. Conference of Mayors 14
Utah Civil Defense 69
Utah Council of Women in Civil Defense 66, 146
Utah Federation of Women's Clubs 65

Veterans of Foreign Wars Auxiliary *see* Women's Auxiliary of the Veterans of Foreign Wars
Vietnam 10, 71
V-J Day 34

War of the Worlds 1
Ward, Florence 62
Warden Operations Conference 92
The Warden Service 87
The Warden's Handbook 5, 37, 87, 108–111
Warner, Dr. William 87
Welles, Orson 1
West, Brig. Gen. J. Wallace 146
Western Technical Training School 92
Western Women's Training Conference 39
What You Can Do Now 61
Whitehurst, Mrs. John L. 36
Whitt, Wayne 154, 201
Wilkinson, Col. Lawrence 117
Wing, Inez 172
Wives, Mothers, and the Red Menace 17
Women in Civil Defense 10, 18, 59
Women in the American Federation of Labor and C.I.O. 14
Women's Auxiliary of the Veterans of Foreign Wars 42, 69, 95
Women's Civil Defense Auxiliary Committee 67; *see also* Civil Defense Women's Advisory Council; National Women's Advisory Committee/Council
Women's Volunteer Civil Defense Coordinating Council 70
World War II 10, 34

Young Women's Christian Association 14
Youth Conference on Civil Defense 42

Zarlengo, Kristina 17
Zedong, Mao 13, 197

www.ingramcontent.com/pod-product-compliance
Lightning Source LLC
Chambersburg PA
CBHW051217300426
44116CB00006B/604